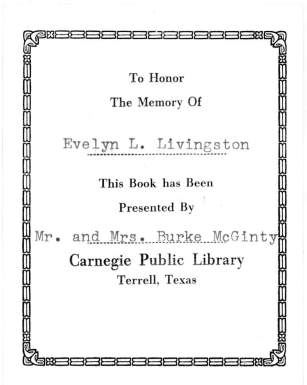

THE LITERARY DECADE ⊛▭⊛▭⊛▭⊛

THE
LITERARY
DECADE

By

Allen Churchill

1982

PRENTICE-HALL, Inc.

Englewood Cliffs, New Jersey

Design by Janet Anderson

Contents ❈▬❈▬❈▬❈▬❈▬❈▬❈

Also including such writers as Willa Cather . . Sherwood
Anderson . . Ben Hecht . . Robert Benchley · · · Will
Durant . . Warner Fabian . . Joan Lowell . . and Milt
Gross . . together with such contemporary phenomena as
literary cocktail parties and the book-banning activities of
vice-crusader John S. Sumner · · · · · · · · · · · · · · ·

It was all rather crazy, rather splendid.

SHERWOOD ANDERSON

It was an age of miracles, it was an age of art, it was an age of excess . . .

F. SCOTT FITZGERALD

"Tell me first, what are the things, the actual concrete things that harm a writer?"

"Politics, women, drink, money, ambition. And the lack of politics, women, drink, money, and ambition . . ."

"But drink. I do not understand about that. That has always seemed silly to me. I understand it as weakness."

"It is an easy way of ending a day . . ."

ERNEST HEMINGWAY

The Bashful Cyclone

The Era . . Sinclair Lewis . . . . . .

The novel known to the world as *Main Street* was published on October 20, 1920. Its author, of course, was Sinclair Lewis, and in those halcyon days copies of his book cost a mere two dollars. Lewis had been a steady scribbler from the tender age of eight, and by the age of thirty-five had published five other novels, together with many short stories for *The Saturday Evening Post* and other mass-circulation periodicals.

His previous books—*Our Mr. Wrenn, Trail of the Hawk, The Job, The Innocents, Free Air*—had been received by the critics with mild approbation and by the reading public with modest purchases. This time, however, he had put an extra amount of skill and determination into his work, as well as the potent distillation of years of supersharp observation of the American scene. The result was a literary achievement which one critic has called "the most sensational event in American publishing history," while another saw it as "less a book than an incident in American life."

Obviously *Main Street* arrived at the proper moment in history. Not only had World War I recently ended, ushering in a new era for all Americans, but the literary atmosphere of the time was permeated with an air of high expectancy. For a generation at least, literature had for the most part been the most sluggish of America's arts, but now the old arbiters of taste were fading away, bringing to younger laborers in literary vineyards the heady feeling that a great era was about to dawn.

William Dean Howells, born in the Presidency of Andrew Jackson, breathed his last in May 1920—and though highly esteemed as the country's first realistic novelist, his longevity made him a representative of the past. As Howells and others disappeared from death or desuetude, aspiring writers seemed to reach a stage of collective impatience which presaged a breakthrough strong enough to drive their craft to the head of the procession of arts in America. Something especially sweet in the ozone promised that these young talents would do their best work in the decade to come—as indeed they did—and that the rewards of authorship and publishing would increase amazingly.

All at once the past seemed unimportant, while the future loomed large. In Chicago, a young critic named Burton Rascoe peered back on the years before 1920 and wrote, "There were only two things for an artist in America to do in those days—stay drunk or commit suicide."

Turbulence was in the air, most of it caused by the disillusionments of World War I. This monumental conflict, calculated to make the world safe for democracy, had created more problems than it solved. Before the war America had been a supremely confident young nation which considered itself the hope of humanity, with enough national vigor and optimism to lead the world into a new day.

Less than two years after war's end, the country had lost this grandiose vision. The American people, once so cocksure, appeared resentful and insecure, the brimming confidence of the past gone sour. Participation in a European war seemed to have been a special mistake for a population whose forebears had largely quit Europe for the New World. Seemingly cheated of hope for a better existence, Americans reacted in different ways. For the first time in history a younger generation had turned on its elders, brazenly flaunting a new independence.

Never had a grown or growing group behaved toward parents in this brutal manner, scorning the advice, wisdom, postulates, and institutions of the old. But this Younger Generation had pounced on the disenchantments of World War I to make them personal property. Nothing that transpired before 1919, they loudly maintained, had any real value, and no one involved in the activities of the past had a right to speak. "We didn't ask to be born," the young snarled in the direction of their elders. "We can do anything we want, provided we don't hurt anyone else."

Determined to go its own inimitable way, the Younger Generation chose a behavior pattern of hectic gaiety as its most conspicuous characteristic. One reason may have been that a million American boys and men had served overseas during the war, and felt the world owed them some kind of reward. Sweethearts and wives who waited at home nursed identical feelings. At first parents and grandparents protested the wildness of youth, then slowly began focusing enviously on the fun involved.

Writers traditionally hold a mirror to their times, although over the previous thirty years America's most popular authors had conspicuously failed to do so. But times were a-change, with the literary pot destined to become the liveliest of contemporary cauldrons. Even now there was much anticipation of the Great American Novel. "In those days, people talked of the Great American Novel as ministers spoke of the Second Coming," one pundit has written. Franklin P. Adams, who shortened his name to F.P.A. when signing his esteemed "Conning Tower" column in the New York *Tribune*, made frequent mention of the Great American Novel, which he characteristically turned into "the G.A.N."

Even before the appearance of *Main Street*, two novels had been candidates for this honor. The first, in 1919, was Sherwood Anderson's *Winesburg, Ohio*, a novel of small-town life which in many ways presaged *Main Street*. But *Winesburg, Ohio* was a pungent work, rather than the sensational effort the times required. It was followed in March 1920 by *This Side of Paradise* by handsome young F. Scott Fitzgerald. An intoxicating novel of college-life-and-just-after, this was dubbed "the Bible of Flaming Youth," while the author found himself hailed as "Laureate of the Jazz Age." Still, *This Side of Paradise* was a flawed, self-indulgent book which did not add up to a major novel. "It has every fault except lifelessness," one critic stated.

So the first summer of the decade unfolded without a true contender for G.A.N. Then Sinclair Lewis and his publisher began showing galleys of *Main Street* to assorted figures in literary circles, and word spread that this book read like a winner. Gossip had it that Sinclair Lewis might just have crashed through with the Great American Novel.

Reviews on publication day all but said the same thing. Heywood Broun, then in charge of the literary section of the New York *Tribune*, accorded the book high praise, as did Robert Benchley (then Robert Charles Benchley) in the New York *World*. In his review, Broun employed words which in years to follow became clichés when writing or speaking of Sinclair Lewis: "He hears even better than he sees. I can't think of anybody who is so unerringly right in reproducing talk. He is right to a degree that is deeper than photographic."

In the New York *Post*, Carl Van Doren also noted Lewis' ear for language, then went on to find "a knack at satire and caustic epigram, with so enormous an acquaintance with the foibles and folklore of the Middle West that he has literally set a new standard for novels." In the pages of the New York *Call*, Clement Wood concluded, "*Main Street* is a book to possess and treasure."

As weeks passed with a joyous progression of critical praise and bookstore sales, all agreed that Sinclair Lewis had made the leap from minor to major novelist with this one book. Inevitably, there was talk of *Main Street* winning the Pulitzer Prize for American Fiction, an honor which, in days before book-of-the-month clubs, created the bonanza Novel of the Year, bought and read by everyone with any pretension to culture. In addition, this author who had stepped overnight from romance to realism was saluted as a new breed of writer. Never in American annals had a novelist dug so deep for material or depended so heavily on the research that filled not only his head but a veritable library of notebooks.

Up to now the country had accepted the American hinterland as offered by such writers as Hamlin Garland and Herbert Quick, along with members of the so-called Hoosier School like Booth Tarkington and Meredith Nicholson. The last named had even written—was the man kidding?—of his native state:

> *It's all pretty comfortable and cheerful and busy in Indiana, with lots of old fashioned human kindness flowing 'round; and it's getting better all the time. And I guess it's always got to be, out here in God's country.*

In his early novels and short stories, Sinclair Lewis had helped perpetuate this blissful legend. But now he had hurled the lie at himself and others by offering pen portraits etched in acid as well as pointing up the vicious aspects of provincial life. The immense gusto of his writing indicated he might even be trying to improve his countrymen by doses of ridicule. His mimicry had a cutting edge close to satire; it was a far cry from the homey vernacular of other chroniclers of the hinterlands. Lewis called his approach "rebellious optimism," but it was hard indeed to locate the upbeat in his slashing attacks on his fictional town of Gopher Prairie.

Finally, Lewis said his novel concerned "the spirit of that bewildered empire called the American Middlewest." Yet he also stated in a foreword that Main Streets existed in all the forty-eight states. So all who perused the novel might well be reading about themselves.

Apparently readers were eager for this. In the words of Mark Schorer, Lewis' foremost biographer, *Main Street* "perfectly met the mood of the post-war, disillusioned American people, and . . . seemed to characterize most strikingly a new national mood of self-criticism and even self-disgust."

Still, it cannot be said that *Main Street* immediately engaged the attention of the majority of book readers in the United States—a nation then boasting a population of slightly over one hundred million.

In days before radio and television, adult America depended heavily on books for relaxation and information. But the larger part of the Great American Public—can it be called the G.A.P.?—preferred its fiction at a somewhat lower level than *Main Street.* On publication of the Lewis novel, the top book business across the country involved *The Portygee,* by Joseph C. Lincoln, an author admired for depicttion of quaint Cape Codders, *Mary Marie,* by Eleanor M. Parker, *Lamp in the Desert,* by Ethel M. Dell, and *Man of the Forest,* by Zane Grey, a onetime dentist whose innate story-telling gifts established him high among outdoor adventure writers like Harold Bell Wright, Peter B. Kyne, Rex Beach, and James Oliver Curwood.

These male novelists of the past and present West were by far the top sellers of the day. In the overall book sales of 1920, Grey's *Man of the Desert* came out ahead, followed by Kyne's *Kindred of the Dust,* Wright's *Re-Creation of Brian Kent,* and Curwood's *River's End.* The enormous sale of books of such rugged virility indicated the odd fact that they also appealed to the female of the species—for they also contained high moral content. Yet the feminine branch of the G.A.P. was no less avid for its own kind of sentimental romance, furnished by ladies like Kathleen Norris, Frances Hodgson Burnett, Gene Stratton Porter, and the newly successful Fannie Hurst, of whom it was said, "She burned with the compulsion of an inner fire."

Yet, alert readers did exist; in fact, the tribe actually seemed to be on the increase. These discriminating types thought of themselves as the "intelligentsia," "cognoscenti," the "intelligent minority," or "civilized minority." The rest of a population which regarded them with combined uneasiness and tolerant amusement preferred the terms "highbrow" or "culture hounds." For a time a merry vogue of highbrow-versus-lowbrow jokes swept the land. By one, the highbrow was the fellow who said *eye*ther, the lowbrow, *ee*-ther. In another, the highbrow asks, "Do you know Ping-Pong?" "No," answers the lowbrow, "who wrote it?"

But whatever the term used, these more discriminating

readers were first to reach out for *Main Street,* a process duly charted in a highbrow magazine named *The Bookman:*

> ◄§ *Lewis' friends all bought the book, then the cognoscenti, then the literati, then the literate. A paltry thousand or so. Then the sleeping beast turned over, rolled its eyes and woke up. Fifty thousand. It howled in ecstacy. . . . One hundred thousand . . . Two hundred thousand . . .*

During this process, a few opposing voices were heard. Heywood Broun, who had reviewed the novel so favorably on publication, returned to it days later to confess that he had found the heroine puerile—a judgment which seems eminently valid fifty years later. Newspaper editors in the Midwest reacted with fury and editorially accused Lewis of base ingratitude toward the area which spawned him. Booth Tarkington, the highly successful creator of such diverse characters as Penrod Schofield and Monsieur Beaucaire, waxed indignant and began to plot a novel titled *Alice Adams,* supposedly an answer to the distortions of *Main Street.*

But angriest of all were residents of the tiny town of Sauk Center, Minnesota, where Harry Sinclair Lewis had been born in 1885. The good folk of this remote community believed Harry had used Sauk Center as the model for Gopher Prairie. Why, he had even underlined this fact in the book by placing the real Sauk Center only a few miles distant from his fictional Gopher Prairie. Citizens of Sauk Center thought they had always showed kindness and understanding to Harry Lewis, who was a son of the local horse-and-buggy doctor. Lewis himself saw things differently. Biographer Schorer calls him a sensitive youth among the insensitive during these days in Sauk Center. For Lewis had been a misfit in his home town, as he would be in many other localities and situations throughout life, and looked back on his growing-up years with a mixture of affection and agony.

One reason was his appearance. Boy and man, Sinclair Lewis was ugly—"*fiercely* ugly," a friend would write. His gangling, six-foot body was topped by a small, skeletal head from which grew darkish red hair—"like a new copper penny," Lewis thought. From late adolescence on, his complexion was pinker than his reddish hair, a phenomenon which never ceased to provoke unwanted comment. The pink skin, blossoming with acne in youth, was deeply pocked (rather than pitted) in later life, possibly because of clumsy x-ray treatments undertaken to cure the youthful acne. "That skin—it seemed to be laid over dirty gravel," a lady who knew him has said. To some, however, the pinkish countenance and ravaged skin were happily subordinate to lively, attractive eyes. Photographer Arnold Genthe recalled, "A pair of remarkable blue eyes, the pupils of which darted with light."

Acutely self-conscious about his looks, Sinclair Lewis was never quite so aware of the effects of his buzz-saw personality. A man of constant—if erratic—enthusiasms, his tense, tight mouth spewed forth a ceaseless torrent of opinion, description, disputation, reminiscence, and satiric observation. One companion paid tribute to him as the most stimulating rapid-fire conversationalist on earth, but others were not so charitable. Embellishing his tireless talk was a brilliant talent for mimicry. "He was gifted—or cursed—with total recall, and his performances could go on for hours," one associate commented. Lewis entirely failed to realize that others might not savor his unusual skills. People who met him were at first attracted by his pyrotechnic personality. Then, wearying of it, they slowly drifted away.

At age seventeen, Lewis wrote of himself, "I am . . . tall, ugly, red-haired, but not, methinks, especially stupid." It was an excellent self-analysis. To get away from Sauk Center and its miseries, he decided to attend a college as far removed from Minnesota as possible. His choice was Yale. Even then, Lewis was a realist who refused to be dazzled by anything. En route to New Haven in 1903, he stopped over in New York, where he was vastly unimpressed by the Towers of Ilium that so delighted other newcomers to the metropolis. Rather, he made note of the noise of trolleys, the dirt on streets, and the visible tensions of New Yorkers.

Some who have pondered the career of Sinclair Lewis feel he should have attended a Midwestern university, and there must have been moments when the Yale undergraduate nursed the same idea. He was always an outgoing chap who liked to use first names directly on meeting his fellowman. Because of his red hair and skin, kindred souls usually responded by calling him "Red," which remained his nickname through life. Yet at Yale, his looks, Middle West heartiness, and nonstop palaver made him a man to avoid on campus. During his first years, classmates gave Lewis the name of "God Forbid"—deriving from the awful possibility of being trapped in his company.

In college, as in adulthood, a vital personality and writing ability enabled him to knock down such barriers, and in time Eli undergraduates more or less accepted him. Tirelessly, he offered contributions to the *Yale Record*, the *Lit*, and the *Courant*, the last edited by William Rose Benét. At the same time the young man boldly sent short stories and verse to national magazines. He also kept a diary, and one entry showed a mind still occupied with Sauk Center: "*the village virus*—I shall have to write a book of how it getteth into the veins of a man good and true." So the idea of *Main Street* was born.

The gawky Lewis usually remained East during summer vacations, signing on cattle boats to England and earning money for his college tuition in other rugged ways. From time to time he dropped out altogether, once to work as a janitor in Upton Sinclair's utopian colony Helicon Hall, and again—for an entire year—to range the Isthmus of Panama in search of construction work on the canal. In this erratic way he completed a university career, graduating in 1908. Almost at once his dreams of a writing career were rendered possible by the miraculous sale of a short story to the popular magazine then known as *Red Book*.

With this, the young man began to travel, and in years to come, Sinclair Lewis, impoverished or flush, always seemed to be on the move—or about to move. At this early moment he journeyed to the burgeoning artists' colony in Carmel, California. Here he visited for a time with the Benét family—William Rose, of course, had been at Yale with him; Stephen Vincent was a boy of ten. Lewis wrote children's verse, mature fiction, and a book for boys on the daring new field of aviation. At the same time, he dipped into the Carmel scene, adding local lore to a mind already stuffed with Americana. Moving to San Francisco, he worked as a newspaper reporter and wrote short stories in his spare time. His restless mind produced so many plots and dramatic situations that he disposed of a few to Jack London, getting paid five to fifteen dollars apiece.

Then, as always, New York was the mecca of book publishing, and Lewis traveled there in 1910, gladly accepting a fifteen-dollar-a-week job as manuscript reader for the esteemed firm of Frederick A. Stokes and Company. Publishing in those days was a courtly profession, where for the most part publisher and editors sat with dignity awaiting the manuscripts writers brought to the reception desk or sent through the U. S. mail. Established authors were treated with courtesy, but seldom with effusiveness, and in offices great decorum prevailed. Lewis, with his loud talk, mimicry, and perpetual motion, was an incongruous figure in the Stokes office, not to say the entire publishing business. One who recalled him said no one ever made more clatter with his typewriter than Red Lewis.

Promoted to the publicity department, he got added responsibility and more money. His personality stayed the same —pleasant enough but still loud and raucous. Edna Ferber, who observed him at this time, saw "a gangling, redheaded, pop-eyed fellow . . . shambling, untidy, uproariously funny." To the English novelist, Hugh Walpole, who met him a few years later, he was, "ugly, harsh-voiced, pushing, but kindly and bursting with enthusiasm." In any group, one friend commented, Red Lewis managed to be "as noticeable as a bashful cyclone."

A self-professed agnostic and pacifist from adolescence, Lewis mingled in off hours with artistic and radical Greenwich Villagers. Yet he was essentially a loner and never really became part of this colorful group which has been designated "Improper Bohemians." One who observed him here was Frances Perkins, later Secretary of Labor in the New Deal Cabinet. "As I remember it," she wrote, "he was at that time tasting of everything that came along, but he always was an outsider." However, Lewis did use his leaping wits to coin the word "Hobohemia" for Village life. Delightedly employing the term in short stories, he finally made it the title of his first play.

"I am a persistent young youth," Lewis set down in his diary. "I keep on writing." Word of extracurricular endeavor reached the ears of his stern employer, Frederick A. Stokes, who undertook to chide his lowly employee. "You are not cut out to be a writer," he warned, "that's all there is to it." Undeterred, Lewis kept on.

In a despondent moment, Lewis had once resolved to teach himself charm, mainly to increase his appeal to the opposite sex. His efforts paid off, for he was capable of a "gawky gallantry" that some girls appreciated. The few females who took time to penetrate the brash surface of the red-headed dynamo discovered an inherent decency and gentility.

But not until an enchanted afternoon in 1912 did Lewis begin to achieve a close relationship with a woman. Then he stepped aboard an elevator in the Stokes building to find himself facing the Girl of His Dreams. She was Grace Hegger, a beauty of vaguely aristocratic background, currently working on the high-fashion magazine *Vogue*. Lewis had always been shy about meeting girls, especially lovely ones like Grace. But instead of striking him dumb, her chic attractiveness seemingly swept aside his inhibitions. "Haven't we met before?" he inquired boldly. Amused rather than insulted by this seasoned gambit, Grace smiled. So began an incongruous courtship.

Next, Lewis moved to *Adventure Magazine* as an editor. At the same time he courted Grace Hegger and found time to write *Our Mr. Wrenn*, a novel about a gentle little fellow whose horizons are broadened by unconventional travel. Grace's feelings toward her cyclonic suitor were ambivalent. His ugliness and uncouth behavior repelled her at times, yet she was ever-fascinated by his geyser of talk and skill at mimicry. Beneath her fashionable exterior lay a childishness which led her to join with Lewis in adolescent pranks and baby talk. The two delightedly invented a private language wherein, for example, adventuring became "daventuring." At other times they actually played at being kids.

Suddenly Lewis had more plus marks in his favor. He had joined a newspaper syndicate where his salary jumped to an incredible sixty dollars a week. Then the house of Harper agreed to publish *Our Mr. Wrenn*. Acceptance, however, was contingent on numerous changes in the manuscript. The job of explaining them to a thin-skinned author was given to a tactful lady editor. Lewis suffered through the long session, then turned to her and said, "Now *praise* me!"

For seven months Grace Hegger held out against a barrage of explosive proposals from her copper-headed swain. Then Lewis showed her galley proofs of his novel, pointing out that the book was dedicated to her. With this Grace decided she had fallen in love, and the two were married in April 1914.

By now the bridegroom was working for the George H. Doran Company, where his strident voice and loud typewriter again disrupted the calm of an old-line publishing firm. He and Grace had taken a house in Port Washington, Long Island, and Lewis commuted daily to his job while also writing an aviation novel, *Trail of the Hawk*. In time he wrote about this in a magazine article which bore the title "How I Wrote a Novel on Trains and Beside the Kitchen Sink."

Lewis had also made the stimulating discovery that his beauteous bride could aid his work. Not only were her editorial comments sagacious, but from her he learned of the difficulties encountered by young ladies in contemporary business. Thus equipped, he wrote *The Job*, his most ambitious novel yet. It told of an intrepid girl trying to forge ahead in a man's world.

Lewis' early novels combined romantic optimism and pungent colloquial dialogue with a dash of caustic observation. This admixture of virtues caught the eagle eye of George Horace Lorimer, potentate-editor of *The Saturday Evening*

Post, whose sizable payments colored the dreams of all who then aspired to write for a living. Lorimer approached Lewis, promising the grandest of rewards. With this, Lewis quit his job and with Grace began to travel. The young couple first visited Sauk Center, where the natives were properly impressed by the stylish sheen of the new Mrs. Lewis. Simultaneously, Lewis saw his home town through his wife's sophisticated eyes—a view which later on was of assistance as he wrote *Main Street*. Next the newlyweds invested in a Model T Ford and set out for Carmel and other distant areas. Long auto trips were rare in those days, and Lewis was able to turn his experiences along bumpy roads into stories and articles for magazines.

Wherever he went, Sinclair Lewis tracked down local writers, not so much for companionship as to pump them greedily for details of local life. In big cities he prowled docks and railroad yards, talking to workmen and jotting down details of odd jobs. Everywhere he took notes. Anna Louise Strong, who watched him operate in Seattle, wrote, "He knew he intended to be a great American novelist, depicting the life of . . . his day and age. He worked toward it always." In most localities he was greeted with pleasure by his fellow craftsmen, but here again his personality came to grate. "He is highly conscious of his own worth and is exceedingly irritated by those who are unable to appreciate his abilities," one writer concluded, after Red departed.

At times Lewis' lack of tact was monumental. On this trip he and Grace paused in Chicago where, among other things, they attended a party given for Sherwood Anderson. Beginning with *Windy McPherson's Son* in 1916, Anderson did much to bring naturalism, colloquialism, and the sex urge to the forefront of American writing. In *The Bookman*, John Farrar said his stories "gave voice to the tragedies of starved lives."

Anderson prided himself on ability as a low-key storyteller, and on this occasion was prevailed upon to spin a favorite yarn. Lewis chafed as Anderson meandered along. The moment the story ended Lewis jumped to his feet to begin one of his own virtuoso performances of mimicry. It drove the Anderson story from the minds of all present, and the author of *Winesburg, Ohio* never quite forgave Red Lewis.

Sinclair Lewis and Destiny began an ardent embrace in the year 1918. Gradually the author of short stories and mildly successful novels had concluded that true success lay in putting his best efforts into one extraordinary novel. He had also felt that the American people would be better off if some of their flaws were sharply pointed out to them. So he began to ponder *Main Street* even while engaged in writing *Free Air*, a novel about auto travel which ran as a serial in *The Saturday Evening Post*. Lewis had, of course, been gestating this small-town novel since the time of his *"village virus"* diary entry in college. Along the way he had picked *Main Street* as the title. With the potboiler *Free Air* out of the way, he sat down to begin what for him was the Big Book. Usually his agile mind ran along commercial channels, ever alert to the possibility of serial sales, play possibilities, and other money-making angles. But with *Main Street* he thought only of the work in progress.

Lewis' major novel was to be published by Harcourt, Brace and Company, a firm more or less the author's own creation. Lewis had long urged his friend Alfred Harcourt to break away from the Henry Holt publishing house to start his own firm, together with another friend, Donald Brace. Lewis promised to be their first author. When Harcourt vacillated, Lewis rushed by train to New York from Minneapolis. "Don't be such a damn fool as ever to work for someone else," he rallied his friend. "Start your own business. *I'm going to write important novels!*"

Most of *Main Street* was written in Washington, D.C., a city for which the footloose author retained a peculiar fondness. By now he and Grace, five years wed, had a son, Wells Lewis, named for H. G. Wells. Early in 1920, with a sultry summer looming, Lewis dispatched Grace and the child to balmy Virginia, while he stayed in Washington. "I am obsessed with the novel," he told a Yale classmate met on the street. "I get my own breakfast and lock myself in a stifling room on the top floor of a rooming house till nine at night to finish the damn thing."

Later he remembered "working eight hours a day, seven days most weeks, though a normal number of hours of creative writing is supposed to be about four. I never worked so hard, and never shall work so hard again."

In mid-July 1920, the 175,000-word manuscript was delivered to the publisher. Alfred Harcourt was immediately impressed and ventured the calculated guess that *Main Street* might sell twenty thousand copies. The firm's experienced sales manager opted for twenty-five thousand. Lewis himself anticipated a sale of ten thousand.

Seldom in history have author, publisher, and sales executive been so thoroughly wrong.

Fiddles Tune Up .. *Dreiser* . . .

Mencken and Nathan . . Others . . . .

⊛⊐⊛⊐⊛⊐⊛⊐⊛⊐⊛⊐⊛⊐⊛⊐⊛⊐⊛⊐⊛

In the twenty years before the turn of the century, American literature for the most part had been swathed in a figurative blanket called by critics the Genteel Tradition.

What was this? Novelist Joseph Hergesheimer, whose first novel came out in 1913, described it by saying: "Our most widely circulated fiction very accurately carries our national defects—an easy sentimentality, pretentiousness, an avoidance of meeting truth squarely, and an almost complete confusion of prudery and purity."

An anecdote from the life of Edith Wharton, who was born into the Rhinelander Jones family of New York aristocracy, better illuminates the Genteel Tradition. At the age of eleven, precocious Edith—then called "Pussy" Jones—wrote a short story which contained the line of dialogue: "If only I had known you were going to call, I should have tidied up the drawing room." The proud moppet showed the story to her mother, who quickly reproved her by saying, "Drawing rooms are *always* tidy."

Tidy was, indeed, the word for the Genteel Tradition. Drawing rooms also fit neatly into the pattern, for, in the words of social historian Lloyd Morris, "American readers of the day preferred life as displayed in the parlor." Romance, sentiment, and polite behavior were enshrined, with heroes brave, heroines pure, villains despicable. Anything realistic, which indicated life might be a grim struggle, was conveniently swept under the literary rug. Bodily contact between the sexes was restricted to fleeting kisses and chaste embraces. Novelists like Herbert Quick, who put an illegitimate child in *Vandemark's Folly*, or Homer Croy, who had a seduction scene in *West of the Water Tower*, risked infamy rather than fame.

By following this cautious Victorianism, novelists like America's Winston Churchill, John Fox, Jr., Paul Leicester Ford, Booth Tarkington, Gene Stratton Porter, Harry Leon Wilson, Rupert Hughes, Owen Johnson, and Robert W. Chambers grew rich and famous by writing romantic historical novels or polite fiction about the modern world.

Faced with this routine fare, discriminating readers were driven to solid English creators like Thomas Hardy, Joseph Conrad, Arnold Bennett, John Galsworthy, H. G. Wells, Compton MacKenzie, and Hugh Walpole. Three big sellers of the era—Conrad's *Arrow of Gold*, Somerset Maugham's *The Moon and Sixpence*, and Blasco Ibáñez' *The Four Horsemen of the Apocalypse*—highlight this foreign orientation.

Still, there did exist a group of American authors trying to probe the soft underbelly of contemporary life. Their number included Theodore Dreiser, Jack London, David Graham Phillips, Frank Norris, Zona Gale, and Sherwood Anderson. Of them Lloyd Morris says, "They had tried to do something for the people's sake, to bring them a little more understanding, a little more wisdom and hope and courage. All of them had a conviction of failure."

By far the greatest here was Theodore Dreiser, that pachyderm of a man who over twenty years had written novels which tried to reproduce the true conditions of living —what the author called "the unsolvable disorder and brutality of life." Back in 1900—when best-selling novels were *Janice Meredith*, *When Knighthood Was in Flower*, *Graustark*, and *Mrs. Wiggs of the Cabbage Patch*—Dreiser's first novel, *Sister Carrie*, had been accepted for publication by Frank Norris and other editors of Doubleday, Page and Company. They did so while publisher Doubleday and his wife were abroad. When the travelers returned to read the galleys, Mrs. Doubleday was outraged by Dreiser's almost photographic realism, her husband horrified. Prodded by his wife, Doubleday tried to squirm out of publishing the book. But the twenty-nine-year-old Dreiser, who had a nonbreakable contract, forced him to proceed. This may have been a mistake. In the words of W. A. Swanberg, Dreiser's chief biographer, "*Sister Carrie*, a literary waif that needed careful nursing, was brought into the world by a publisher who detested the book and its author."

Most reviews of *Sister Carrie* followed the Doubleday line of damning the novel on moral grounds. There was also something inflammatory about the author himself, and critics who branded *Sister Carrie* immoral usually placed Dreiser personally in the same category. One particular enemy—a lady—castigated him as "the tomcat of literature." Not only did bookstores refuse to handle *Sister Carrie*, but friends of the author cut him dead on the street or refused to let him inside their homes.

From then on, the craft of authorship brought Dreiser enough heartbreak to shatter a less monolithic man. In time, fellow craftsmen like John Dos Passos would salute "the ponderous battering ram of his novels [which] opened the way through the genteel reticences of America fiction." But for the moment, few gave Dreiser credit for anything. Between 1900 and 1920 he published the novels *Sister Carrie*, *Jennie Gerhardt*, *The Financier*, *The Titan*, and *The "Genius."* Each was greeted with sound and fury from would-be moral elements. A critic in the New York *Herald* flatly stated that anyone who wrote such filthy trash should be shot. *The New York Times*, covering the death of Emile Zola, dealt Dreiser a gratuitous by-blow, saying Zola "died in his own vomit [and] it would be well for an American writer named Dreiser, a disciple of Zola, to take note."

Yet the Dreiser novels, so widely accused of immorality, were never aphrodisiac in the sense of an eroticism which aroused to lustful thought or deed. Rather, the author's offense lay in freely mentioning married men with mistresses, girls who enjoyed the sex act, males in promiscuous pursuit of women, whorehouses, and other aspects of life which the post-Victorians considered taboo.

Further ammunition against Dreiser came from a clumsy, groping style which was often as elephantine as the author himself. Of it one critic wrote, "He came into this world with an incurable antipathy for the *mot juste*." His detractors asked how a writer who produced such turgid prose could possibly be considered a major author. Dreiser, who stood steadfast before the world as a man certain of his own greatness, was inwardly ashamed of his murky prose and envious of others with stylistic grace. He showed this (and revealed his own feelings about the literature of the Genteel Tradition) in a comment about Booth Tarkington: "He does not know reality, does not know life, work, the average human being, or sex. If he . . . dealt only with the raw realities, what a marvel he would be with his exquisite style!"

The "Genius"—350,000 words at $1.50 a copy—had been published in 1915 and immediately branded "an orgy of lust" by one paranoid critic. A Montreal editorialist opined that only a man who had himself plumbed the depths of depravity could write such a book. Paul Elmer More, a highly respected essayist, saw Dreiser's writing as "the mongrel sort to be expected from a miscegenation of the gutter and the psychological laboratory." Stuart P. Sherman, a vibrant professor at the University of Illinois, was permitted the pages of the liberal *Nation* to call Dreiser and his work "barbaric."

In New York John S. Sumner, successor to Anthony Comstock as head of the vigilant Society for the Suppression of Vice, threatened to arrest any bookseller who dared vend a copy of *The "Genius."* Cowed, the publisher withdrew the novel, allowing it to remain in a peculiar limbo, neither banned nor up for sale.

Thus it seemed, as the second decade of the century drew to a lingering close, that Dreiser's army of detractors had at last brought the titan to bay. The monumental man had not published a novel since *The "Genius"* and was existing like a wounded lion in the depths of Greenwich Village.

In the first dozen years of the century, culture hounds had to be content with the heavy fare provided by Dreiser and the few others who in individual ways wrote of American life as seen through their own honest eyes. In this group were three ladies who in their fashion wrote realistic fiction. They were Edith Wharton, who had turned author as therapy when her Boston Brahmin husband lost his mind, then produced books exposing the shams of New York society as well as the authentic New England masterpiece *Ethan Frome*; Ellen Glasgow, who used irony rather than sentiment to delineate her native South, and Willa Cather who, after an amazing career as girl reporter and lady magazine editor, wrote books which dealt fondly with the past and conveyed deep disillusionment with the present. . . .

Then, all at once, American literature began erupting to a degree that all but turned the true culture hound into a member of the avant garde. The shock waves came initially from poetry, where Edwin Arlington Robinson had been a lonely pioneer. In 1912, Edna St. Vincent Millay's poem "Renascence," part of an anthology called *The Lyric Year*, burst on the public consciousness. "It startled our ravished ears," enthused artist Lee Simonson. A year later, Vachel Lindsay emerged with his resounding "General William Booth Enters into Heaven," the author prepared to chant his work publicly whenever asked, preferably against a musical background of "kettledrums, piccolo, flute, and birchbark moosecall."

In 1915, Carl Sandburg's *Chicago Poems* appeared, with a reviewer exulting, "He breathes Chicago, he *is* Chicago." Sandburg informed the world he depended on "language, lingo, slang," and in New England, Robert Frost did the same by utilizing Yankee vernacular for his *North of Boston.* Edgar Lee Masters with his verse *Spoon River Anthology* antedated both *Winesburg, Ohio* and *Main Street.* Meanwhile from postwar Europe sounded the exciting notes of the American expatriates Gertrude Stein, Ezra Pound, and T. S. Eliot.

Best-selling fiction of this era might encompass *Seventeen* by Booth Tarkington, *V. V.'s Eyes* by Henry Sydnor Harrison, and *Pollyanna* by Eleanor Porter. Nonfiction included *The Education of Henry Adams,* Theodore Roosevelt's *Letters to His Children,* and *White Shadows in the South Seas* by Frederick O'Brien. But the culture hound dined on richer fare. Writings by Freud, Jung, and Havelock Ellis were beginning to reveal the mainsprings of human behavior. Sections of James Joyce's *Ulysses,* running in Margaret Anderson's *Little Review,* had a thunderbolt effect on young writers like Djuna Barnes who exclaimed, "I shall never write another line— who has the nerve to after this!"

Sprightly old Jack Yeats, transplanted Irishman and father of William Butler Yeats, stated it this way: "The fiddles are tuning up as it were all over America." He referred specifically to poetry, but his buoyant words applied to the full literary spectrum.

Only a few years before, the simple indication of a highbrow was that he or she preferred the novels of Dreiser to the slick formula fiction in the glossy pages of *The Saturday Evening Post, Delineator, Pictorial Review, Red Book,* and *Ladies' Home Journal.* Now the status of culture hound required a knowledge of, it not familiarity with, such names as Sigmund Freud, Ezra Pound, Bertrand Russell, Marcel Proust, D. H. Lawrence, Oswald Spengler, Edna Millay, John Dewey, Isadora Duncan, and Carl Sandburg. Latest additions to the list were Eugene O'Neill and Sherwood Anderson.

It all produced a feeling of heady excitement, causing e. e. cummings, a young man determined to experiment with poetry of lower-case letters and extravagant punctuation, to write to his sister, "When I see you next, I shall expect you to be conversant with two books: The Interpretation of Dreams and WIT and the Unconscious. Both are by Freud.—!! GET WISE TO YOURSELF!!—"

Catering especially to the appetites of culture hounds were a gaggle of magazines and a few book supplements of metropolitan newspapers.

Among the magazines were *Harper's, Scribner's, The Atlantic,* and *The Century,* each of which pursued a time-honored tradition of satisfying fiction and informative, if lofty, fact—a policy which in each case attempted to grow livelier as the decade progressed. *The Bookman,* recently invigorated by the appointment of John Farrar as editor, carried literary gossip and bright, unsigned pen portraits of newly arrived talents. *The Dial* and *The Freeman* were literary magazines (*The Dial* carried the poems of Ezra Pound) whose influence ebbed and flowed with various editorial regimes. *The Nation* and *New Republic* carried excellent book-review departments, though main emphasis was on the political scene. *The New Masses,* stemming from the Village-oriented *Masses* suppressed during World War I, enjoyed a brief flowering. *The Little Review,* founded in Chicago, moved to New York and gained immortality by printing the first excerpts from *Ulysses,* for which it was haled into court.

The most sophisticated of current periodicals was *Vanity Fair,* published by Condé Nast and impeccably edited by Frank Crowninshield, a much respected bachelor about town who once said, "Married men make poor husbands." One friend called him "a delicious man."

Under Crowninshield, *Vanity Fair* was commendably quick at printing the works of new writers, American and English. Among them already were Dorothy Parker, Robert E. Sherwood, Robert Benchley, Gertrude Stein, Michael Arlen, Anita Loos, P. G. Wodehouse, Edna St. Vincent Millay, Edmund Wilson, Aldous Huxley, and Noel Coward. Yet *Vanity Fair* was never a magazine to stir the blood. At best, its high-quality pages might agitate a few brain cells with examples of urbane cleverness. (One was the stunt of having well known writers pick the Ten Dullest Books.) Yet as a literary catalyst *Vanity Fair* best played a part by calling attention to upcoming authors—usually in its Hall of Fame—by portraits and witty captions.

A magazine that did agitate the blood and arouse the imagination was *Smart Set*. Edited by Henry L. Mencken and George Jean Nathan, this monthly was at times subtitled the Magazine of Cleverness, at others the Aristocrat Among Magazines.

Mencken, forty years old in 1920, a newspaper reporter from the age of nineteen when his father's death ended his formal schooling, was a solid fellow with a square Teutonic face ("You kept looking for dueling scars," said a friend) lighted by twinkling blue eyes. "Picture a butcher's boy with apple cheeks, who parts his hair in the middle and you have a fair idea of the facial aspect of Heinie Mencken," a contemporary wrote. He dressed unobtrusively and spent as much time as possible in his native Baltimore, making no more than two quick trips to the *Smart Set* office in Manhattan during a month. "Trying to be a philosopher in New York," he once explained, "is like trying to sing in a boiler factory."

George Jean Nathan, Indiana-born, two years younger, was the beau ideal of the contemporary man-about-Manhattan. A highly respected and much-imitated drama critic, Nathan was as suave and good-looking as any of the theatrical leading men whose performances he so shrewdly evaluated. He puffed cigarettes through an ivory holder and dressed impeccably with the aid of a handsome wardrobe which Mencken described as "seventy-five winter overcoats, twenty-five spring coats, six hundred suits, a thousand neckties, and eleven jock straps for both fast days and feast days." In his writing Nathan was partial to smooth epigrams like "An actress has to be something more than a woman, an actor something less than a man."

It is a mistake to assume that the influence of Mencken and Nathan began with *The American Mercury,* which did not commence publication until 1924. They were a force long before. The pair had met for the first time on an afternoon in May 1908, toasting an immediate rapport in a forgotten concoction known as the Tavern cocktail. Interesting is the fact that the cocktails were doubles. Mencken lived and breathed books and writing, Nathan's world was theater. Together they formed an immensely formidable editor-writer-critic team. Both existed to smash idols—Mencken with words that struck like fists, Nathan with phrases as elegant as his silver-headed evening cane. "Criticism and progress, to be effective, must be iconoclastic and pugnacious," wrote Mencken. It was the credo of both.

In 1914, Mencken and Nathan grasped the helm of *Smart Set*, and promptly began to shake, rattle, and rock the cultural cosmos. During America's actual involvement in World War I, the Magazine of Cleverness operated under a cloud because of Mencken's stubborn partiality for things Germanic. But with the Armistice, it bounded back in full, rambunctious glory. In days before *The American Mercury* and *The New Yorker*, the only magazine for a sophisticated young writer to aim at was *Smart Set*. One such discovery was S. N. Behrman, who dubbed Mencken and Nathan "Their Majesties, whose personalities enhaloed the magazine."

In *Smart Set* years, these two editors bought the first works of Eugene O'Neill, F. Scott Fitzgerald, and Dashiell Hammett. Others who found an early haven in *Smart Set* were Dorothy Parker, Damon Runyon, Carl Van Vechten, Thyra Samter Winslow, and Edna St. Vincent Millay. Along with them appeared older writers like Dreiser, James Branch Cabell, D. H. Lawrence, and James Joyce.

In his *Smart Set* writings—most of them quickly reprinted in his books titled *Prejudices*—Mencken used words like "pap," "slobber," "hocus-pocus," "softies," "popinjay," "flapdoodle," "flubdub," "poppycock," "balderdash," "pishposh," and "sissy." He praised Dreiser, extolled James Branch Cabell and Joseph Hergesheimer, fought Prohibition, ridiculed the Middle West and the Bible Belt South, mocked religion and its evangelist practitioners like onetime ballplayer Billy Sunday. Not only did Mencken find flaws in the American scene, but he recognized the barren minds responsible. He wrote scathingly of "boobus Americanus," "the booboisie," and "homo boobiens," while lamenting an age of "oafish faiths, of imbecile enthusiasms . . . of incredible absurdities." One of his favorite phrases was "the bilge of idealism." Of Clarence Darrow, he once wrote, "He likes to make men leap." He should have said it about himself.

Any Mencken sentence was likely to be an invigorating succession of unlikely words. A man he disliked was "a noble swine"; romantic fiction "moony mush." Once he called Nathan "a horse's asterisk." Writing his own books, he vowed, made him "suffer like an elephant dancing the mazurka." Mencken's paragraphs were bound to contain two surprises: first, what he said, second, the way he said it. His wit was Brobdingnagian and often Rabelaisian. Perhaps his finest tribute came from an anonymous fellow who said, "You'll never fall asleep reading Mencken." It is also likely that his prose stands forth as the most thoroughly masculine ever produced by an American, not excluding that of Jack London or Ernest Hemingway.

If Mencken was a gourmand of life, Nathan was a gourmet —or epicure. Mencken viewed his elegant sidekick as "the *Smart Set* Scaramouche, the ribald fellow, the raffish mocker . . . his naughty enthusiasm for pretty legs." Then he went on to praise:

> ᵉᵍ *His refusal to take imbecilities seriously, his easy casualness and avoidance of pedagogics, his frank delight in the theatre as a show shop—above all, his bellicose iconoclasm and devastating wit.*

Aspiring male writers—what female could hope to write like these two?—had difficulty deciding which of these talents to emulate. Should he follow the robust, irreverent Mencken, whose words exploded in the mind like bombs, or would it be better to be the urbane Nathan, whose prose was more elegant but no less shattering? Of a fellow drama critic who depended on his emotions more than his intellect, Nathan wrote:

⊸§His style is either a gravy bomb, a bursting gladiolus, a palpitating missa vanata, *an attack of psychic hypochondria, or a Roman denunciation [caused by] a too high blood pressure perhaps, an unfortunate chronic costiveness: something of the sort.*

Mencken and Nathan had a vastly stimulating effect on the literate folk of the land, driving provincialism from the atmosphere and drawing belated attention to domestic culture. Yet the impact of the pair on the Manhattan literary scene was equally great. For these two men obviously loved the business of living, and their ebullient buffoonery removed much of the stuffiness from the publishing sphere. Mencken was one of the topmost practical jokers of all time. Usually he conceived the japes with Nathan a delighted co-conspirator. But sometimes the latter was the one kissed by inspiration. For their efforts as jokesters, the two were dubbed the Katzenjammer Kids of Literature.

The busy Mencken managed to devote several hours a day to japery. He began gag letters to friends with salutations like "Dear Wolfgang," "Dear Rupert," "Dear Llewelyn," or "Dear Gottfried," and ended, "Yours in Christ," "Yours in the One True Faith," or "In His Blessed Name." The final fillip came as he scrawled the signature "Heinrich" across the page.

At other times he stuffed envelopes with religious tracts, cures for venereal disease, or the gelatinous poems of Edgar A. Guest. These he sent to sobersided pals like Theodore Dreiser. Once Mencken returned from lunch clutching a pamphlet of the Tobacco-Chewer's Protective and Educational League of America. His pleasure in this rose to the heights as the text revealed that Henrik Ibsen had chewed tobacco!

Around Mencken and Nathan, sun and moon of the literary heavens, clustered a galaxy of subordinate newspaper and magazine talents. It was a time—who can visualize it today?—when most large newspapers across the country featured amusing, mellow, and sometimes erudite daily columns. In New York, the peerless Don Marquis, parent of archy and mehitabel, conducted "The Sun Dial" in the *Evening Sun;* F.P.A. presided over "The Conning Tower" on the *Tribune,* where sterling light verse alternated with pithy, witty comments and occasional civic crusades; Christopher Morley had just undertaken "The Bowling Green" in the *Post;* H. I. Phillips contributed daily humor to the *Globe;* man-about-town Karl K. Kitchen transcribed his daily activities in the *Evening World.* Kitchen was locally famous as the first American to be granted a passport to Europe after World War I. Told to write down the purpose of his projected trip, he wrote, "Pleasure—if possible!"

All at once the author of a new book might anticipate an intelligent, understanding review from Mencken in *Smart Set,* Robert Benchley in the *World,* Heywood Broun or Ben Ray Redman in the *Tribune,* William Rose Benét, Henry Seidel Canby or Christopher Morley in the *Post,* Francis Hackett, Ernest Boyd, or Walter Lippmann in the *New Republic,* Van Wyck Brooks, Mary Colum, C. Hartley Grattan, or John Farrar in *The Bookman,* William Lyon Phelps in *Scribner's,* Edmund Wilson, Lewis Mumford, Gilbert Seldes, or Llewelyn Powys in *The Dial,* Floyd Dell in *The Liberator,* Ludwig Lewisohn, Carl Van Doren, and his wife Irita in *The Nation.*

Publishing was also involved in the revolution after World War I. Old-line houses like Harper, Doubleday, Appleton, Stokes, Century, Holt, Putnam, Dutton, and Dodd Mead had profitably dominated the field for years, but now newcomers like Alfred A. Knopf, Ben Huebsch (who had published Joyce's *Portrait of the Artist as a Young Man* in 1916), Alfred Harcourt, Albert and Charles Boni, and Horace Liveright rose as challengers. Like Mencken, they were more anxious to publish native talents than British novelists or practitioners of America's own Genteel Tradition. One night excitable Red Lewis, drinking a little more than necessary, lifted his glass to cry. "I toast the day when Harcourt, Boni, Knopf, and Huebsch will dominate the publishing world."

Of these publishers, Alfred Knopf—only twenty-seven years old in 1920—was by far the most remarkable. This young man loved the appearance of books as much—if not more—than the contents. As a result, his Borzoi line became the best-looking books on the American market, featuring striking dust jackets and covers, individual type faces, and top-quality paper. Out in St. Paul, Minnesota, a young F. Scott Fitzgerald, his first novel just accepted by Scribner's, fondled a Borzoi book and thought, "I grow envious every time I see a Knopf binding." Knopf's excellence forced other publishers to emulate him, and in so doing he improved the appearance of all American books.

Horace Liveright, tall, intense, handsome, with a Barrymore profile, was living proof that book publishing offered excitement. A plunger-gambler by nature, Liveright had quit Wall Street at age forty to join Albert and Charles Boni in the firm Boni and Liveright. If the rewards of publishing appealed to this man's blood, he still respected books and authors. His greatest admiration was accorded Theodore Dreiser, the stricken giant of Greenwich Village. Though Dreiser had not written a novel for years, Liveright had faith in him. He became Dreiser's publisher, and his intuitions advised him to be patient.

With publishers came receptive new editors. Maxwell Perkins joined the encrusted firm of Scribner's and began the process of becoming a legend in his time. Eugene Saxton at Doran, T. R. Smith at Boni and Liveright, Robert Linscott at Houghton Mifflin, Guy Holt at Robert M. McBride—these were only a few of the young editors prepared to preside over a dawning era.

Nor was New York the only exciting literary locale. Chicago, which Mencken considered America's most civilized metropolis, was also in happy ferment. The Windy City boasted the Kroch Bookstore, where the volumes of Zane Grey, Harold Bell Wright, and other Western authors were not allowed to sully the shelves. The literary sections of the Chicago *Tribune* and *Daily News* were, if anything, livelier than their Manhattan counterparts.

Among the talents writing, criticizing, or arguing literature in Chicago were (or until recently had been) Carl Sandburg, Floyd Dell, Ben Hecht, Maxwell Bodenheim, Harry Hansen, Burton Rascoe, Janet Flanner, Will Cuppy, Marquis James, Lloyd Lewis, Percy Hammond, Charles MacArthur, Edgar Lee Masters, George T. Bye, Henry Blackman Sell, J. P. McEvoy, Lewis Galantière, John V. A. Weaver, Sherwood Anderson, and Gene Markey.

Even more than New York, this Midwestern cultural center displayed what Robert Browning once called "the faculty of wonder"—the very ingredient that would make the book world of the Twenties unique. In vital Chicago, bookish sensations seemed to explode like strings of giant firecrackers. Burton Rascoe, the wiry, euphoric editor of the *Tribune's* book pages, found on his desk one morning an advance copy of *This Side of Paradise*, an unheralded novel by an unknown Scott Fitzgerald. Dipping into it, Rascoe remained enthralled far beyond his lunch hour. "Here was something fresh, vital, sparkling new," he recalled later. "Here was a *discovery!*"

At last Rascoe set out for lunch. En route he encountered John V. A. Weaver, a rival book reviewer whose "In American" vernacular verses had been hailed by *Smart Set*. Weaver, too, had just put down *This Side of Paradise*. "Have I read a book," he yelled at Rascoe. "Wow! Boy! HAVE I READ A BOOK!"

But with only a few exceptions (Carl Sandburg, for one) these Chicago literary talents dreamed of shining amidst the brighter lights of Manhattan. "I know I really belong in New York," Rascoe told himself at a moment of peak accomplishment and personal happiness in Chicago. Ben Hecht, Chicago's wonder-boy reporter and author of the about-to-be-published *Erik Dorn*, was preparing to abandon the city for the more exciting East. Floyd Dell, author of *Moon-Calf*, had long preceded him, to become one of the colorful figures in Greenwich Village.

Such was the literary scene in America as *Main Street* stood poised for publication on October 20, 1920.

Up to this moment in history, Sinclair Lewis had been somewhat suspect to the intelligentsia of the land. Not only had he written romantic novels and popular short stories for slick magazines, but he had also named his son after H. G. Wells.

Yet his name was a familiar one in the literary business, and thus it seems surprising that in 1920 Mencken and Nathan appeared unaware of him. This is especially strange since Lewis had contributed the short story, "I'm a Stranger Here Myself," to *Smart Set*, while Nathan had reviewed the Lewis play *Hobohemia*, which ran for eleven weeks at the Greenwich Village Theatre. The imperturbable critic had damned it in somewhat mystifying terms as "exquisitely—if I may be permitted so critically indelicate a word—epizoötic." ("Epizootic" is a term used of animal diseases.)

Nevertheless, the Katzenjammer Kids of Literature were totally unprepared the night they were invited to meet the author of the forthcoming *Main Street* at the home of T. R. Smith, top editor of Boni and Liveright. Prohibition had gone into effect a short time before, and Smith had prepared for a doleful future by removing the books from his shelves and jamming the space with bottles of liquor.

In these surroundings, Mencken and Nathan were introduced to Sinclair Lewis. As Nathan recalled the meeting, he barely had time to register "a tall, skinny, paprika-haired figure," before Lewis coiled one arm around his neck and the other around Mencken's. Then the author began to bellow:

 So you guy's are critics, are you? Well, let me tell you something. I'm the best writer in this here gottdamn country and if you, Georgie, and you, Hank, don't know it now, you'll know it gottdamn soon. Say, I've just fin-

ished a book that'll be published in a week or two and it's the gottdamn best book of its kind that this here gott-damn country has had and don't you guys forget it! I worked a year on the gottdamn thing and it's the goods, I'm a-telling you! Listen, when it comes to writing a novel, I'm so far ahead of most of the men you two think are good that I'll be gottdamned if it doesn't make me sick to think of it! Just wait till you read the gottdamn thing. You've got a treat coming, Georgie and Hank, and don't you boys make no mistake about that!

Lewis' brash performance may have been what a later generation called a put-on. But who could be sure? Hank and Georgie got away as fast as possible, leaving Lewis behind. On the safety of the sidewalk, Mencken erupted, "Of all the idiots I've ever laid eyes on, that fellow is the worst." Nathan, his sensibilities still in shock, only mumbled, "Numbskull."

Even in those distant days, authors were not supposed to praise their own work loudly, especially in the hearing of book critics. When Alfred Harcourt learned of this episode, he lectured his favorite author severely. But *Main Street* had too much to be downed by anyone. A few days later, Nathan received a note from Mencken in Baltimore. It read:

ᴥᔤ DEAR GEORGE: *Grab hold of the bar-rail, steady yourself, and prepare yourself for a terrible shock! I've just read the book of that* Lump *we met at Schmidt's and, by God, he has done the job! It's a genuinely excellent piece of work. Get it as soon as you can and take a look. I begin to believe that perhaps there isn't a God after all. There is no justice in the world. Yours in Xt.,* M.

The Younger Generation

Main Street . . This Side of Paradise . . The Sheik

*M*ain Street may have been the literary blockbuster of its time, but read today it seems almost as dated as the Genteel Tradition fiction it did so much to displace.

For one thing, it is almost impossible to imagine an era when a doctor, even in a small town, had difficulty making a living. Nor in our time of fast travel is it easy to conceive of a young woman in St. Paul marrying a fellow in not-so-distant Gopher Prairie without first visiting his hometown to meet his friends.

Yet the crux of *Main Street* lies in the impact of Gopher Prairie, Minnesota (population three thousand), on Carol Kennicott, who arrives there as a bride. Carol is twenty-four, mildly pretty, and well brought up. Thanks to a New England father, she had been more alert and broad-minded than her classmates at Blodgett College, "a bulwark of sound religion." After graduation she spent a year at library school in Chicago, then returned to work in the St. Paul Public Library.

Carol meets Dr. Will Kennicott, Gopher Prairie physician and surgeon, at a party. To make conversation she inquires about his hometown, and he tells her Gopher Prairie is "a good hustling burg." She asks if life there is "nice," at which Dr. Will grows eloquent:

&§ *"Nice? Say honestly—. Of course, I may be prejudiced, but I've seen an awful lot of towns—one time I went to Atlantic City for the American Medical Society meeting, and I spent practically a week in New York. But I never saw a town that had such up and coming people as Gopher Prairie. . . . And it's a darn pretty town. Lots of fine maples and box elders, and there's two of the dandiest lakes you ever saw, right near town. And we've got seven miles of sidewalks already, and building more every day."*

Yet to Carol, arriving there a year later as Mrs. Kennicott, Gopher Prairie seems barren, small, and ugly, as had the other "burgs" where the train stopped on the way from St. Paul. Waiting to welcome her at an unimposing depot are Dr. Will's friends, the same folk he considers so up-and-coming. One of them steps forward to speak for all:

&§ *"Welcome, little lady! The keys of the city are yourn! I'm Sam Clark, dealer in hardware, sporting goods, cream separators, and almost any kind of heavy junk you can think of. You can call me Sam—anyway, I'm going to call you Carrie, seein' 's you've been and gone and married this poor fish of a bum medic that we keep round here. . . . The fat cranky lady back there beside you, who is pretending that she can't hear me giving her away, is Mrs. Sam'l Clark; and this hungry looking squirt up here beside me is Dave Dyer, who keeps his drug store running by not filling your hubby's prescriptions right—fact you might say he's the guy that put the 'shun' in 'prescription.' So! Well, leave us take the bonny bride home. Say, doc, I'll sell you the Candersen place for three thousand plunks. Better be thinking about building a new home for Carrie. Prettiest Frau in G. P., if you asks me!"*

That night, at a party in their honor, Dr. Will gives his bride word pictures of others in their set:

&§ *"Well, the nice-looking couple over there are Harry Haydock and his wife, Juanita. Harry's dad owns most of the Bon Ton, but it's Harry who runs it and gives it the pep. He's a hustler. Next to him is Dave Dyer the druggist*

—you met him this afternoon—mighty good duck-shot. The tall husk beyond him is Jack Elder—Jackson Elder— owns the planing-mill, and the Minniemashie House, and quite a share in the Farmers' National Bank. Him and his wife are good sports—him and Sam and I go hunting together a lot. The old cheese there is Luke Dawson, the richest man in town. Next to him is Nat Hicks, the tailor."

It takes Carol little time to discover that Dr. Will's friends are older folk, and that Gopher Prairie lacks a true social set—the working merchants of Main Street and their wives form the elite of the town. She considers the men loud and uncouth, the women smug and dowdy, both sexes as soulless as the town itself. Citizens of Gopher Prairie are also a pure lot, if total disinterest in the subject of sex on the author's part can be deemed purity. Avoidance of this sordid subject was, of course, a plus for *Main Street* in the eyes of most readers of the time. But Lewis does not even hint at the ecstacies or agonies of Carol's nuptial night.

A librarian herself, young Mrs. Kennicott had expected to find Gopher Prairie's librarian a particularly compatible soul. But after Carol expatiates on the joys of seeing children read, this worthy female snaps, "You feel so? My feeling is that the first duty of a conscientious librarian is to preserve the books." When Carol asks the richest man in town for financial aid toward a plan to create a more attractive locality, he gives this answer:

> *"Why now, child, you've got a lot of notions. Besides, what's the matter with the town? Looks good to me. I've had people that have traveled all over the world tell me time and again that Gopher Prairie is the prettiest place in the Middlewest. . . ."*

Against this wall of smug satisfaction, Carol Kennicott beats like an eager moth. Inevitably, she manages to antagonize nearly everyone in town. The local furniture dealer, a big wheel, is offended when she goes to Minneapolis to buy her bridal parlor and dining-room sets. No one, not even Dr. Will, likes the broad sofa and other modern pieces she brings home.

In truth, Carol gets little aid from her husband, who also believes she should buy her furniture in Gopher Prairie. "I make my money here, and they naturally expect me to spend it here," he explains. When she speaks of waking up the townsfolk, he asks, "Wake 'em up? What for? They're happy!"

Eventually Dr. Will sells a parcel of land, providing the couple with enough money to have a child. For a while, a son takes Carol's mind off the torments of local life. Then a girl schoolteacher appears in town, to be accorded the same suspicious, hostile treatment Carol received at first. It is too much for Carol, who flees with her child to postwar Washington, where she gets a job in the Bureau of War Risk. Life in the nation's capital interests her, but she is still dissatisfied— Sinclair Lewis, aware of it or not, has devoted a multitude of words to etching a shallow woman.

Slowly Carol realizes that, with all its multifarious faults, Gopher Prairie at least offers roots to herself and little Hugh. After two years of freedom she decides to return—*she* is different now, perhaps the town has changed. "I'll take back the sound of Yvette Guilbert's songs and Elman's violin," she tells herself. "They'll be the lovelier against the thrumming of crickets and the stubble on an autumn day. I can laugh now and be serene. . . ."

As she travels homeward, her mind bubbles with fresh ideas for improving her Minnesota town. In line with postwar "cynicism," Carol is not much changed. Neither, she will discover, is Gopher Prairie.

The main thrust of the Lewis novel seemed to be that Carol was a woman with a brain but no incentive to use it in "that bewildered empire called the American Middlewest." Yet she was also a strangely weak character, little more than a mild-spirited idealist, empty of the guile, resourcefulness, intuition, or devious skill at intrigue that might have helped attain her ends. It was this which brought complaint from Heywood Broun in his second review of the book, and caused a later critic to say, "Carol's idealism is at least as superficial and worthless as the faults of Gopher Prairie."

Dr. Will Kennicott is hardly better. He seems to have none of the inquiring spirit desirable in a physician, nor had a college education plus medical school brought him perceptible culture or refinement. He is no more than a nice, well-intentioned guy.

With these flaws, *Main Street* resembles a Hollywood epic with the leading roles portrayed by rank amateurs, while subordinate parts are in the hands of professionals of rich experience. Throughout the book Lewis devoted his best efforts to delineating the townsfolk who revolve around the Kennicotts instead of the couple themselves, and it was the sharpness and ruthlessness of these secondary characterizations that turned the Genteel Tradition into a corpse. Lewis showed no mercy whatsoever to Gopher Prairie folk pleased with material possessions rather than those of mind and spirit—citizens who dealt in *things,* not ideas.

Such was *Main Street,* a novel for which it almost became necessary to coin fresh English-language adjectives. By January 1, 1921, it was the top-selling novel in the United States, and by maintaining this eminence throughout the year it became the first American book of its calibre to sell 400,000 copies. Meantime, critical praise rolled in, the consensus being that *Main Street* had brought the nation a new conception of itself. The author himself assumed a position as successor to William Dean Howells as America's most respected author of realistic fiction.

Main Street was also phenomenal in the way it hauled other books aboard the bandwagon. Because they were mentioned in reviews of *Main Street,* Sherwood Anderson's *Winesburg, Ohio,* Floyd Dell's *Moon-Calf,* Zona Gale's *Miss Lulu Bett,* and Dorothy Canfield Fisher's *Brimming Cup* received unusual attention and enjoyed unusually large sales.

On other levels, *Main Street* proved to be the catalyst which united the tastes of highbrows, mediumbrows, and some lowbrows, at least during the period of its sensational success. In so doing, it focused the gratifying attention of the nation on the universe of books. The novel also altered the popular conception of authors, for in red-headed Sinclair Lewis the Great American Public perceived a writer willing to be one of them. Here at last was a teeming talent ready to be crusader, critic, and commentator. Theodore Dreiser had tried the same thing and failed. Lewis not only came along with the right book at the right moment, but cleverly coated his pungent social dosage with amusing mimicry and broad satire.

Only one thing marred *Main Street*'s overall impact: it failed to win the Pulitzer Prize. On the 1920–21 selection committee were Hamlin Garland and other writers associated with the Genteel Tradition. Nonetheless, they voted *Main Street* the outstanding work of the year. With this, the trustees of Columbia lumbered forward to abrogate the award and bestow it on Edith Wharton's *Age of Innocence,* a novel about the 1870's. Five years later, Lewis evened things by refusing a Pulitzer Prize for *Arrowsmith,* but for the moment the tumult and outrage only served to increase already large sales.

Yet amidst this hoopla, there was one block of Americans who dutifully perused *Main Street,* then shrugged its shoulders and muttered the contemporary equivalent of "So what" —perhaps saying, "So's your old man." And, having thus contemptuously dismissed a towering best seller, members of the group blithely returned to their own foxtrotting affairs. Naturally, this indifferent band was the widely publicized Younger Generation, to whom *Main Street* was strictly an I-told-you-so proposition. The Younger Generation believed it already possessed all the knowledge necessary about the elders who had produced a nation barren, empty, and culturally bankrupt. Of the Younger Generation, Van Wyck Brooks, then rather young himself, had this to say:

    They find themselves born into a race that has drained away all its spiritual resources in the struggle to survive

*and that continues to struggle in the midst of plenty
because life no longer possesses any real meaning.*

But there was a far greater reason why the Younger Generation felt no need for *Main Street,* or any other novel bringing a new concept of America. In Scott Fitzgerald's *This Side of Paradise,* the young had found precisely the book necessary. The pages of this slender novel were studded with smart phrases supporting the me-first attitude and general rebelliousness with which the young embraced postwar life. To a Scott Fitzgerald character, life was a subjective matter, involving personal pleasure. The author's best creations were these "wild" young girls just becoming famous as flappers—in large part because of Fitzgerald's skill at portraying them. (Fitzgerald always credited Mencken with applying the term "flapper" to peppy young girls, but never fortified the claim with facts.)

In his writings, Fitzgerald charted the course of the pretty, popular American girl who began as the "belle," then advanced to the "flirt," to the "baby vamp" of World War I, and finally to the "flapper." Out of their bee-stung lips, the young novelist most clearly articulated the philosophy of the Jazz Age. One of his pretty, pretty girls said the name of the game was

> ✍§ *Not to be sorry, not to loose one cry of regret, to live according to a clear code of honor toward each other, and to seek the moment's happiness as fervently and persistently as possible.*

Another uses more personal terms:

> ✍§ *No one cares about us but ourselves. It'd be ridiculous for me to go about pretending I felt any obligations toward the world, and as for worrying what people think about me, I don't, that's all. Since I was a little girl in dancing school, I've been criticized by the mothers of all those little girls who weren't as popular as I was, and I've always looked on criticism as a sort of envious tribute.*

Naturally the young got most out of *This Side of Paradise*
—the critic who called it "a chronicle of youth by youth" hit
the nail right on the head. But the older generation was ir-
resistibly drawn to it by shock effect. From the pages of this
$1.75 novel, parents at last began discovering what darling
sons and daughters were doing after borrowing the family car
for an evening, or when disappearing into leafy shadows at a
country-club dance. In the past, boys had traditionally pro-
posed marriage first, then kissed the girl for the first time after she accepted. Now, it appeared, the flapper allowed herself to be kissed without giving the slightest thought to marriage. "I've been kissed by dozens of men," burbles one girl in
This Side of Paradise, "and I suppose I'll be kissed by dozens
more."

Fitzgerald also revealed that the flapper who kissed without
coaxing was known as "a speed" or "speedy." "None of the
Victorian mothers—and most of the mothers were Victorian
—had any ideas how casually their daughters were kissing,"
one of his speedies gloated.

Most of this promiscuous kissing was done during "petting
parties," another phrase brand new to the world. Fitzgerald
disclosed that wealthy boys and girls had been petting before
and during the war, but not until the postwar era did the
young really begin. "Only in 1920 did the veil finally fall," he
opined. "The Jazz Age had begun."

Scott Fitzgerald was unusual in that he unabashedly dipped
into real life for his material. Tirelessly he combed episodes in
his own life, as well as incidents recounted by others. In *This
Side of Paradise* he also made use of letters by and to him, as
well as youthful short stories and poems. This brought the
novel a scrapbook quality and caused a few critics to dismiss
it as flawed. Edmund Wilson, Fitzgerald's mentor at Princeton, was one who could not take it seriously. He called it "a
phantasmagoria of incident . . . immaturely imagined . . .
verging on the ludicrous."

But if Fitzgerald borrowed from real life, he invariably
gave his pilferings an unusual twist. It was as if each remembered moment were transmuted by a talent which some say

amounted to genius. Those intimate with the author marveled at his ability to take actual events and breathe rare life into them. Of Fitzgerald a friend said, "His mind is undisciplined, but he guesses right, his intuitions are invariably marvelous." A reviewer complimented his "uncanny ability to see life through the eyes of his characters."

This last has been called double-vision by Malcolm Cowley, who continues, "It was as if all his novels described a big dance to which he had been taken . . . and as if at the same time he stood outside the ballroom, a little Midwestern boy with his nose to the glass." Says biographer Arthur Mizener, "His work was the major interest in his life, for he was a natural writer if only in the sense that . . . nothing was ever quite real to him until he had written about it."

Fitzergald was twenty-three when he wrote *This Side of Paradise*; twenty-four when it came out. So his first novel was something of a distillation of his life to that point. Like him, the book's Amory Blaine came from a socially obscure background and did not begin to savor life until reaching Princeton. Like Scott, Amory quit college when America entered the war, going to officer's training school. After the war, Amory-Scott worked at a puny job in a New York advertising agency. Still, his Princeton contacts enabled him to be part of the bourgeoning Jazz Age, as one of "the gilded youth who danced around the young Connie Bennett at the Club de Vingt."

Amory had learned to drink and kiss at Princeton. Now, stepping out on Manhattan blind dates, he was all a-tingle because the girl he met before eight would probably be kissing him before midnight. When progress was slow, he had techniques of acceleration. "I'm always afraid of a girl before I've kissed her," he tells one jazz baby. She promptly sets about dispelling his fears. Along with kissing in the novel went hints of subsequent petting parties and drinking from hip flasks that might lead—well, anywhere. In those days, the ultimate sex act was known as "going all the way."

Amory Blaine falls madly in love with Rosalind Connage, a Park Avenue debutante. It was her jazzy, pleasure-first philosophy which sent shivers down middle-aged spines. Indeed, it was eighteen-year-old Rosalind (she was patterned after Zelda Sayre, the Alabama girl Scott met and loved as an Army officer) who admitted kissing dozens of men, and was planning to kiss dozens more. Rosalind kisses Amory within five minutes of meeting. More shocking, perhaps, is the fact that her sixteen-year-old sister surreptitiously puffs cigarettes in the next room.

The apparently flush Connage family is slowly running out of funds, and racy Rosalind fully realizes her obligation to wed a wealthy man. So a bitter-sweet aura of futility hovers over this Flaming Youth romance. At one point she tells Amory, "It may be an insane love affair, but it's not inane." When inevitably it ends, Amory reacts in proper Jazz Age fashion by going on a three-week drunk.

While writing his book, Scott Fitzgerald believed he had forever lost the love of Zelda Sayre, who could see no husband-potential in a young man anxious to write fiction. Most of the Amory-Rosalind scenes in the novel are based on the actual courtship of Scott and Zelda, following their love-at-first-sight meeting at a wartime officers' club dance in Alabama. With his fictional love affair dead like his real-life one, author Fitzgerald floundered. Amory Blaine does not return to his ad agency job, but drifts in aimless circles. In life, Scott returned to his native St. Paul, where he wrote *This Side of Paradise*. When it was accepted by Maxwell Perkins of Scribner's, Zelda changed her mind about marrying Scott.

The final chapter of *This Side of Paradise*—the one the Younger Generation seized on most avidly—is given over to what might be called a search for larger meaning. In it, Amory begins to walk—yes, *walk*—from New York to Princeton where he had once been so happy. After awhile the footsore young man turns hitchhiker, and to older men who pick him up, expatiates on the manifold disillusionments of the young. The result is a grab-bag of downbeat philosophy which greatly inspired the young readers of the time. Amory provides fodder for a new state of mind by saying, "Here was a new generation . . . destined finally to go out of dirty gray turmoil to follow love and pride . . . a new generation grown up to find all gods dead, all wars fought, all faiths in man shaken." World War I, he states flatly, "ruined all the old backgrounds . . . killed individualism." He salutes the Younger Generation as "the chosen youth from a muddled, unchastened world, still fed romantically on the mistakes and half-forgotten truths of dead statesmen and poets." All this was summed up in a verse Scott wrote later—

> Victorians, Victorians, who never learned to weep
> Who sowed the bitter harvest that your children
> go to reap.

On the outskirts of his beloved Princeton, Amory Blaine finds that his sentimental journey has acted as a fortuitous purge, changing him from empty egotist to real individual. "I know myself, but that is all," he tells himself.

Finis. . .

This Side *of Paradise* sold fifty-two thousand copies—roughly one to every eight of *Main Street*. Yet the two books stand proudly forth, arms entwined, as milestones in American literature. From both—you might say—the Turbulent Twenties learned the score. In the words of Burton Rascoe:

> With Main Street *and* This Side of Paradise, *the literature of the Twenties was inaugurated, and these two books, so unlike, were to represent the two main characteristics of the Twenties—the protest against the smugness of the American mores and the provincialism of the American culture on the one hand and, on the other, the so-called post-war disillusionment on the part of the young, which was less a disillusionment than an attempt to catch a new illusion in drinking, dancing, promiscuous flirtation and lovemaking and excitement.*

Both books, so widely read and discussed, were the kind of fiction highbrows approved—which brings up the question of whether their joint popularity raised the level of American reading taste.

It's a moot point. Some members of the G.A.P. bought *Main Street* less from literary appreciation than because of the controversy it aroused. Across the nation Good Citzenship Leagues branded Sinclair Lewis an anti-American radical and tried to keep his books from local libraries. There was no public outcry about *This Side of Paradise,* but parents hid it from children who might be polluted by its nonchalant kissing and fun-first philosophy. Others bought the books merely because it was considered smart to display them on parlor tables—and at those prices, who could go wrong?

Intellectuals who took pride in the two novels' success also had to face the unpleasant fact that the most popular authors in the country remained members of the "outdoor moral" school typified by Zane Grey and Harold Bell Wright, the latter a writer Lewis had gone out of his way to ridicule in *Main Street.* As for Zane Grey, he was on the verge of releasing no fewer than three books; a reviewer of *Wanderer of the Wasteland,* best of the trio, would express the opinion that such books were vastly popular because those who read them were not required to think. Highbrows pointed out that the same could be said of every other writer in this genre.

The women of America, having just won the right to vote, had also started to bob hair, roll stockings, and apply rouge to cheekbones. They were equally free to read—husbands permitting—books by Freud and Havelock Ellis, which were deemed daring at the time. But women were equally able to demand their own kind of mass-reading thrill. They got it in *The Sheik,* a book for women also read by men for sex-thrills. *The Sheik* ran a scorching second to *Main Street* in 1921 and spilled across the next two years as a major seller. Written by Edith M. Hull—not Ethel M. Dell, as some sources have it— this can be called the romantic success of the era, as opposed to the realistic.

In one way, though, *The Sheik* stands triumphant. Both *Main Street* and *This Side of Paradise* were sold to the expanding Hollywood movie industry. *Main Street* was turned into an anemic film with Florence Vidor, while *This Side of Paradise* never reached the grinding cameras. Yet *The Sheik* achieved true immortality when Rudolph Valentino, great lover of the silent screen, popped his eyes and panted out his love in a movie version and the sequel *Son of the Sheik*. Meanwhile, the danceable fox-trot tune of the day was "The Sheik of Araby."

The Sheik was in the shimmering tradition of Elinor Glyn, a novelist who since 1907 had written seduction scenes so coated with effulgent prose and stilted sentiment that the results were shocking but never censorable. Edith Hull (like Mrs. Glyn, she was English, her novel an import) followed this pattern so skillfully that one reviewer called the book "poisonously salacious."

The Sheik proved that England, too, had flappers. It recounts the story of Diana Mayo, who for obscure reasons has been raised more like a boy than a girl. If nothing else, this gives her the slim, boyish figure which was the ideal of females on both sides of the Atlantic.

Diana is a spoiled, willful child who gives servants orders like, "Fly, Stevens, and fetch the soup." At nineteen or twenty, she has yet to be kissed and grows irritated when males make passes or whisper of love. "When God made me He omitted to give me a heart" is the excuse she offers one injured swain.

Diana, parentless and filthy rich, is bent on crossing the Sahara Desert at the head of her own caravan. Relatives and friends object, but the imperious brat starts out anyway. On the first day, another caravan is spotted across the sandy wastes. A figure on a fine horse disengages and gallops toward her. Sensing evil intent, Diana jabs spurs into her own mount and attempts to escape. Slowly the man gains and finally, in the most palpitating scene of contemporary fiction, draws up beside her—"rising in his stirrups and leaning toward her, he flung a pair of powerful arms around her, and with a jerk, swung her clear off the saddle and on to his own horse in front of him."

Her abductor turns out to be Sheik Ahmed Ben Hassan,

thirtyish, educated in Europe, conveniently versed in English and French. In his opulent desert tent, he informs the beautiful child that he spotted her on the streets of Biskra and waited on the desert to abduct her. Ahmed has "the handsomest and cruellest face" Diana has ever seen, and this girl who has never known fear grows alarmed. Plainly he is accustomed to treating women like slaves, and "his fierce burning eyes swept her until she felt the boyish clothes that covered her slender limbs were stripped from her, leaving her beautiful white body bare under his passionate stare." (Can this be the first time "beautiful white body" ever appeared in print?)

Curtly, the Sheik orders Diana to remove her riding habit and leaves the room. When he returns, the girl is still dressed. His lips part in a sneer, while his eyes express sardonic amusement. "Must I be valet as well as lover?" he demands. Then he moves toward her. . . .

Diana fails to enjoy this rude deflowering. Nor, as days pass, does she relax enough to enjoy her life as a white slave in the midst of Oriental luxury and European comfort. Especially humiliating to her is the fact that she and Ahmed share the same bathroom. Yet her proud spirit never cracks. "Curse you," she screams at him. "When will you let me go?" Ahmed smiles his cruel smile and answers, "When I am tired of you." Aware that he has failed to arouse her sexually, he increases his master-slave demands, "Kiss me, my little piece of ice," he orders.

When angered, Sheik Ahmed whips servants until they bleed to death. He personally tortures Arab horses he cannot break. He never exactly strikes Diana, but his fingers dig cruelly into her delicate shoulders when she is slow to respond. "I can make women love me when I choose," he boasts, and proves it in spades by suddenly winning Diana. All at once the girl is his love slave, as eager to serve him sexually as to win him mentally. "I love him," she admits to herself. "And I want his love more than anything in Heaven and earth."

Into this intimate picture steps Raoul de Saint Hubert,

Ahmed's former schoolmate. "The best friend a man ever had," the Sheik informs Diana. She leaves the two to reminisce and takes a daring gallop across the burning sands. Riding too far, she is captured by the henchmen of a rival sheik, who drag her to their master. As gross as Ahmed is handsome, the rival rips off her blouse, leaving her bare to the midriff. When she spurns his further advances, he puts a knife to her throat and applies pressure.

At this moment Ahmed and his faithful men appear. In the ensuing fracas Sheik Ahmed is seriously wounded. As he hovers between life and death, Raoul de Saint Hubert tells Diana that—wonder of wonders!—Ahmed is an Englishman. The reasons for this are complex, requiring a full twelve pages of tight print to explain. The gist is that Ahmed's father had once discovered a pregnant English girl wandering in the desert. Falling in love with her, he made her child (Ahmed) his own. It may have been this elaborate revelation that caused one critic to write, "Such a story, viewed from a sane literary standpoint, is preposterous."

When Ahmed recovers, he has learned humility. Gone is the arrogant he-man; now he cannot imagine a girl like Diana loving him. After Saint Hubert's departure, he informs her that she must go as well. The words are like daggers in her thumping heart. "Ahmed! Ahmed!" she cries. "You are killing me, I cannot live without you!"

Slowly Ahmed realizes that this heedless London flapper really loves him. He relents and takes her in his arms. Diana's paroxysms of grief have brought the girl to a pitiable state, and she is barely able to whisper, "I am not afraid of anything with your arms around me, my desert lover."

Rocky Road to Immortality . . *Cabell* . . *Hergesheimer* . . *Van Vechten* . . *Dos Passos* . . . .

In his first "Bowling Green" column in the New York *Post* for the year 1921, Christopher Morley offered the following tongue-in-cheek prognostication for the upcoming year:

> *In January, Sinclair Lewis will be hailed as the greatest*
>   *living writer*
> *In February he will be supplanted by Joseph Hergesheimer*
> *In March, D. H. Lawrence*
> *In April, F. Scott Fitzgerald*
> *In May, Robert Charles Benchley*
> *In June, George Santayana*
> *In July, James Joyce*
> *In August, Marcel Proust*
> *September 1–5, Sherwood Anderson*
> *September 15–30, James Branch Cabell*
> *October 1–10, Heywood Broun*
> *October 10–31, Thomas Mann*
> *November 1–15, T. S. Eliot*
> *November 15–17, Ben Hecht*

November 17–30, Harry Kemp
December 1–4, Ellen Glasgow
December 4–13, Stuart P. Sherman
December 18–23, Willa Cather
December 23–31, Will Rogers

To the highbrows and mediumbrows who perused it, this seemed little more than an amusing commentary on the vagaries of critical and popular approbation. Yet like all good satire, it contained a nugget of truth. For no less than other citizens of the Twenties, book readers were displaying an ability to leap from one celebrity to another of the literary circus. Already the process had begun with Sinclair Lewis and Scott Fitzgerald. Simultaneously, the public was developing a brand-new respect for native writers. Until recently, of course, Americans had looked to England for titans among authors; now, prodded by the exhortations of Mencken, Burton Rascoe, and others, they had begun regarding with interest the homegrown talents who suddenly seemed to stand as tall as, or taller than, scribbling Englishmen.

Indeed, this surge of native pride had grown so great that Americans scanning the cultural scene at the beginning of the 1920's—and even at the end—found it difficult not to place Joseph Hergesheimer and James Branch Cabell in the exalted category of literary immortal.

If nothing else, forty-one-year-old Joseph Hergesheimer lived in the manner the American public expected of prominent authors. Success, which came to him in 1917 with publication of *Three Black Pennys*, had enabled him to live the life of a country author-squire in the especially pleasant town of West Chester, Pennsylvania, his wife's birthplace.

The Hergesheimers occupied Dower House, a historic Pennsylvania Dutch homestead built of local boulder stone, with original timbers intact. The interior was tastefully crammed with American antiques and a priceless collection of glass. These and other facets of the Hergesheimer home life were frequently and lovingly detailed in articles by the author in *The Saturday Evening Post*. When he sold one of these articles—getting top *Post* prices—Hergesheimer bought additional antiques and glass, then wrote about *them*. This was a self-renewing process which left him and the public content.

Hergesheimer was a bustling, cherubic man, whose heavy horn-rimmed glasses brought him an owlish look. He possessed a controlled, productive energy which to one friend was "incalculable . . . almost appalling." Not only did he live in extreme comfort, but he was—if the word may be used—a florid dresser, partial to rich suitings embellished by purple or crimson cummerbunds and other touches of unlikely color. At home his wardrobe ranged from velvet smoking jackets to ruffled silk evening shirts which he donned for dinner. Of him, Mencken said, "Hergy belongs in a cosy corner, draped in scarlet."

This was no superficial pose in the owl-eyed novelist, who valued himself as an important man of letters. Having labored with single-minded intensity to become a writer, Hergesheimer let it be known that he had reached the top of the heap, with only the Englishmen Joseph Conrad and Edmund Gosse qualified to criticize his work.

Born in Philadelphia, Hergesheimer had first tried to be a painter, a small income allowing him to study abroad. Passage of time brought the realization that he could never really succeed at the easel, and a nervous breakdown resulted. With returning health, he began to write and did so for thirteen years before selling a word. As a prospering novelist, he still worked hard. The industrious squire of West Chester liked to publish a book or two a year, moving neatly from contemporary novels, to historical fiction, to collected short stories or articles.

Joseph Hergesheimer's dreams of being a painter were still reflected in his prose, for he tried to make each sentence a brush stroke. Ever alert to the *feel* of words, he considered style more vital than character or motivation. According to gadfly Burton Rascoe, "He has assignations with adjectives, love affairs with nouns, and capricious liaisons with adverbs and prepositions." Hergesheimer was equally enamored of punctuation, obsessed by qualifying clauses, asides, and divagations which in turn spawned a welter of commas, colons, semicolons, dashes, and parentheses. Of one character on her deathbed, he wrote, "Savina was rapidly growing, at last, cold."

He was also a tactile author who described attire and decor with the loving fondness of a salesperson in a luxury shop. This ability to evoke mood and texture was perhaps the chief reason for his success. George Jean Nathan complimented "the rich and countless ornamentations and embroideries with which he intricately embellishes [his] novels and makes them flash and glitter like so many fricaseed rainbows."

Yet Hergesheimer was no stuffed shirt, not even a ruffled silk one. Among colleagues in the literary game, he was cherished as a dining and drinking companion. Like most authors, he talked as he wrote and was capable of profundities like "There are two courses of conduct superior to all others—to be profoundly serious with charm, or to be as charming as a fresh muslin gown very profoundly." Once he described his ideal person as either "lightly serious or seriously light." And he could be witty. Hergesheimer may have been the first ever to say to a young lady whose aspirations disappointed him, "You have hitched your star to a wagon."

As a novelist, Hergesheimer was rated second only to Dreiser by H. L. Mencken. The public ranked him higher, for Dreiser had never written a popular novel, while Hergesheimer was the author of *Three Black Pennys, Java Head, The Bright Shawl, Linda Condon,* and other successes. Now, in 1921, he was making the strongest bid of his career to be considered a "modern" writer. In *Cytherea*—his tenth book —he emerged as the first novelist to chronicle that the middle-aged not only envied Younger Generation its jazzy fun, but had set about emulating it.

The revelation of *Cytherea*—the name of a wise-eyed doll who watches with sardonic amusement from a mantelpiece— was that amidst prosperity and disillusionment, middle-aged marrieds were bored with themselves and each another. The novel goes on to depict an older generation chasing boredom by adopting the drinking and promiscuous kissing of Flaming Youth. The country-club dance in *Cytherea* is, in fact, wilder than any in *This Side of Paradise*. One drunken gent, passing out in the middle of the dance floor, grabs at his partner for support and rips the dress from her body!

Hergesheimer displayed added modernity by putting a clever young Hollywood actress on his pages. Of the female sex she boldly declares, "We are not made of sugar and spice and other pleasant bits, but of two: prostitute and mother." The author also proves that he has been reading Freud and Krafft-Ebing by featuring a mature woman who successfully fought nymphomania for years! When her iron resolve crumbles at last, she shrieks, "I want to be outraged"—this, of course, in the sense of violated. All of which earned Hergesheimer an accolade from Henry Seidel Canby in the *Post:* "He is so much and so lusciously at home with cocktails, limousine drinking parties, stair-sitting, and intra-marital kissing!"

James Branch Cabell was the second author of the time who seemed destined for literary immortality. Born in 1879, he was a man of medium stature topped by the distinguished head of a Roman senator. Cabell's eyes were sleepy, his manner bored. At work and elsewhere, he loved toying with words, and gave as his personal philosophy, "I burn with generous indignation over the world's pigheadedness and injustice at no time whatsoever." Of his literary ambitions, he declared, "My aim is to write perfectly of beautiful happenings." Of Cabell, his fellow craftsman Hergesheimer once murmured, "James is so delicately balanced."

As a member of a First Family of Virginia, Cabell lived with gentlemanly decorum in the city he loved to designate as Richmond-in-Virginia. By his side stood an aristocratic wife who referred to him as "Mr. Cabell." Yet Cabell's life had its moments of vigor. For two years, he had worked in New York as a rough-and-tumble reporter on the *Herald*. Returning to the South, he labored for two additional years in coal mines.

With this hard-core living behind him, Cabell began to act as if harsh reality were more than he could endure. He started writing novels that wafted him and his readers back into an imaginary medieval land named Poictesme. Amusing himself while teasing readers, he accompanied his books with maps, family trees, and other shreds of "proof" that his characters actually lived—many were convinced by it all. Cabell planned to write no fewer than twenty books as an overall Chronicle of Manuel of Poictesme, each volume a mere chapter in the whole. Some of his tomes bore fanciful titles like *The Rivet in Grandfather's Neck*; some of his sentences ran like this:

> *Henceforward you must fret away much sunlight by interminably shunning discomfort and by indulging tepid preferences. For I, none but I, can waken that desire that uses all of a man, and so wastes nothing, even though it leave that favored man forever like wan ashes in the sunlight.*

Amazingly, no one seemed to relish this highfalutin prose more than Henry Mencken, who hailed Cabell as a "penetrating ironist, a delicate virtuoso of situation, an anatomist of character, one who sees into the eternal tragi-comedy of hope and striving, above all, a highly accomplished doctor of words."

Fame came to James Branch Cabell with *Jurgen*, the fourteenth novel in his ambitious saga. Like the others, this read like a rendering into prose of Tennyson's *Idylls of the King*, and exposed an author ever delighted by intricate word games. At the beginning came "A Foreword: Which Asserts Nothing." Readers then pressed on to the adventures of the incautious amorist, Count Jurgen, who tries to seduce every female available in the placid land of Poictesme.

Jurgen was published without fanfare late in 1919. Soon after a letter to the New York *Tribune* denounced it as "naughty . . . [with] thinly veiled episodes of all perversities, abnormalities, and damn foolishness of sex." With this, the Society for the Suppression of Vice, under the command of John S. Sumner, surged into action. Raiding the offices of Cabell's publisher, police seized plates, sheets, and copies of the novel. In court proceedings *Jurgen* was denounced as "offensive, lewd, lascivious, and indecent."

Since then the *Jurgen* case had been on the treadmill of the courts, while the fortunate few who had bought copies turned into "bookleggers" cautiously lending them to friends, just as *Ulysses*, *Lady Chatterley's Lover*, and *Tropic of Cancer* would be booklegged later on. As a result of this notoriety, thousands panted to buy *Jurgen*, which would be available again if the judge's verdict favored author and publisher. The forces of virtue had not learned—have they ever?—that suppression of a book automatically creates a best seller.

Readers who searched Cabell's involuted paragraphs for sex had little difficulty finding it. Indeed, a reading of *Jurgen* today brings the impression that, for a Virginia gentleman, Cabell possessed a considerable knowledge of, and interest in, pornography. In one scene, Jurgen is bathed by four bare, nubile girls, the nipples of whose tits tickle him excitingly. At such moments one feels James Branch Cabell would love to break loose and become the John Cleland of his day.

But the laws, if not the temper, of the times prevented him, and Cabell was obliged to clothe his pornography in terms of high symbolism. Thus, while his intent is obvious, the spice is lacking. The sexiest part of *Jurgen* comes in the chapter "As to a Veil They Broke," which details an act of intercourse in elaborate obscurity. Elsewhere, Jurgen embraces Dorothy La Desirée, sex symbol of Poictesme: "He was touching her everywhere, this horrible lascivious woman, who was certainly quite old enough to know better than to permit such liberties." It has been noted that Cabell, whose heroines were the most wanton of the time, always seemed shocked by their wantonness.

Cabell reached a crest of popularity in 1922, when *Jurgen* was at last cleared by the courts, allowing the reading public to gorge on its obfuscated sexuality. Yet even before *Jurgen*,

Cabell as well as Hergesheimer had been highly regarded by fellow writers; Sinclair Lewis dedicated *Main Street* to both, plainly considering them his peers in the craft.

More surprising was Mencken's wholehearted support. Ordinarily, this Katzenjammer Kid might be expected to despise two such velvety authors, but in his infinite perversity Mencken said of Hergesheimer, "I venerate the man," and praised Cabell's "novel and ingenious ideas." In fact, the reputation of the two men was largely attributable to hosannas from Mencken. It was Mencken who persuaded Cabell to write *Jurgen*, which first saw light as a short story in *Smart Set*.

Today, fifty years later, these novelists once marked for immortality are little more than footnotes in our cultural history. Mark Schorer calls Cabell's novels "foolishly tenuous allegories," while few bother to remember Joseph Hergesheimer at all. Yet in their fashion, the two played a role in the liberation of native authors, of whom Van Wyck Brooks was saying, "There is no doubt that for half a century the American writer has gone down to defeat."

Cabell and Hergesheimer lived like victors on the battlefield of life, and did so by writing novels different from the Genteel Tradition and the Hoosier School. They also wrote prose as polished as any British author, which has caused Malcolm Cowley to say in tribute:

> *They made it possible for young Americans to write without a side-glance at London or Oxford, to speak in their own language about everyday matters, to be accurate, coarse, even bawdy without too much fear of having their books suppressed.*

By this alone, they gave other authors an amount of courage. Theodore Dreiser had dug the vein of deep realism, relentlessly exposing the forces dragging men downward. By his standards Cabell and Hergesheimer wrote escape fiction—yet at the time it was considered serious escape reading and offbeat as well. Thanks in part to these two contemporary titans, young writers (and some not so young) felt free to be different, to experiment by being elegant, effete, rough, ready, or eccentric.

One who gaily tripped the Cabell-Hergesheimer path was Carl Van Vechten, whose first novel, *Peter Whiffle*, now made its appearance. Van Vechten's birthplace was Cedar Rapids, Iowa, a community the sensitive youth loathed from boyhood. "I'm so damned bored with this town," he told a playmate, "that I'd like to put on a bath towel and run through the streets naked. I'd do anything to create some excitement!"

He never did, but as soon as possible lighted out for the University of Chicago. From there he went to New York, to become music critic of the *Times* and for a while its Paris correspondent. No matter where Van Vechten lived, or (as it turned out) whatever his age, he was a dauntless partisan of the avant-garde, bubbling with enthusiasm for everything new, amusing, bizarre, or beautiful. At the time of *Peter Whiffle* his raptures were lavished on the daring, innovative jazz of George Gershwin and the purple-hued novels of England's Ronald Firbank. Van Vechten also adored cats; his *Tiger in the House*, which Alfred Knopf considered the handsomest book he had published to date, was hailed as the definitive word on felines.

Tall, silver-haired, puffy, and (to use one of his own favorite words) pinguid, Van Vechten affected rings, bracelets, and ruffled shirts; some thought it was to distract attention from unaesthetic buck teeth. He had worked to cultivate an immobile countenance, and his basilisk stare disconcerted many. In talk and writing, Carlo—as friends called him—employed esoteric words like "egrimony," "inspissated," "ipitumetic," "peccant," "moriegation," "epigone," "sapidity," and "oppugnacy." At the same time, he could flatter a young lady by telling her, "You look like a child of Sarah Bernhardt by a yellow panther." Despite an apparently compatible marriage to actress Fania Marinoff, Carl Van Vechten evinced an uncommon interest in the gilded, precious world of the elegant homosexual.

Van Vechten's style had been influenced by Cabell and

perhaps (recently) Ronald Firbank. His years as a newspaper critic and *aficianado* of culture enabled him to insert in his work esoteric oddments about art, music, and literature. *Peter Whiffle*, the alleged biography of an imaginary person, led unsuspecting readers into a grotesque artistic half-world, where life for both sexes was amoral, sumptuous, and debauched. To the poetess Elinor Wylie, his book was

> *a strange fantastic creature, not quite tamed and grown into a novel perhaps, but possessing a charm which . . . other books may excel but never duplicate. . . . A heavier mesh of plot might have crushed the butterfly, but Mr. Van Vechten has caught it alive and shining for the enchantment of all.*

Despite his perennially youthful state of mind, Van Vechten had been born in 1880, making him the same mellow vintage as Mencken and Hergesheimer. What, then, of younger writers who were also inspired by the sudden surge of energy in the literary sphere? One of the most promising was Ben Hecht, until recently the Bad Boy of Chicago journalism. Hecht's first novel, *Erik Dorn*, had just emerged as one of the early successes in a decade destined to abound in promising first novels. The twenty-seven-year-old author had arrived in New York for his publication day, and *The Bookman* promptly subjected him to a capsule psychoanalysis:

> *He cocks his hat on the side of his head, cultivates a repertoire of gestures and facial expressions, and speaks with a swagger that has overtones of insolence. This is because at bottom he lacks self-confidence.*

Where Dreiser and Sinclair Lewis were inclined to blame a wicked world for the miseries of characters, young Hecht in *Erik Dorn* had chosen to reverse this by suggesting that the demons of discontent inside a man might be the real culprits. His Erik was a brilliant Chicago journalist (just like Hecht) with an adoring wife and a tempting mistress. Even so, his life was drab and empty. "I must go away," he groused to friends.

Dashing to Europe, Erik gets entangled in postwar socialist uprisings in various countries—and also unearths another girl. Yet life continues dull, and he returns to Chicago, expecting to find wife and mistress eagerly waiting for him. Neither is—in postwar days this surprise development was considered beautifully cynical! Unhappy Erik, apparently his own worst enemy, winds up in the company of an elderly father, who on hot nights likes to sit outdoors "making love to the stars."

Ben Hecht had been a boy acrobat in vaudeville and was something of an acrobat with words. Yet his overblown prose —to him the press was "a blind old cat yowling on a treadmill"—was well in key with literary experimentation of the era. Critics favored it, with Burton Rascoe finding in Hecht "our finest epithetician." However, another reviewer found "a surfeit of cleverness." *The New York Times* believed, "When Ben Hecht gets himself in hand, America will have another great writer of novels." Oddly enough, the best comment on Hecht's style was to be found in the novel, where a character calls Erik "an amusing writer, sometimes violent, and always empty."

Hecht's greatest jolt as a first novelist, however, came from Sherwood Anderson, a man he had come to revere. Following publication, the author sought out Anderson to learn his opinion of the novel. The two met in a pleasant barroom over foaming steins of beer. Hecht expected praise from the man he considered a master, but Anderson began, "Ben, boy, we've been friends now for seven years. That's a long time to be friends. It kind of wears off and loses its point, friendship does. My idea is that we become enemies from now on. Real enemies. I'll begin with your book *Erik Dorn*. . . ."

No fewer than fourteen publishers turned down the manuscript of *Three Soldiers* by twenty-five-year-old John Dos Passos. Finally, it was accepted by the stodgy firm of George H. Doran.

In his *The Best Times,* published forty-five years later, Dos Passos indicates his wartime experiences as an overseas ambulance driver and a domestic draftee were rather pleasant. No such impression can be gained from *Three Soldiers*, the story of three young Americans of diverse backgrounds. "This ain't no war," grumbles one, "it's a goddam madhouse." Critics called the pioneering war novel a terrible indictment of war, notable for "savage energy" and "the harmonious expression of well-chewed rage."

Even so, *Three Soldiers* was not as pungent as it could have been, for Doran editors insisted on laundering much of the profanity used glibly by Dos Passos' doughboys. At first the author objected, then gave up. "Do what you goddam please," he said in doughboy parlance, and went abroad as a traveling expatriate. In his absence *Three Soldiers* had only a moderate sale.

The same fate befell e. e. cummings' *The Enormous Room*, a book whose reputation has grown with the years. This detailed the author's Kafkalike experiences in a French detention camp. Dos Passos and cummings, close friends, were for the moment praised by critics, neglected by the public.

If the contemporary world of fiction was in a state of flux, so was the more literal field of nonfiction.

Here a new category had appeared with books of behind-the-scenes revelations. Before the war, the memoirs of royalty and diplomats occasionally offered indiscreet glimpses of the great and near-great. Now the widespread belief that World War I had been bungled created a demand for more revealing books about policy making and battlefield performance. *Now It Can Be Told*, by war correspondent Philip Gibbs, was the first sensation in this field. More discreet (and less successful) were *The Mirrors of Downing Street* by a Gentleman with a Duster, *Mirrors of Washington* by Clinton W. Gilbert, and *Peace Negotiations* by Robert W. Lansing, former Secretary of State.

Yet the public was also interested in the distant past. For the major seller—by far—in nonfiction was H. G. Wells's *Outline of History*. This encompassing work was first published as a two-volume set for $10.50, then cut to one volume for $5.00—both sums appallingly high for books in the 1920's. In any case, *The Outline of History* performed the monumental feat of remaining the nation's top nonfiction book over four long years. Describing this ambitious work in proper Yankee verbiage a critic called it "The first systematic attempt to round up all human history, wrestle it to the ground, and hog-tie it." The popularity of *The Outline of History* on this side of the Atlantic proved not only that Americans had more time to read, but that many had developed a desire to know about the past and its mysteries. It has been noted that before the discontents resulting from World War I, Americans had been satisfied to savor only the present.

Inevitably, *The Outline of History* caused other authors to produce compact run-through histories of other aspects of days gone by. Among them were *The Outline of Science*, by J. Arthur Thomson, *The Story of the World's Literature*, by John Macy, *Outline of World Literature* by John Drinkwater, and *Outline of Man's Knowledge* by Clement Wood.

Yet no book approached the popularity of *The Outline of History* until the Land of the Free produced its own flavorsome historian in the bulky person of Hendrik Willem Van Loon. Dutch born, American educated, Van Loon resembled a much-inflated cigar, his frame rising more than six feet in height, covered by nearly 250 pounds of flesh. Moving with ballet-dancer agility on tiny feet, this man mountain radiated ebullient zest for life.

Up to now Van Loon had used his multitalents to write bright books for children, illustrating them with jagged, amusing pencil sketches. The labor had not paid off, and legend has it that the author was reduced to washing dishes in a Greenwich Village restaurant, while living off the cuff at the Harvard Club. Then Horace Liveright persuaded him to combine his erudition, light-touch prose, and wispy sketches into a book for both grown-ups and children. Titled *The Story of Mankind*, it became the first great success for both author and publisher.

The popularity of nonfiction also reflected the sudden interest of Americans in their own personalities. For the first time a reading public was showing concern about what made people tick, a curiosity perfectly expressed by a book title of some years hence—*Why We Behave Like Human Beings.* The writings of Freud and Jung, together with those of American psychoanalysts like Dr. A. A. Brill, offered the most profound answers, but readers desiring less depth had *The Mind in the Making* by James Harvey Robinson, *Human Nature and Conduct* by John Dewey, *Outwitting Our Nerves* by Josephine Jackson and Helen Salisbury, and (even) *The Dance of Life* by Havelock Ellis. Americans just beginning to display an interest in personal appearance and physical well-being were buying the pioneering *Diet and Health* by Lulu Hunt Peters. Manners were also attracting attention, with Emily Post's newly published *Etiquette* right on hand.

Human beings had begun wondering about other human beings, especially famous ones, and so commenced an era rich in biographical writing. From England came advance word of Lytton Strachey's *Queen Victoria*, a book which cast a jaundiced eye on a venerated monarch. This volume, published in America in 1922, changed the course of the world's biographical writing. Yet it must be pointed out that the United States was already doing fairly well in that department. Nineteen hundred and twenty had seen publication of Albert Beveridge's excellent biography of John Marshall, as well as Van Wyck Brooks's *Ordeal of Mark Twain.* Also *The Education of Henry Adams*, appearing just before the beginning of the decade, had been a milestone in the field of autobiography.

With all this, however, the most stimulating nonfiction writing was found in the area of culture. Critics and essayists— where is the breed now?—jubilantly demolished old reputations, while enshrining the young and the new. Prominent among such writers was Mencken, whose volumes of *Prejudices*, six in all, covered such topics as his cohort Nathan, his beloved Beethoven, Criticism of Criticism of Criticism, and "the Sahara of the Bozart," a stinging attack on the culture— if any—of the South.

A far gentler essayist was Ernest Boyd, a transplanted

Irishman who emerges as one of the most staggeringly erudite figures ever to take a bow on a literary stage. Ernest Boyd seemed familiar with every known language, and obscure dialects as well. Not only did he appear to have read every book published but every magazine, pamphlet, brochure, and broadside. Carl Van Vechten, a man not easily awed, saluted his fellow litterateur in these enraptured words:

>One of the most interesting literary figures in America is an Irishman. I pause after this word and wonder if any man can be an Irishman who speaks eight languages fluently, and reads sixteen others, including Danish, Zend, and Hawaiian, with a fair degree of accuracy. . . . He informs himself (and others) about everything from Dadaism to the Samoan Secessionists and the Salon d'Automne of Helsingfors. In his easy, fluent style, he passes in comparative review from George Moore to the Kama Sutra. He reads the new books of d'Annunzio and those of Francis Carco and Baroja. He is acquainted with Knut Hamsun in the original. I don't suppose there is anything he doesn't know; he puts the proper accents on Magyar substantives; he is aware of the burial place of Kryloff; he can tell you what John Eglinton likes for dinner and the name of André Gide's tailor. He is privy to the feminine endings in Pennsylvania Dutch; he can conjugate the Yiddish irregular verbs; and he can order alligator pears in Persian. Withal he is a delightful and charming companion and can spin a sullied yarn with the best spoken longshoremen and drink a cup of anti-legal ambrosia with the habitual gobletman. If his qualifications were essential to membership in the Academy of Arts and Sciences, he would be the only member.

Slender, of distinguished bearing, Boyd was a debonair soul who invariably dressed in brown (even to evening clothes) to match a spruce russet beard. With ladies he was a charmer, among men a cherished carouser. "A combination of urbanity and humanity," one smitten lady breathed. Boyd had crossed the ocean with his French wife Madeleine to become British consul in Baltimore, but switched to the literary life after matching *Bierstube* wits with Mencken in that city.

If Mencken's hearty prose functioned as a fist which kayoed enemies, Boyd's possessed the sharpness of a stiletto. Two of his books were titled *Appreciations and Depreciations,* and *Literary Blasphemies.*

Admirers of less erudite essays found a favorite in Christopher Morley, conductor of "The Bowling Green" column in the New York *Post.* Not that Morley lacked erudition—he belonged to an intellectual Pennsylvania family where all the sons were Rhodes scholars. As an author he first found a public with the whimsical novel *Parnassus on Wheels,* about a lovable ambulatory bookseller. Now he was beginning to contribute genial essays to literary periodicals—"playful but responsible," one critic thought them. Morley once described the ideal life as one spent in "learning, earning, and yearning." His readers adored such homey aphorisms.

In person, Christopher Morley was the very image of the tweedy, pipe-puffing bookman, a twinkle in his eye and a Niagara of literary fact and opinion at tongue tip. Here was an author objective enough to evaluate his own work: he called it "embroidered, with [too much] loving fondling of words." His books at the beginning of the twenties were *Mince Pie, Chimneysmoke,* and *Plum Pudding and Other Essays.*

By the 1920's, two Van Dorens had emerged from the Midwest to make an impression on the universe of books. Carl, the elder, had written *The Roving Critic* and *Many Minds.* He was literary editor of *The Nation,* to which his wife Irita also contributed reviews. Brother Mark was a professor at Columbia who wrote book reviews for literary magazines.

In the bubbling world of humor, Ring Lardner had just won fame by his *You Know Me, Al* baseball stories. A step behind him was H. C. Witwer, who utilized contemporary slang so effectively that his prose was dubbed "slanguage." Witwer's most appreciated efforts were his Leather Pushers books, about prize-fighting.

Among intellectuals, Robert Benchley rated high because his fanciful humor was "pure"—it had no homey roots in the

American scene. This onetime editor of the *Harvard Lampoon* had first won attention with his "Social Life of the Newt" in a 1919 Vanity Fair. An indication of his unique humor is found in the title of the first story he ever wrote: "No Matter from What Angle You Looked at It, Alice Brookhansen Was a Girl Whom You Would Hesitate to Invite into Your Own Home."

Beside Benchley—or perhaps ahead of him at this time—stood Donald Ogden Stewart, noted for his *Parody Outline of History* and *Aunt Polly's Story of Mankind*. Next, Stewart invented the hilarious American couple Mr. and Mrs. Haddock. Don Marquis hopped into the parody field with *The Old Soak's History of Mankind*—he was author of a highly successful play about the Old Soak. Irvin S. Cobb, who was uncannily able to duplicate his deep Southern drawl in prose, was recognized as a master story teller. Stage comedian Will Rogers heeded the advice of friends to put his pithy comments between covers.

Yet it's possible that the most admired book-humorist of the time was George S. Chappell, currently riding the crest with the adventure-travel spoofs *Cruise of the Kawa* and *My Northern Exposure: the Kawa at the Pole*. Both were signed with the pretentious pseudonym Walter E. Traprock, F.R.S. S.E.V., N.L.L.D., and each included mock action illustrations posed by the author's friends and fellow writers, along with a bevy of pretty girls.

From across the Canadian border came the nonsense of Stephen Leacock. Also, readers were just beginning to relish the early P. G. Wodehouse stories of Jeeves, Bertie Wooster, Psmith, and Stanley Featherstonehaugh Ukridge. After appearing as magazine serials, these inevitably emerged in books.

Mystery readers of the time were a small, self-conscious group. True, Mary Roberts Rinehart had written *The Man in Lower Ten* a full decade before, and she and a few others had continued to produce excellent whodunits. But not until the late 1920's, with S.S. Van Dine and his ineffable Philo Vance, did the mystery novel attain true respectability. In the meantime American leaders in the field were ladies: Mrs. Rinehart,

Carolyn Wells and Anna Katherine Green. Louis Joseph Vance gave the public the Lone Wolf, while Arthur Train dominated the legal-courtroom area with Ephraim Tutt, of the firm Tutt & Tutt. Soon Frances Noyes Hart scored with *The Bellamy Trial*.

From England came mystery masterpieces of all kinds. The Sherlock Holmes stories of Conan Doyle still had a wide following. Agatha Christie and Mrs. Belloc Lowndes provided intricate bafflers with English atmosphere. London's scary Limehouse was the province of Sax Rohmer and his sinister Dr. Fu Manchu. John Buchan combined high adventure and mystery. Two of the most popular Englishmen in the field were E. Phillips Oppenheim and the superprolific Edgar Wallace, both of whom usually wrote about white-tie crime. Wallace's book of the moment was *The Hairy Arm*.

The Erle Stanley Gardner of the era was J. S. Fletcher, an Englishman published in America by the classy firm of Alfred A. Knopf. Fletcher wrote three or four books a year, employing such titles as *False Scent*. The true mystery addict of the time had to be a Fletcher fan. Yet Fletcher, like so many authors, is a forgotten man today.

There were all these books, and more. In distant Richmond-in-Virginia, a lady named Emily Clark had, with the encouragement of James Branch Cabell and others, started the literary magazine *The Reviewer*. She wrote:

> ☙ *The literary scene . . . was quivering with undeveloped and unexploded personalities. The post-war insurgence was nascent and exciting. . . . There was no Literary Guild and no Book of the Month Club. People who liked books were spontaneous and excited about discovering them for themselves.*

Flappers and Philosophers

Scott and Zelda Fitzgerald . . . .

F. Scott Fitzgerald and Zelda Sayre of Montgomery, Alabama, had been married in the chapel of St. Patrick's Cathedral in New York on the Saturday afternoon following publication of *This Side of Paradise.*

After the ceremony, the newlyweds shed relatives and friends to amble slowly up a Fifth Avenue on which, Scott later recalled, lay "a rippling sun." At a specialty shop, Scott bought a Patou suit for the bride—he thought it made her look like Justine Johnson of the *Follies,* reigning beauty of the town. Scott Fitzgerald had literally become famous overnight, and the shop was overjoyed to let him charge this purchase; it was the first time in his life he had charged anything, and the delightful simplicity of the process beguiled him.

Resuming a magic promenade up Fifth Avenue, the young Fitzgeralds walked as far as the Plaza Hotel on Fifty-ninth Street, then went inside to join the Connie Bennett set at a tea dance. After fox-trotting to "Stumbling," "The Sheik of Araby" and other contemporary tunes, as well as downing Bronx cocktails from flasks, they accompanied tipsy friends to the hit play *Enter Madame.* Occupying the entire front row of the orchestra, the giggling group set out to disconcert the actors by laughing uproariously at serious lines and sitting stonily through funny ones. Later, they repaired to *Ziegfeld's*

Midnight Frolic on the New Amsterdam Roof, where Scott admired the statuesque, bare-thighed showgirls and Zelda the taffeta pyramids.

Scott had taken the bridal suite of the Hotel Biltmore for the honeymoon. Zelda had never before visited New York, and Scott spent most of the week showing her the sights of the city. Over the weekend they went to a Princeton house party. Drinking from hip flasks was becoming the favorite indoor sport of the restless young, and the Fitzgeralds imbibed gloriously en route, to step from the train lurching and wobbling. Leaving Zelda, Scott draped an improvised laurel wreath across his brow and cavorted drunkenly across the campus as if playing the pipes of Pan; for this public display he was summarily dropped from his cherished Princeton club.

Later, at a cocktail party given by alumnus Harvey Firestone in his robin's-egg-blue private railroad car, Scott acquired a black eye. Presumably it was an indication that his flirtatious bride was as attractive to Northern males as she had been down South.

Returning to New York, Fitzgerald found his fame increasing by leaps and bounds and decided the Biltmore was not good enough. Moving to the Commodore, they celebrated by whirling around in the hotel's revolving door for a hilarious half hour. Soon the Commodore was beneath them and they moved to the stately, atmospheric Plaza, which Scott called "an etched hotel." From now on this hallowed hostelry always seemed their spiritual home.

So began the amazing Jazz Age saga of F. Scott Fitzgerald who, as time rolled by, appeared to turn into a living symbol of his gaudy era rather than just a successful contemporary novelist.

Along with his peppy, short-skirted Zelda, Scott stood proudly poised atop a fox-trot world, both of them resembling characters straight out of his own fiction. Scott's early books have been praised for giving "the pitch and beat" of the time, yet the Fitzgeralds themselves—newlywed, newly famous, newly prosperous—danced to precisely the same beat. Giddy, popular, and always (it seemed) to some degree drunk, the bright pair were achieving an uncommon distinction. Overnight this young—oh, so young!—couple became that rarest of phenomena: a legend in their own time.

Seldom, in fact, has an author been so much a projection of his own work. Numerous writers have spoken for a generation, as did Scott. But how many have also played—or overplayed—the principal role in the emergence of that generation? Everything this gilded pair did seemed to breathe life into the image of a Younger Generation. *This Side of Paradise* was the starting gun of the flamboyant Jazz Age, and immediately Scott and Zelda began to shine as living embodiments of Flaming Youth. Future critics might rate Scott's reign as laureate of the Jazz Age as the least important part of his career, but the Jazz Age had no such objectivity. In far-off Paris, Gertrude Stein observed that Scott had created the Jazz Age by *being* it. It was just as simple, as innocent, and as monumental as that!

If, by a single novel, Scott became the spokesman of the Younger Generation, he was equally able as a married man to establish the ideal boy-girl image of the 1920's. Zelda, just turned twenty, was only too glad to act a prototype flapper by bobbing her hair, applying cheek-rouge and lipstick, cutting off skimpy dresses at her dimpled knees, and sprinkling her talk with shocking "hells" and "damns."

But how was it—it may be asked—that the personality, philosophy, and antics of these fresh residents of mid-Manhattan became so well known in a world then blissfully free of personal press agents, gossip columnists, and peephole journalism?

The answer lies in the word *Extravagance*. In 1920, Scott's first year of success, he earned $18,000, a considerable sum for those days. Yet with Zelda's enthusiastic aid he spent every penny. The sales of *This Side of Paradise* failed to supply the quantities of money these two seemed able to squander, nor did those of *Flappers and Philosophers*, a collection of Fitzgerald short stories hastily rushed into print. To keep pace with his own extravagance, Scott was forced to write short stories for markets from *The Saturday Evening Post* to *Smart Set*. In one of them was a sentence which haunted him later on: "She was a faded but still lovely woman of twenty-seven."

Slick short fiction was exactly the sort of writing Scott Fitzgerald despised, and his anger increased as it began to seem that the worse the story to him, the more he got paid for it—usually by the *Post*. In his individual fashion, Scott based his stories on episodes straight out of his or Zelda's past, or on episodes currently happening to both—"plagiarizing their existence," one critic has called it. He also polished and perfected the image of the flapper by writing not only about Zelda, but also Princeton-prom girls who had preceded her in his life.

In this way, a wide magazine public easily learned what the mad young Fitzgeralds were up to. Soon, a vast movie audience had the same data, for the couple's financial recklessness was vastly aided by sale of short stories to Hollywood. Names and stars of these films provide an exercise in deep nostalgia —*The Chorus Girl's Romance* (Scott's "Head and Shoulders"), with Viola Dana and Gareth Hughes; *The Off-Shore Pirate*, with Viola Dana and Jack Mulhall; *The Husband Hunter*, with Eileen Percy; *Grit*, with Glenn Hunter. The average sale price of these stories was $2,500; in addition Famous Players paid $10,000 for *This Side of Paradise*, which never achieved production, perhaps because of its inchoate story line.

In every sense, it seemed, the glittering Fitzgeralds became the personification of Jazz Age youth. Zelda, of course, was the perfect flapper, while twenty-four-year-old Scott displayed the accepted handsomeness of the time. His profile was straight in the manner of the much-admired Arrow collar ads of the day. Yellow, curly hair was parted severely in the center in true Twenties style; in a pale face, conspicuous eyelashes drew attention to penetrating green eyes—did all the exceptional writers of the time have remarkable eyes? Now and forever Scott looked the perennial college youth—"sophomore face and troubadour heart," Ben Hecht said. Five-feet-eight, with broad shoulders and a solid body, his dispropor-tionately short legs were the only physical flaw. One observer thought his overall appearance added up to that of a "faun"; another saw an "archduke."

Scott personified the Jazz Age in more ways. Take away his talent and he stood revealed as a vaguely upper bracket young male of the new age. Minus his gift for writing, he probably would have become one of the young brokers or junior executives who appeared in his stories. The same was true of Zelda. Had it not been for the lucky accident—if, in the end, it *was* lucky—of meeting Scott, she would have re-mained the routine wild flapper, petting in parked cars, nip-ping bootleg gin, and creeping up the stairs at 3 A.M. with shoes in hand, trying not to wake her parents. In time she would marry a solid young provider, to become the kind of flapper wife whose thrill was the country club dance.

Scott was of special interest to his age because he was a poor young man who had managed to attend an Ivy League col-lege. Thus he epitomized the golden dream of contemporary parents and growing boys. Born in St. Paul, Minnesota, he was the son of an ineffectual father whose chief distinction was a blood line from Francis Scott Key of "Star Spangled Banner" fame; indeed, Scott was christened Francis Scott Key Fitzgerald. His mother, domineering and eccentric, was the daughter of a father born in Ireland. "Half black Irish, half old American stock," was Scott's description of his heritage.

As an aimless father moved from job to job, the Fitzgerald family lived in genteel poverty, or near it. So it was something of a miracle for Scott to reach Princeton at all. Yet he showed little gratitude for his rare good fortune—and this too was typical of the Twenties-to-come. Careless of the Princeton curriculum, he devoted his energies to writing stories and verse for Nassau literary magazines and lyrics for the Triangle Club shows. Such glamorous activity, with his good looks and attractive personality, enabled him to mix with rich boys whose fathers gave them Stutz Bearcats. It turned Fitzgerald into a bit of a snob, ashamed of his mother's closeness to

Ireland and vastly impressed by the wealthy, whom he always considered a breed different from the rest of humanity.

Scott not only achieved the Ivy League in the best success-story tradition, but also fell in love in approved contemporary style. Heretofore boy-weds-girl fiction in the *Saturday Evening Post* and such popular periodicals had leaned heavily on stern parents refusing permission for darling daughters to marry. Now, as in real life, the parental menace was gone, to be succeeded in popular fiction by couples falling in love at first sight and eloping without thought of daddy's wrath.

Scott and Zelda Fitzgerald did not elope, but they certainly tumbled into love at first sight. The memorable moment came after Scott, impelled by patriotism, had quit Princeton in his junior semester to attend one of the officers' training camps of World War I. Graduated as a second lieutenant, he was sent to an army camp outside Montgomery, Alabama. Here, at a dance, he spied a golden-haired girl surrounded by ardent admirers. Recalling this initial glimpse years later, he itemized "glorious yellow hair . . . the eternal kissable mouth, small, slightly sensual and utterly disturbing . . . her vivid, instant personality." Others recall the hair as honey gold, and add a pink and white skin ("The skin you love to touch") lighted by deep blue eyes. The eternal kissable mouth was the cupid's bow of current magazine covers.

Zelda Sayre—her unusual first name derived from a gypsy in a romantic novel—was the daughter of a local judge. Already in July 1918, she projected the outline of the flapper of the Nineteen Twenties. Her figure was supple and boyish, with tapered legs just made for rolled stockings and high heels. Ever an undisciplined spirit, Zelda felt free to do whatever appealed to her; when dances grew dull she livened things up by turning cartwheels around the floor. Into the life of this man-crazy eighteen-year-old, the fortunes of war had deposited a camp full of army officers, young and old, rich and poor, handsome and homely. No doubt this pioneer jazz baby was even now kissing and petting, as well as puffing cigarettes and sipping corn-likker from proffered flasks.

At first sight of zippy Zelda, Scott felt his legs turn to marshmallow. Oddly enough, the baby vamp felt identical sensations as he elbowed his way toward her. Already they had fallen in love, and knew it. Yet Zelda wanted fun and luxury out of life—in that order. Scott might be able to supply the fun, but a young man who talked vaguely of being a writer failed to meet her high standards as a lifetime provider. So Zelda continued to date other men.

When she did Scott got desperately drunk, even though initial samplings of alcohol at Princeton had brought the realization that he was unable to hold his liquor like a gentleman. A few swallows of the hard stuff altered Scott's pleasant personality, making him antic, annoying, and morose before he passed out. Yet this inability to hold liquor failed to deter him from a drink-drenched life.

After the Armistice, Scott bypassed his two remaining Princeton years to go to New York where, in an effort to impress Zelda with his earning potential, he took a job writing slogans in an advertising agency. Earning less than one hundred dollars a month, he lived in a furnished room on Claremont Avenue in the Bronx. He made several long railroad journeys to see Zelda in Montgomery, and during the last the pair fought so violently that all seemed over between them. Back in New York, Scott (like Amory Blaine) took off on a three-week bender—"Hating the city, I got roaring, weeping drunk on my last penny." Then he returned to his native St. Paul to write *This Side of Paradise.*

When word reached him in St. Paul that Scribner's had accepted his manuscript, Scott's immediate reaction was to dash into the middle of the street, stopping the autos of friend and stranger alike to report the glad tidings. Not only was he ecstatic at the fate of his brainchild, but he was jubilant about his own future. Somehow the intuitive young man sensed what the Roaring Twenties would be like and realized that he was in a position to become foremost chronicler of the decade. As he eventually put it—

. . . there seemed little doubt about what was going to happen—America was going on the greatest, gaudiest spree in history, and there was going to be plenty to tell about it. The whole golden boom was in the air.

So Scott Fitzgerald began following his star. After making sure Zelda would marry him, he went to New York alone and began acting the King of the Jazz Age. Acceptance of his novel had brought him luck, and his short stories began selling to magazines. Taking a suite in the Hotel Knickerbocker on Times Square, he summoned bellboys to assist him in dressing and—some say—to scrub his back in the tub. He attended Ivy League parties, at which he was a celebrity, with hundred dollar bills ostentatiously peeking from pockets. Grandly intoxicated by love, success, and money, he downed his Bronx cocktails with the finest of flourishes.

Publication of *This Side of Paradise*—a title purloined from Rupert Brooke—added fame to his fortune. The novel failed to win the unalloyed praise given *Main Street*, but it was completely in focus with the mood of the young, catching superbly the rootlessness and (even then) desperations ruling the decade. Scott neither caricatured nor ridiculed like Sinclair Lewis, but told his story in natural fashion, as if it were normal and amusing. Later Glenway Wescott wrote, "*This Side of Paradise* haunted the generation like a song, popular but perfect."

So Scott became famous, recognized, admired, interviewed. To one reporter, he said his novel was "a book about flappers and philosophers." Delighted by this offhand remark, he chose *Flappers and Philosophers* as the title of his short story collection.

With all this, Scott was still amazed at the enthusiastic way sophisticated New York reached out to embrace the boy from Minnesota and with him Zelda, the sleepy time gal from Alabam'. The young-married Fitzgeralds were, he concluded, "the archetype of what New York wanted." High Society dowagers, the Ivy League rich, book publishers, and fellow authors inundated the pampered pair with invitations. Shining symbols of youthful rebellion, as well as of the growing older-generation opposition to the Eighteenth Amendment, they began to lead a gilded existence where, in Zelda's fragrant phrase, "It was always tea time, or late at night." Scott put it more prosaically: "We felt like small children in a great bright unexplored barn. . . . [we] were at one with New York, pulling it after us through every portal."

Among those doting on the golden pair were the Katzenjammer Kids of Literature. Mencken quickly dubbed Scott "Fitzheimer," an indication of solid acceptance. The sleek Nathan preferred Zelda, caressingly addressing her as "Dear Blonde." Ernest Boyd did not seem bothered by Scott's lack of pride in his mother's Irish blood, though it annoyed the Padraic Colums and others among the Erin-born; the Fitzgeralds were often honored guests at bookish soirees given by Boyd and his French wife Madeleine. So great was the glamour of the couple that they were permitted on the set while D. W. Griffith directed Dorothy Gish in a movie. This experience began Scott's lifelong infatuation with film making, but his thoughts about it at the moment indicated a personal uneasiness as a Gotham celebrity. "The role of the motion picture actor," he wrote, "was like our own in that it was in New York and not of it—it had little sense of itself and no center."

In the Teeming Twenties, steady drinking was considered more play than problem. The Fitzgeralds helped establish this heedless pattern by getting happily soused—to use Scott's favorite term of the moment—by lunchtime on some days, teatime on others. The trick was to be so drunk by nightfall that it grew hard to remember what happened the rest of the night. Drinkers of Scott and Zelda's calibre spent a good part of the morning after trying to discover what transpired the night before.

At various times, these pampered pets of the town rode up and down Fifth Avenue on the roofs of taxicabs, dunked in the Plaza fountain and the one downtown on Union Square. Aroused by the nude showgirls of naughty George White's *Scandals,* Scott rose in his favorite front row seat and began to disrobe. At a dance in downtown Webster Hall, he took a wild swing at a uniformed guard and miraculously landed. Next morning's newspaper headlines read, "KNOCKS OFFICER THIS SIDE OF PARADISE."

History books are inclined to report that the speakeasy era did not begin until mid-decade, but Scott Fitzgerald knew better. There were plush speakeasies in 1920, and he and Zelda all but supported a few. Zelda did the shimmy atop cabaret tables while Scott, rendered truculent by gin slings, exchanged punches with patrons and waiters. The two danced until dawn to the music of Paul Whiteman, Brooke Johns, or Vincent Lopez, then reeled up Fifth Avenue to the Plaza clutching full bottles of champagne. Sometimes it was their drunken caprice to smash these bottles against curb stones before the eyes of astonished wage slaves hurrying to work.

Invited to elegant Fifth or Park Avenue parties, they sometimes greeted host and hostess with deep alcoholic dignity, then advanced on the nearest sofa and fell asleep in each other's arms. At one literary gathering the radiant duo burst in two hours late, announcing they had not seen a bed for two nights. With this, they sat down and fell asleep—or was it passed out? Zelda, in her handkerchief-size flapper dress, was carried into the bedroom and deposited on a bed, "where she lay asleep like a silky kitten."

Scott, slumbering in an easy chair, suddenly awoke to denounce the party as a bore. Lurching to the telephone, he contacted a bootlegger and ordered two cases of champagne sent to the premises. Then he roused Zelda to tell her. She irritably countermanded the order and told him to round up enough taxis to transport the entire party to a nightclub. In episodes like this, we are told, the enchanted couple was high-spirited, wayward, and perverse—but never vulgar.

Not all was fun and frolic, however. Liquor often turned rancid in the early morning hours, and the two engaged in ugly fights. On other occasions Zelda's compulsive flirting precipitated verbal brawls. Both were subject to wicked hangovers, and Scott wrote of "two days of gaiety, two days of moroseness—an endless, almost invariable round."

Scott's friends blamed Zelda, for the frail flapper seemed

able to drink as much, if not more, than her spouse. One of Scott's Princeton classmates wrote in his diary: "Zelda increasingly restless—says frankly she simply wants to be amused and is only good for useless, pleasure-giving pursuits." Doing this, she kept pulling Scott deeper and deeper into the madcap whirl. One day he made the unhappy discovery that their money had run out. "Well," Zelda said brightly, "let's go to the movies."

During the summer of 1920, the couple took a house in Westport, Connecticut. If nothing else, the quest for a summer home and the hot-weather sojourn in the country provided Scott with material for the second novel on which he had embarked.

Now the all-night revels took place in woodsy surroundings. After a drunken battle with Scott, Zelda began walking to New York along the railroad tracks and narrowly missed being hit by a train. During one wild party Scott turned in a fire alarm. "Where's the fire?" the arriving fire laddies shouted at Zelda. "Right here," she said, indicating a boyish breast. Scott stepped forward to explain that he had summoned the apparatus because his friends were "lit." Local authorities took a dim view and haled him into court.

One weekend guest was George Jean Nathan, who arrived bearing bottles of Milshire gin. The puckish critic was tickled to find his hosts employing a Japanese houseman named Tana, and pretended to recognize the Oriental as a disguised German agent Lieutenant Emil Tannenbaum. Throughout the weekend he gleefully kept his jape alive.

In the *Smart Set* office, Nathan regaled Mencken with his weekend inspiration. Mencken began sending postcards in German to Lieutenant Tannenbaum, care of the Fitzgeralds. One told the spy to advise if the cellar of the house was big enough to hide a two-ton cannon. "Reply in Code 24-A," the card instructed. Said Mencken to his fellow Katzenjammer Kid, "Let me know if Fitzheimer is killed when the Westport American Legion raids his house."

Mencken also mailed copies of the *Berliner Tageblatt* to

Leutnant Tannenbaum. In them, harmless ads were circled in meaningful fashion. "This will agitate the Westport burlesons," Mencken stated. (Albert Burleson was then Postmaster General.)

By autumn, the Fitzgeralds had returned to the city, living at 51 West 59th Street, where meals could be delivered from the kitchens of their adored Plaza. Otherwise the arrangement was not too happy, for Zelda was a hopeless housekeeper who never emptied an ashtray and hid dirty laundry in closet corners and suitcases. Their frantic round of parties and speakeasy nights was immortalized by Scott in verse:

> *There's on orchestra*
> > *Bingo! Bango!*
> *Playing for us*
> > *To dance the tango,*
> *And people would clap*
> > *When we arose*
> *At her sweet face*
> > *And my new clothes.*

Gossip of the moment said Scott had grown jealous over the intensity of flirting between Zelda and George Jean Nathan, that an argument ensued, with the drama critic abruptly departing the frivolous circle.

Nathan tells a different story. He claims to have been rendered uneasy by Zelda's "Godiva act." That is, he found her an exhibitionist who enjoyed undressing in public. The mellow folklore of the Twenties lists Zelda as taking at least two drunken dives into public fountains, supposedly while attired in her skimpy flapper's dress. Nathan declares that before leaping into the Union Square fountain, at least, she peeled to the skin. He also recalls Zelda summoning the guests at a party to look at her in the bathtub, and further reports that she once started to take off her clothes in—of all places!—Grand Central Station.

For Scott the first full winter of success was bittersweet. One evening he rode up the canyon of Fifth Avenue in a taxi under a mauve and rose sky. "I began to bawl because I had everything I wanted and knew I would never be so happy again." Around him other members of the Younger Generation were exhilarated because "It seemed only a question of years before the older people would step aside and let the world be run by those who saw things as they were."

At the same time he instinctively felt that the gaudy spree could not last, either for him, the Younger Generation, or average citizens of the United States. One symptom of danger was that "young liquor was taking the place of young blood." Later he wrote of this period, "All the stories that came into my head had a touch of disaster to them. In life these things hadn't happened yet, but I was pretty sure living wasn't the reckless carefree business people thought."

In other ways, Scott was a man divided. The sensible part of him knew the all-night drinking and carousing dulled his talent and cost him precious hours of work. He was making progress with his second novel, but always had to concentrate on popular short stories in order to pay the bills. Usually he wrote through a shimmering hangover, while Zelda sat in a rumpled bed, impatiently buffing her nails, or soaked for long periods in the bathtub. On her part, Zelda never got over being impressed by sales to *The Saturday Evening Post*. Once she said, "I always thought a story for the *Post* was tops, a goal worth seeking."

In this atmosphere the giddy pair lived and loved, drank and battled. Through the madness, they remained star-crossed lovers. "Of all the things possessed in common," Scott wrote once, "the greatest of all was their almost uncanny pull at one another's hearts." In time, Carl Van Vechten put these shining symbols of the Jazz Age into a novel aptly titled *Parties*. "They love each other . . . desperately, passionately," he wrote. "They cling to each other like barnacles cling to rocks, but they want to hurt each other all the time to test their feeling."

By March 1921, Scott had managed to finish the first draft of *The Beautiful and Damned*, a title already used on a short story. Simultaneously Zelda discovered herself pregnant. In those days authors who were successful usually took a trip to Europe. The young Fitzgeralds, who had already talked Grand Tour, decided to go there before the birth of the baby.

In his biography of Fitzgerald, Andrew Turnbull re-creates the night before their scheduled sailing. Long after midnight a lurching Scott appeared at the portals of a gilded speakeasy known as the Jungle Club, where the doorman refused him admittance on grounds of drunkenness. Suddenly a furious Zelda materialized, to berate Scott for walking out on her at the last club. Quickly taking in the new situation, she shrilly informed Scott that no blankety-blank doorman had the right to keep a man of his fame out of a cheesy speakeasy.

At this, Scott aimed a clumsy blow at the doorman, who responded with a shove that sent Scott sprawling. Zelda, momentarily absent, returned to shriek, "Scott, you're not going to let him get away with *that!*" Scott struggled to his feet and moved forward belligerently. . . .

On the morning the Fitzgeralds were supposed to sail for Europe, Scott lay abed, head bandaged, an eye swollen shut, body aching from a severe beating. A barber from the Plaza was trying to shave him as gently as possible. Zelda was absent, having rushed downtown to make goo-goo eyes at clerks in the steamship office in an effort to exchange their tickets.

A week later the Fitzgeralds, legends in their time, were able to board the ship, temporarily leaving the Jazz Age behind.

But the melody lingered on. . . .

A Panorama of the
Literary Scene in the
Nineteen Twenties

Sinclair Lewis radically changed the course of American fiction with his novel *Main Street*. Seemingly the most informal of men, Lewis loved to doll up after success hit him, and was caricatured in full plumage on the cover of *Smart Set*, edited by his friends Mencken and Nathan. (*Photo credit:* UPI; *Magazine credit: Beinecke Library, Yale University*)

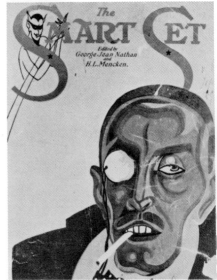

Mr. and Mrs. Sinclair Lewis and son Wells, named after the author of *The War of The Worlds*. (UPI)

By F. Scott Fitzgerald

THIS
SIDE OF PARADISE

"A Novel about Flappers
Written for Philosophers"

"It is probably one of the few really American novels extant."—HARRY HANSEN in the *Chicago Daily News*.

"A very enlivening book, indeed; a book really brilliant and glamorous, making as agreeable reading as could be asked."—*New York Evening Post*.

"The glorious spirit of abounding youth glows throughout this fascinating tale. . . . It could have been written only by an artist who knows how to balance his values, plus a delightful literary style."—*New York Times*.

"It is abundantly worth while; it is delightful, consciously and unconsciously, amusing, keenly and diversely interesting; cracking good stuff to read, in short."—*New York Sun*.

Twelfth Printing

CHARLES SCRIBNER'S SONS

Scott Fitzgerald's *This Side of Paradise* was a sensation among the young, a shocker to older folk. Overnight Fitzgerald and his flapper wife Zelda became archetypes of Flaming Youth. Most of Scott's short stories appeared in popular magazines like *The Saturday Evening Post* and *Hearst's International*—the latter boasted of signing him exclusively in May 1923. But his better efforts usually appeared in small-circulation periodicals like *Smart Set*. (*Beinecke Library, Yale University*)

"The Diamond as Big as the Ritz"
By F. Scott Fitzgerald

Most photos of Henry L. Mencken
show him stolid as a butcher—as
here, where the Sage of Baltimore is
in custody of officer Oliver B. Garrett
after being arrested for selling a copy
of the suppressed *American
Mercury* on Boston Common. (UPI)
But the caricature by William
Gropper which appeared in *The
Literary Spotlight* catches the
shrewdness, resilience, and informality
that were his. It also shows he was
once a thin man! (*Sketch by William
Gropper from* The Literary
Spotlight, 1924) *Permission of the artist*

Ernest Boyd was called the most erudite figure on the literary scene of the Twenties. Charming, witty, and handsome, he was a bit of a showman who wore brown attire matching his hair, eyes, and beard.

George Jean Nathan, senior editor of *Smart Set* (because he had been hired first), was a drama critic as handsome as the leading men in plays that opened under his scrutiny. Boulevardier, epicure, epigrammatist, and connoisseur of sweet young things, Nathan was coeditor of *The American Mercury* with H.L. Mencken when it began publication in 1924. But his active tenure was short. (*Erik S. Monberg*)

MY CITY
BY THEODORE DREISER

ΛΛΛΛ

ILLUSTRATED
WITH EIGHT ETCHINGS
IN COLOR BY
MAX POLLAK

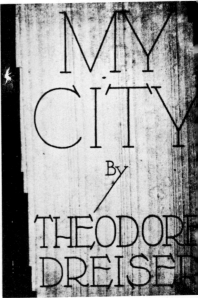

NUMBER

THIS EDITION IS LIMITED TO
TWO HUNDRED SEVENTY-FIVE COPIES,
EACH SIGNED BY
THE AUTHOR

Limited editions were a publishing staple of the Twenties. Expensive, decorated and illustrated by noted artists, they were printed in small, exclusive runs, with the type broken up afterward. The limited edition of Theodore Dreiser's *My City* measures 15 by 11 inches and contains a sampling of metropolitan poetry and prose. The Pollak etchings are full page and in full color; Liveright was the proud publisher. (*Courtesy Mrs. Ad Schulberg*)

The novels of Theodore Dreiser (whose *Sister Carrie* was published in 1900) served as battering rams, allowing American literature of the 1920's to enter into unprecedented realism and honesty. At first, authors like Sherwood Anderson and Sinclair Lewis reaped the rewards of his determined frankness. Then Dreiser himself scored in 1925 with *An American Tragedy*.

ALL THE SAD
YOUNG MEN

F·SCOTT FITZGERALD

CLEON

Scribner's and its editor Maxwell Perkins had done so well with Scott Fitzgerald's novels and short story collections (see jacket above) that Ernest Hemingway left Liveright, his first publisher. This is how he looked in Scribner's promotion photographs for *The Sun Also Rises,* his third-published book in America. (*Credit for Hemingway only: Erik S. Monberg*)

JOSEPH HERGESHEIMER

JAMES BRANCH CABELL

Joseph Hergesheimer and James Branch Cabell were among the top novelists of the early Twenties—it was impossible to believe their fame would not last forever. Sherwood Anderson's *Winesburg, Ohio* predated *Main Street* and resembled it in content. The mellow Anderson's influence over young writers like Hemingway and Faulkner was amazing—and sometimes sadly unappreciated. (*Sketches by William Gropper from* The Literary Spotlight, 1924)

SHERWOOD ANDERSON

BURTON RASCOE

Burton Rascoe, literary catalyst
extraordinary. First in Chicago,
then in New York, he wrote
about books with electrifying
enthusiasm and delighted in uncovering new talent. His
"Bookman's Daybook" in the
New York Tribune carried the
first bright gossip of literary
goings-on. (*Sketch by William
Gropper, from* The Literary
Spotlight, 1924)

NO SIRREE!
An Anonymous Entertainment by the Vicious Circle of the
Hotel Algonquin
49TH STREET THEATRE
SUNDAY EVENING, APRIL 30TH, 1922
(Theatre by courtesy of the Messrs. Shubert)

Spirit of the American Drama ....Heywood Broun

OPENING CHORUS
Alexander Woollcott, John Peter Toohey, Robert C. Benchley, George S. Kaufman,
Marc Connelly and Franklin P. Adams

"THE EDITOR REGRETS——"
Mabel Cenci .... Marc Connelly, '25
George Medeci ....J. M. Kerrigan, '26

A Composer-Author ....Donald Ogden Stewart, '25
Dante .... Harold Gould, '23
An Average Male Reader...........................Henry Wise Miller, '22
An Average Female Reader...............................Mary Brandon, '30
        Venice at the time of Dante. The editorial offices of "Droll Tales,"
        a popular twice-a-month magazine which flourished at that period

THE FILMLESS MOVIES
Baron Ireland and F. P. A.

THE GREASY HAG
An O'Neill Play in One Act
CAST
(In the order of appearance)
Elizabeth Inchcape, known as Coal-Barge Bessie, a retired water-front
        prostitute .... John Peter Toohey
The Murdered Woman .... Ruth Gillmore
First Agitated Seaman ....George S. Kaufman
Second Agitated Seaman ....Alexander Woollcott
Third Agitated Seaman ....Marc Connelly
                        Scene
    Vote
    for
    One
Backroom of Billy the Bishop's saloon, near Coentie's Slip, New York
Firemen's forecastle on a freighter bound east from Rio.
                Time—The present
        Incidental music by Arthur H. Samuels

HE WHO GETS FLAPPED
With Robert E. Sherwood and the following ingenues: June Walker, Winifred
        Lenihan, Juliet St. John-Brenon, Tallulah Bankhead, Mary Kennedy, Ruth
        Gillmore, Lenore Ulric, Helen Hayes and Mary Brandon.

BETWEEN THE ACTS
The Manager ....Brock Pemberton
The Manager's Brother .... Murdock Pemberton
And the following first nighters: Dorothy Parker, Alice Duer Miller, Neysa
        McMein, Beatrice Kaufman, Jane Grant, Heywood Broun, Alexander
        Woollcott, Robert C. Benchley, George S. Kaufman, Marc Connelly, Kel-
        cey Allen, Arthur Bachrach.

"JOHNNY WEAVER," a Ballad
Sung by Reinald Werrenrath

BIG CASINO IS LITTLE CASINO
A Samuel Shipman Play
(In Three Acts)

James W. Archibald (a Rich Man)........................John Peter Toohey
Dregs (a Butler)..Alexander Woollcott
Mr. Harper (a Broker)..J. M. Kerrigan
John Findlay (a Young Attorney)........................George S. Kaufman
O'Brien (a Detective) ....Franklin P. Adams
Margaret (Archibald's Daughter) .... Mary Kennedy
A Convict .... Marc Connelly
The Broker's Boy..David H. Wallace
The Governor of New York............................Robert E. Sherwood
Guests ....Alice Duer Miller, Neysa McMein, Jane Grant

Synopsis of Scenes

ACT   I—The Home of James W. Archibald
ACT   II—The same. A week later
ACT III—A Wall Street Office. Two days later
Offstage Music by J. Heifetz

INTERMISSION

MARC CONNELLY
"That Somewhat Different Cornettist"
—in—
"A NIGHT AT FRANK CAMPBELL'S"
Scene—Frank Campbell's   Time—Night

ZOWIE
Or The Curse of an Akins Heart
(A Romanza In One Act)
"Nor all your piety and wit"—*From the Persian*

CAST
(In the order of appearance)

Marmaduke LaSalle (a Stomach Specialist).................John Peter Toohey
Lady friend of LaSalle's.................................. Neysa McMein
Another lady friend of LaSalle's..........................Louise Closser Hale
Dindo (a Wandering Busboy)..............................J. M. Kerrigan
Zhoolie Venable (a Suppressed Desire*)........................Ruth Gillmore
Mortimer Van Loon (a Decayed Gentleman)..............George S. Kaufman
Archibald Van Alstyne (a Precisionist)...................Alexander Woollcott
Lemuel Pip (an Old Taxi Driver)............................Harold W. Ross
Scene—A Capitol Lunch.   Time—Printemps, 1922.
    * Suppressed in Humansville, Mo., sometime in April, 1908.
Offstage Music by J. Heifetz

MR. WHIM PASSES BY
An A. A. Milne Play

Cynthia .... Helen Hayes
Nigel .... Sidney Blackmer
Uncle Tertius ....J. M. Kerrigan
The scene is the morning room at The Acacias, Wipney-cum-Chiselickwick

---

SONG: "KAUFMAN AND CONNELLY FROM THE WEST"

BEATRICE HERFORD
—in—
"The Algonquin Girl"

F I N A L E
by the entire company

On a Sunday night in 1922, members of the Algonquin Round Table hired a Broadway theater and presented a revue called *No Sirree!* Its cast was a who's who of literary and theatrical glamour.

Dorothy Parker seems young and defenseless in this 1922 portrait by Neysa McMein, fellow member of the Algonquin Round Table. Five years later Mrs. Parker again sat for her friend; but then, says her biographer John Keats, she looked tense and neurotic. (*Erik S. Monberg*)

Edna Ferber, a writer from childhood, had to wait until *So Big* in 1924 before changing from a writer of magazine fiction to noted novelist. She then went on to even greater glory with *Show Boat*.

To the amazement of all involved, Anita Loos' *Gentlemen Prefer Blondes* became one of the sensational sellers of the decade. This caricature of Miss Loos by Ralph Barton, who illustrated *Gentlemen*, shows her at the typewriter—though she writes in longhand. (*Courtesy Anita Loos*)

The Book-of-the-Month Club and the competing Literary Guild were controversial topics of the day. Booksellers opposed them, claiming that cheaper hardcover editions cut into their business. The clubs countered with claims of having opened the market to new readers who were not lucky enough to have a bookstore within browsing distance. Bruce Bairnsfeather poked gentle fun at this idea in humor magazine *Life*.

Crossword-puzzle books put the fledgling firm of Simon and Schuster on its feet. The fad swept the country to such an extent that even commuters atop Fifth Avenue buses were diverted. (*Drawing by Herb Roth in the New York* World)

THE ARRIVAL OF THE BOOK-OF-THE-MONTH

Trader Horn (Alfred Aloysius Horn, né plain Smith) appeared to be the author of the most exceptional adventure-biography of the latter Twenties. But after his arrival here (with his combination spear/walking stick), doubts were engendered as to the book's authenticity. While pleasant enough, the old Trader did not seem overly bright, and distinguished himself at cocktail parties by gulping every drink in sight.

Could Joan Lowell be a prevari-
cator? Simon and Schuster,
publishers of *Trader Horn*
didn't think so and encouraged
Joan to write her own adventure
yarn, *Cradle of the Deep.*
Exposed as more fancy than fact,
it continued its brisk sales as
fiction. (UPI)

Despite heavy competition, Louis Bromfield remained the most personable and charming author of the Literary Decade. After his first success, however, he departed for France to become the most dazzling of expatriates. (*Woodcut from* Mirrors of the Year, 1927)

Perhaps New York's most colorful literary figure in the 1920's was Carl Van Vechten, pictured here in 1925. Author of super-sophisticated novels, ardent espouser of the avant-garde, and rare discoverer of talent both white and black, Van Vechten also gave celebrated parties which brought together every variety of art and artist. (*Courtesy Bruce Kellner*)

Hail the conquering author! Michael Arlen, whose novel *The Green Hat* had triumphed in England, arrived in America to duplicate his success. The book was a landmark in sexually permissive fiction of the Twenties. (UPI)

Blanche and Alfred Knopf brought flair to publishing and beauty to books. Each Knopf book closes with a note giving details of its physical format. The one illustrated here comes from the volume commemorating Knopf's tenth year of publishing. (*Photo credit:* UPI; *colophon from* Borzoi 1925)

Of the BORZOI 1925
*there were printed in the month of December
five thousand copies on laid India tint paper
made by The Tileston-Hollingsworth Co.*

*The book was designed by Elmer Adler
and the composition, printing & binding
done by the Plimpton Press, Norwood*

*The halftone plates were made by The
Walker Engraving Co., and printed on
S. D. Warren's ivory cameo paper.*

Horace Liveright, buccaneer among publishers, loved authors and saw the publishing business through a gambler's eyes. He won with Theodore Dreiser, lost heavily with others, while presiding over the swinging mid-Manhattan firm of Boni & Liveright. Incongruously, its trademark was a cloistered monk. (*Photo credit: Erik S. Monberg*)

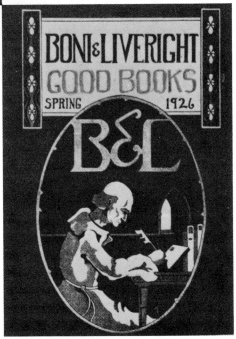

Publishers like Liveright enjoyed doing business in gilded speakeasies similar to this one pictured (with slight cubistic overtones) in the painting *Speako Deluxe* by Joseph

Golinken. But writers themselves
were inclined to prefer the informal,
all-night atmosphere of Tony's on
West Fifty-second Street. (*Museum
of the City of New York*)

Triumph and tragedy at decade's end. Scott Fitzgerald, the ravages of drink and his wife's dementia apparent on his face, returns to the United States from Paris. Sinclair Lewis departs in glory to receive the Nobel Prize for Literature—clutching *Swedish in Ten Lessons.* (UPI)

At the end of the decade, Carl Van Vechten abruptly ended his career as a novelist to become a distinguished portrait photographer. One of his first subjects was H.L. Mencken, who had just astounded the world by taking a bride. (*Carl Van Vechten, Courtesy Van Vechten Estate and Bruce Kellner*)

A Bookman's Daybook

Burton Rascoe . . Christopher Morley . . .

Strange to relate, the young Fitzgeralds did not enjoy Europe. These darlings of mid-Manhattan not only lacked friends overseas, but apparently bore no letters of introduction. Nor did they make efforts to contact the handful of American expatriates who had begun to stake a claim to the Left Bank of Paris. More responsive to persons than to places, the Fitzgeralds could not fall back on the simple pleasures of sightseeing. Drifting from London, to Paris, to Rome, they amused themselves largely by tormenting the staff of hotels in which they stayed.

In Paris, they scattered pornographic postcards around their rooms, left ice cream to melt, and used a belt to secure the hand-pull elevator to their floor during changes of attire. Once they purchased an uncured Armenian goatskin which stank up the entire premises. They found Rome dull, but were briefly diverted in Venice. Wrote Scott, "We had fun in a gondola feeling like a soft Italian song."

Having "done" the Continent in two dismal weeks, they returned to London and lodged at Claridge's, where an elderly room waiter provided their sole contact with the outside world. When this worthy failed to be amused by their inimitable antics, Scott went to the local Scribner representative and borrowed passage money home. Two hours later the

Fitzgeralds were on the boat train. Back in New York, Scott exclaimed to Maxwell Perkins, "What an overestimated place Europe is!"

In this antipathy, the Fitzgeralds appeared to constitute a minority of two in the literary community. Since 1920, Young America's dream had involved departing the country, preferably for the Left Bank of Paris. From this stimulating spot it would be easier to write the G.A.N.—"to do one honest novel in an atmosphere free of Puritan inhibitions." Intellectuals lacking the ability to write, paint, or compose would be content to mingle with those who did. The human beacons charting this merry course were Gertrude Stein, Ezra Pound, and T. S. Eliot. Americans all, they stoutly maintained that an artist's best work could only be done in transatlantic climes.

Even as the Fitzgeralds came home, twenty-two-year-old Ernest Hemingway was in Chicago percolating plans for leaving the United States. In 1919, Hemingway had returned from the war as something of a minor hero. Unable to enlist in the army because of poor eyesight, he had volunteered as a Red Cross ambulance driver, and was said to be the first American wounded (237 fragments of Minnie shell in his leg) in the Italian campaign.

After the war, he labored as a reporter on the Kansas City *Star* and other newspapers, his mind gestating a lean, crisp writing style which was unlike any other ever attempted. Quitting newspapers, he moved into a Chicago boarding house full of aspiring writers like himself. Simultaneously he was preparing to marry Hadley Richardson, an attractive woman eight years his senior. Hadley had a small income which made living in Europe feasible, and she opted for Rome. Sherwood Anderson, who liked to visit the colorful rooming house, had convinced Ernest that Paris was the only city where genius could flourish. Hemingway talked Hadley around, and the two picked December 1921 as target date for crossing the ocean.

Other writers and would-be writers toying with the idea of Europe were sharply propelled in that direction by publication in January 1922 of *Civilization in the United States*. This five-hundred-page epic was the brainchild of the picturesque Greenwich Villager, Harold Stearns, who had been an outstanding undergraduate at Harvard, but done little exceptional since. Dwelling in a damp cellar, he made a meagre living by writing book reviews for *The New Republic, Freeman,* and *Dial.*

Yet Stearns managed to regard himself with high approval; a friend characterized his swollen ego as "a refreshing lack of modesty." With his towering self-confidence, Stearns believed that male companions were under obligation to buy him unlimited drinks. Females, he thought, should freely offer their charms; his attitude toward women was described as "the pleasure is *hers.*" Once Stearns said, "For some reason, I collect myths about myself as easily as a snowball gathers snow rolling down a hill." Van Wyck Brooks saw in him "an element of the medieval vagabond student who is known, in contemporary parlance, as the literary bum."

His personal foibles notwithstanding, Stearns had sold the firm of Harcourt, Brace an idea which sounded earth-shattering at the time. His notion was a symposium by American writers and scholars which would examine contemporary America in stimulating depth. Said Stearns portentously, "This is a book that must be done."

The contributors he set out to corral were a Who's Who of living writers. Oddly, youth was no criterion. The oldest contributor turned out to be fifty-seven, the youngest twenty-seven, with thirty-six the mean age. Twenty-seven American males, two females, and three foreign critics ultimately provided the articles and essays. H. L. Mencken wrote on Politics, Nathan on Theater, Lewis Mumford on the City, Van Wyck Brooks on Literary life, Deems Taylor on Music, Conrad Aiken on Poetry, Hendrik Willem Van Loon on History, Thorne Smith on Advertising, Ring Lardner on Sports, and so on. Stearns assigned himself Intellectual Life. Some of the other topics were Economic Opinion, the Small Town, the Alien, Racial Minorities, Nerves, Medicine, and Humor.

Two provocative subjects—Family and Sex—were daringly parceled out to the females Katherine Anthony and

Elsie Clews Parsons. As Mencken sat in Stearns' cellar perusing their manuscripts, he thumped fist on table and shouted, "Why, God damn it, Stearns, the gals are doing better than the men!"

The chore of compiling *Civilization in the United States* took honest effort on the part of the hitherto dilatory Stearns. When finally finished, the book was properly cynical and disillusioned, giving the impression that, contrary to its title, life in the United States was really uncivilized. Nowhere on its many pages did readers find hope for present or future, and no contributor provided a remedy for improving this sad state of affairs. Each contributor seemed driven to damn his subject, making the book "a curious document of disaffection, failure of culture, family life, religion . . . of everything but science." Rereading it years later, Malcolm Cowley found a similarity to "an inquest over a man everyone disliked. . . . They [came] forward to tell us that life in this United States [was] joyless and colorless, universally standardized, tawdry, given over to the worship of wealth and machinery."

In his essay on politics, Mencken accused the politicians of

> *incurable cowardice and venality. . . . Go into their debates, and you will discover what equipment they bring to their high business. What they know of sound literature is what one may get out of McGuffey's Fifth Reader. What they know of political science is the nonsense preached in the Chautauqua and on the stump. What they know of history is the childish stuff taught in grammar schools. What they know of the arts and sciences— of all the great body of knowledge that is the chief intellectual baggage of modern man—is absolutely nothing.*

About American shools, Clarence Britten felt:

> ⊷§ *We discipline a rash instructor who carries too far his private taste for developing originality; we pass acts that require teachers to sink their own individuality in our own unanimity.*

After detailing America's lack of sympathy for abstract thought, Harold Chapman Brown ended:

> ✣ *If [its] philosophy can find freedom, America can find philosophy.*

Anent the intellectual life of the country Stearns pleaded:

> ✣ *Surely one can hope that the America of our natural affections rather than the present one of enforced dull standardization may some day snap the shackles of those who today keep it a spiritual prison.*

As for the nation's other aspects, Lewis Mumford called America's growing cities sorry examples of material success and spiritual failure. Much-respected John Macy branded native journalism corrupt and controlled by advertisers, upbraiding the public for uncritically accepting the news printed. Despite the upsurge in American writing, Van Wyck Brooks thought the literary life "a very weak and sickly plant." Garet Garett, who made good money writing on finance for *The Saturday Evening Post*, nonetheless detected a lack of morality in business and concluded "man's acquisitive instinct [is] acting outside of humanistic motives."

Civilization in the United States was a sensation among intellectuals, its doleful conclusions acting as the final catalyst that drove young men and women to Paris. This was especially true in the case of Harold Stearns, who naturally felt the full impact of his volume before anyone else. On the day after giving his magnum opus to the publisher, Stearns boarded ship and quit his native land, an episode enshrined by Malcolm Cowley in the essay, "The French Line Pier, 1921." On the Left Bank, Stearns became a charter member of the group which then or later included Americans like Matthew Josephson, Ernest Hemingway, Harry and Caresse Crosby, Kay Boyle, Laurence Vail, Gorham Munson, Kenneth Burke, Djuna Barnes, Malcolm Cowley, Lewis Galantière, Robert McAlmon, Harold Loeb, e.e. cummings, Glenway Wescott, John Dos Passos, Morley Callaghan, Allen Tate, Archibald

MacLeish, Samuel Putnam, Horace Gregory, Ludwig Lewisohn, and a host of others.

These young intellectuals, branded self-pitying and self-indulgent by disapproving elders, were fully aware of their unique status in the cultural cosmos. At first they self-consciously referred to themselves as the Lost Battalion, after an epic episode of World War I. Then Gertrude Stein studied them and rendered an opinion. "You are all a lost generation," she said. So the designation "Lost Generation" came into being, to the obvious satisfaction of its members.

As if to fill the void created by so many departures, Burton Rascoe arrived in New York. This one-man cyclone was known to friends as Rapid Rascoe because of his speedy movements and quicksilver mind. Tense, thin, so fast a talker that he seemed to stammer, Rascoe almost visibly burned energy. "His conversation resembles the outpouring from a decanter abruptly inverted," a friend thought. Rascoe had always dreamed of working in New York City, and had even chosen in advance the ideal spot for his labors. It was the New York *Tribune*, founded by Horace Greeley, which boasted on its pages F.P.A.'s "Conning Tower," book, drama, and sports coverage—has there ever been such a troika of duties?—by Heywood Broun, the foreign reportage of Frazier "Spike" Hunt, pungent sports column by W. O. McGeehan, and the "Mr. & Mrs." cartoons by Clare Briggs.

Yet Rascoe's summons to New York late in 1921 was not from the *Tribune*. Rather, he was lured from Chicago to assume the post of associate editor of *McCall's*, the women's magazine whose two million circulation was gained by short stories and serials by Kathleen Norris, Robert W. Chambers, Fannie Hurst, Mary Roberts Rinehart, and Irvin S. Cobb. Its slick pages also carried illustrations by Neysa McMein, John La Gatta, Henry Raleigh, Dean Cornwall, and Howard Chandler Christy.

In this potent editorial post, Rascoe was able to cement friendships with men like Dreiser, Hergesheimer, Cabell, and

Fitzgerald, but otherwise he was far from content. At a time when starched white collars were *de rigueur* for men in business, Rascoe got in immediate hot water by wearing unstarched blue. He then invited further wrath by refusing to punch the office time clock.

Rapid Rascoe was sprung from this uncongenial spot when his friend Julian Mason arrived from Chicago to become managing editor of the *Tribune*. Heywood Broun and F.P.A. had just left to become pillars of the rival *World*, and as a consequence the *Tribune* was in cultural doldrums. It is hardly surprising, therefore, that Mason offered Rascoe the job of the *Tribune*'s literary editor and chief book reviewer— precisely the job he had dreamed of filling.

Rascoe was twenty-nine at his moment of apotheosis, too old to belong to the Younger Generation, but young enough to have plenty of what the Twenties called pep. He also looked much younger than his years. From boyhood he had been gobbling up Kant, Schopenhauer, and Spinoza, so that people meeting him for the first time were dazzled by the immense erudition of a man who had, one said, "a deceptive air of juvenescence." His youth also impressed *The Bookman*, which pictured him as a

> smooth-faced, elegantly leggy lad, to whom at sight one would hardly credit more than twenty-four summers. His hazel eyes have the wandering alertness of a fox terrier's; his remarkable long nose emphasizes this impression of pouncing inquisitiveness . . . and its owner is never still.

Inevitably Rascoe was an opinionated fellow, and *The Bookman* went on to cite "an affable arrogance." Immoderate enthusiasm was the main attribute of his frequent literary crusades, and it was said that as a critic he had preferences rather than standards. One observer put it this way, "As a critic he is a wonderful newspaperman."

Obviously not everyone appreciated Rascoe, though he apparently wished to be liked by all. One false friend caught him in action at a bookish gathering:

◄§ *Posing on tip-toe, like a dawn new-lighted on some heaven-kissing hill, he bows from the waist, gestures with his hands, straightens his tie; he beams and blushes engagingly.*

Rascoe's chosen place in the literary procession seemed to be that of running footman, clearing the way for a bandwagon. The year 1922, when he took over at the *Tribune*, was ideal for such efforts. In the spring the Scott Moncrieff translation of *Swann's Way* was published in the United States, beginning the Proust vogue; in the summer returning travelers began slipping copies of James Joyce's *Ulysses* past unwary customs inspectors; in the fall T. S. Eliot won the two thousand dollar *Dial* prize for *The Waste Land*, which first appeared in that magazine.

More important to Rascoe, however, was the fact that the literary world seethed with talk of writers like Cabell, Lewis, Sherwood Anderson, Willa Cather, Hergesheimer, Ben Hecht, and poets like Edna St. Vincent Millay, Edwin Arlington Robinson, Edgar Lee Masters, Vachel Lindsay, Elinor Wylie, e. e. cummings, Carl Sandburg, and Conrad Aiken. All these and more were Rascoe enthusiasms, and in his first column he warned *Tribune* readers: "I should like to herald in these pages the work of the men and women whose writings are worthy in our own age and country. My belief in the American literature of the present and the future is profound."

Even so, the new critic in town was full of surprises. Having prepared readers for his preoccupation with modern American talents, he peppered columns with references to Stendahl, Nietzsche, and Anatole France. Readers who opened the pages of the *Tribune* one morning found this sentence, "Today I read Swift again; he is to me a constant source of delight."

A culture hound himself, Rascoe made others like him wince by declaring, "I think *The Saturday Evening Post* is more authentically literary than *The Atlantic Monthly*." He approved best-selling Gertrude Atherton by finding her "a bit opinionated perhaps, but with quite interesting ideas which do not assume the dead weight of convictions." He quoted Ben Ray Redman on young-expatriate type critics: "They have achieved senility before reaching maturity." He fomented literary feuds, one with Heywood Broun, of whom he wrote, "As a person I admire him this side of idolatry; but though he writes a lucid prose, I think, as a critic, he is nix."

Rascoe hired as helper Isabel M. Paterson, a small, waspish, scholarly young lady he had disliked on first meeting. She exacerbated him further by approving literary talents he disapproved. Yet she proved an excellent balance for his rampant enthusiasms, and eventually became an important figure in the book world as I.M.P., conductor of the weekly "Turns with a Bookworm." Rascoe traveled to the lonely stretches of Long Island's High Hill Beach (now Jones Beach) where Will Cuppy, a man he had admired in Chicago, lived like a hermit in a shack crammed with books on psychoanalysis, neurology, psychopathology, and love. To his few visitors Cuppy would say, not without pride, "I have every symptom mentioned in those books." Cuppy professed to hate the world and all in it, but Rascoe persuaded him to write book reviews and, in time, humorous pieces.

Rascoe reviewed a book a day for the *Tribune,* and was also responsible for a weekend literary supplement. When he took charge, this last was merely part of a "Review of the Arts." Rascoe began building a stable of reviewers like Mrs. Paterson, Ben Ray Redman, John Cournos, Bruce Gould, Stanton Coblentz, C. Hartley Grattan, Elinor Wylie, Thomas Beer, Edmund Wilson, Gilbert Seldes, Ben Hecht, John Macy, and Carl Van Vechten. He then became an innovator by printing caricatures of authors and using other drawings; his artists were Ralph Barton, Helen Hokinson, Miguel Covarrubias, Gene Markey, Reginald Marsh, and Hans Stengel. All this spelled success. Within a few months. Rascoe's literary supplement had become so popular that it was turned into the special tabloid insert, "Book News and Reviews."

Rascoe's master stroke, though, was a column called "A

Bookman's Daybook," in which he told on a more or less daily basis what he read, those he met, what people said to him, and what he said in return. Written hurriedly, often at the end of a hard day, the column skimmed brightly over multifarious personalities and topics, often deviating into lively, pre-Winchell gossip.

But if Rascoe adumbrated Walter Winchell, he owed a particular debt to F.P.A. who as far back as 1911 commenced a Saturday column called "The Diary of Our Own Samuel Pepys," which detailed his own activities during the week. F.P.A., however, told mostly of the people he met, seldom what they said. Rascoe was not often guilty of a similar omission.

In "A Bookman's Daybook," Rascoe revealed personal things. He considered himself unusually in tune with what Spengler called "the megalopolitan culture." He approved the smooth jazz of Paul Whiteman and could equate George Gershwin with T. S. Eliot—"*The Waste Land*, like the wailing pathos of Gershwin's 'Rhapsody in Blue,' is a thing of haunting beauty, indicative of a mood." He lifted the curtain on his own private life by admitting daydreams of being a drummer in a jazz band. He carried through on this by practicing with drumsticks, real and imaginary. Uneasily he confessed this weakness to the psychoanalyst Dr. Smith Ely-Jelliffe, who reassured him in the best jargon of the day: "There is nothing psychoanalytically sinister about your case—just a harmless outlet of muscular eroticism and a satisfaction of a profound sense of rhythm. Keep it up!"

Like Gilbert Seldes, Rascoe viewed popular entertainment as art, and praised Ed Wynn, Joe Cook, and W. C. Fields. At this moment in time, Fields was the pet of intellectuals, and it became the smart thing to visit the great man backstage after a performance of *Poppy*.

Rascoe also detected high art in the lowly comic strip and stated, "I think George Herriman, who draws Krazy Kat, has genius of an exquisite and original sort." In the same vein, he branded the German artist George Grosz "an imitation Rube Goldberg."

Eventually, Rascoe devoted a considerable part of his autobiography to proving that the gossip in "A Bookman's Daybook" was a minor part of the overall column. But there can be no doubt that—rightly or wrongly—his light and sometimes malicious tattlings became its most popular feature. Rascoe's gossip not only flattered the folk mentioned but made the literary world seem exciting to the public. Who, for example, could fail to feel sharp pangs of envy after reading:

> *Went to a lunch today, given by Alexander Woollcott for Hilaire Belloc. Others present were Robert C. Benchley, Heywood Broun, Christopher Morley, Laurence Stallings, Herbert Bayard Swope, and Father Duffy.*

Or:

> *Went for drinks at the office of Horace Liveright. There met Ford Madox Ford, Hendrik Van Loon, Carl Van Vechten, C. Hartley Grattan, T. R. Smith, Konrad Bercovici, Madeleine Boyd, and actress Carrol MacComas.*

And who would not change places with the Rascoe family on the night of July 25, 1922:

> *About nine o'clock a taxi drove up and there came trooping up the stairs Mary Blair dressed in pajamas, house slippers, and raincoat; Tallulah Bankhead in bathing suit and cutaway coat; and Edmund Wilson in brown dressing gown and top hat. They gave us forthwith a superb vaudeville performance.*

In the gossipy "Bookman's Daybook" nothing was too trivial. Devoted readers learned that Carl Sandburg could play the jew's harp, guitar, and cello, Ben Hecht was skilled at the violin, the ethereal poetess Elinor Wylie could toss her thumbs out of joint, James Branch Cabell was capable of exhibitions of shadow swordsmanship, and that Edmund Wilson, later the very essence of literary propriety, had great skill as an amateur magician plus a rare ability to turn sudden handsprings in limited space.

Rascoe delighted in unearthing nicknames and revealed

that Mencken was Harry to Joseph Hergesheimer, who in turn was Joe or Hergy to Harry. Nathan called Mencken Menck or Heinie, while he was Chorge or Chorgie to Heinie. Few folk had the audacity to call Cabell by his first name, but absolutely no one dared use Jim. For unknown reasons, Sherwood Anderson was Swatty to intimates.

"A Bookman's Daybook" kept track of the practical jokes of the Katzenjammer Kids of Literature. When Professor Archibald Henderson made the long trip from North Carolina to consult the *Smart Set* editors about the chances of a book on George Bernard Shaw, the two men took him to dinner and let him outline the project. Then Mencken wagged his head sadly. "Shaw's as out of date as a velocipede," he stated mournfully. Disconcerted, Henderson broached the subject of Ibsen. "No one reads Ibsen any more," Nathan chimed in. It was a bad night for Henderson, who in time became Shaw's first biographer.

The Katzenjammer Kids even played jokes on each other. One night drama critic Nathan endured a play translated from the Hungarian; it was so abysmal that he decided use could be made of it. Knowing Mencken hated the theater and loathed evening clothes, he wired Heinie in Baltimore reporting the debut of a masterpiece by a playwright who rivaled Shaw and Ibsen. "You must see it," he declared, adding the playwright wished to give a party in Mencken's honor after the performance.

Mencken grudgingly set out for New York. Attiring himself in uncomfortable evening dress, he joined Nathan and play producer John Williams, who was in on the joke, in a stage box. After ten minutes he leaned over to whisper, "This sounds like a lot of pishposh to me." Nathan was upset. "It's an indubitable work of genius," he whispered back. Mencken began to fall asleep, but his two companions nudged him awake with the warning that the playwright was in the wings observing his reactions.

"Either you two are terrible imbeciles," Mencken burst out, "or I'm going crazy—this is the cheesiest play I ever saw." Nonetheless, he remained awake. Only when he caught a smile flitting over Nathan's usually bland countenance did the peerless practical joker realize he had been flummoxed.

"A Bookman's Daybook" also paid tribute to George Jean Nathan's fame as a boulevardier, epigrammatist, and wit by reporting that one night the critic climbed into a taxi and gave the address of the Hotel Royalton, where he lived. "Forty-four West Forty-fourth Street," he directed. "What's that?" the driver inquired. "Some kind of epigram?"

Rascoe revealed lumbering Theodore Dreiser in a mood of unusual hilarity. At an all-male luncheon, the author of *Sister Carrie* drank so much bootleg alcohol that he happily began rubbing salad oil in the hair of other midday boozers. While he was engaged in this, Arthur Vance, editor of *Pictorial Review*, called out, "I'll make you a proposition, Theodore! If you will write a story that hasn't a prostitute or a kept woman in it, I promise to buy it and pay our top price."

"You're on," Dreiser shouted back, and returned to his salad-oil shampoos. At home he wrote "Glory Be, McGlathery," and sold it to Vance.

Proust, Ezra Pound, Joyce, and T. S. Eliot—"Tears" Eliot, e. e. cummings called him—were the overseas names currently most stimulating to the American literary world, and Rascoe recounted any stories concerning them that traversed the Atlantic. He told of Nora Joyce berating James Joyce about his indifference to their children. "You pay no attention to them," Nora stormed. "Why, you've never done a single thing for them."

"You forget, my dear," replied Joyce with dignity, "that I was responsible for their conception."

T. S. Eliot, London's literary lion, was asked by a fluttery female at a party if he did not think the gathering interesting. "Yes, it is," Eliot replied, "if you concentrate on the essential horror of the thing."

Then in his early thirties, Eliot, too, was handsome as the popular Arrow collar ad. Yet the painter Marie Laurencin was taken aback on meeting him at a London soiree. "Eliot?

Eliot the writer?" she queried. "But they told me you were a woman!"

"No, I assure you," Eliot replied, "the facts are the other way."

"But surely I can't be mistaken," the lady persisted. "I was given to understand that you were a woman."

"No, no," Eliot assured her, "I have known myself for quite a long time, and I am convinced that I am not and never have been a woman."

"But aren't you *George* Eliot?" the painter demanded.

Stories about these men were fun, but at the same time, Joyce, Eliot, and Pound provoked literary battles. Opposition from men like the popular novelist Rupert Hughes was to be expected, but how to explain Robert Frost, who went around saying, "I hear that James Joyce wrote *Ulysses* as a joke"? The first issue of the weekly newsmagazine *Time* said, "It is rumored that *The Waste Land* was written as a hoax." Ultra-erudite Ernest Boyd dared call Eliot "merely amusing," for which Rascoe labeled Boyd "an elegant reading machine." And Alexander Woollcott, drama critic of *The New York Times*, invited wrath by declaring, "Reading Proust is like bathing in someone else's water."

Rascoe and others were unsettled when Harry Leon Wilson, author of *Merton of the Movies* and *Ruggles of Red Gap*, returned from London to tell of a dinner party at which Eliot supposedly admitted writing *The Waste Land* with tongue in cheek. This calumny was so widely believed that Eliot was forced to write a letter of denial. He did so with good humor, but was infuriated when Ernest Hemingway, recently arrived in Paris, assailed *The Waste Land* in Ford Madox's Ford's *transatlantic review*. To be attacked by a newcomer on the literary scene was just too much!

Despite Rascoe's fascination with expatriates, he was primarily interested in America. In one bright "Daybook" paragraph he tells of making a train trip to visit e. e. cummings and amusing himself en route by counting the number of first-rank lyric poets since Poe:

◄§ Emily Dickinson, yes, on the evidence of two or three lyrics alone—Sara Teasdale, darn near it, darn near first rank anyhow . . . Edna St. Vincent Millay, absolutely, because she is one of the few poets who have been able to breathe life into the sonnet since Shakespeare; Arthur Davison Ficke is another, and Cummings! But we'll come to him—Wallace Stevens for a certainty . . . and there's Conrad Aiken, ecstatically and imperishably lyrical when you excavate—and T. S. Eliot, poet laureate and elegist of the jazz age . . . Ezra Pound; now Pound's a talent, but has he written more than one lyric?

. . . Put him down anyway—Comes then who? Sandburg? Bodenheim, Lindsay, Masters, Lowell (Amy), Kreymborg—let's keep Kreymborg in. . . . Robinson, Wheelock . . .

Who remains? Who indeed, but the chap we're to meet this afternoon. If there is a finer lyricist since Keats and Swinburne (I include them both), forgetting Yeats, in the English language, I wish you would introduce me to him. Uneven? Yes, I grant you! So was God.

In May 1, 1923, Joseph Conrad arrived on the liner *Tuscania* for a first visit to the United States. This novelist's influence on American writers of thirty years of age and more had been great—much as Hemingway would be a few years hence. So a welcoming delegation headed by Rascoe and Christopher Morley headed down the bay in the early dawn with the ship-news reporters and photographers who in those days met all incoming liners to interview the celebrities aboard. Both Rascoe and Morley, who conducted the rival "Bowling Green" column in the New York *Post*, clutched a Conrad novel to be autographed.

Aboard the cutter, Morley delivered a lecture on Conrad's importance and otherwise showed such reverence for the arriving author that he was appointed unofficial spokesman for the group. Conrad suffered from gout, and because of poor health and general sensitivity was terrified of being interviewed by an uncouth American press. Suspecting this, Morley warned the reporters and photographers—whom he considered "barbarians, restless and independent"—that they must accord Conrad deep respect.

Conrad awaited the news-hungry group in the captain's quarters adjacent to the bridge. He wore a stiff-bosom shirt, high starched collar, heavy overcoat, and derby hat. In one eye glinted a monocle. The pain of gout had etched lines on his face, and to Rascoe, he looked "shy, modest, and frightened." Morley's reactions were on a higher plane. "How lovely he is," he thought, "the frankness of his smile underlaid by an uneasy terror." One barbarous member of the working press thought Conrad resembled "a perplexed physician."

The interview began smoothly. One of the newsmen addressed the seafaring novelist as "captain," which obviously pleased him. Yet Morley was vexed. "Of the conduct of the photographers one does not like to speak," he wrote later. When one of them called out to Conrad to take off his hat, Morley became enraged and declared the interview ended. On the return trip, he announced himself in such a state of "ecstatic pleasure" that it would be impossible for him to write of the experience for some time. Rascoe wrote his story right away, and it was so detailed and warm that the *Tribune* placed it on page one, a most unusual spot for the by-line of a literary editor.

In time Christopher Morley felt able to write his account, and began like this:

> ◆§ *Happiness consists in finding the right words. How is one to find those that will express the feeling of being on the* Tuscania's *bridge, that May Day morning, with Joseph Conrad? I suppose my tone of voice now lays me open to the charge of idolatry (there are worse charges, incidentally) . . . The feeling of the reporters, as they stood decently apart while Mr. Conrad got a tranquil view of New York rising from the hyaline dimness of the spring sky, was not the mere admiration of an individual, however brave, sensitive, or potent. It was a sense of doing*

honor, through this man, to a certain phase of the human spirit; a sense of homage to one who had found the right words; who had, through long and patient years, tried to utter the unsayable tremors of the mind. At a time when we are repeatedly and wearisomely assured that The Saturday Evening Post *kind of thing (admirable enough in its own innocent way) is the ultimate benison of human success, there is something purging in contemplating achievement of a different sort. . . .*

Bunk—and Debunk

Babbitt . . William Woodward . . Elinor Wylie

Among the novels published during the 1922–23 season were *One Man in His Time* by Ellen Glasgow, *Gentle Julia* by Booth Tarkington, *One of Ours* by Willa Cather, *Gargoyles* by Ben Hecht, *The Glimpses of the Moon* by Edith Wharton, *If Winter Comes* by A. S. M. Hutchinson, *Black Oxen* by Gertrude Atherton, *Lummox* by Fannie Hurst, *The Able Mc-Laughlins* by Margaret Wilson, *The Covered Wagon* by Emerson Hough, *Captain Blood* by Rafael Sabatini, *The Breaking Point* by Mary Roberts Rinehart, *To the Last Man* by Zane Grey, *The Dim Lantern* by Temple Bailey, and *The Mine with the Iron Door* by Harold Bell Wright.

But with all these, the big literary news was that Sinclair Lewis had done it again.

The gangling, garrulous man with the pink face and coppery hair had scored with *Babbitt*, a novel projected even as the manuscript of *Main Street* was put in the hands of the printer. Just before the publication day of *Main Street*, Lewis had discarded George T. Pumphrey and Jefferson Fitch as possible names for the main character of a book about a go-getting realtor in the bustling community of Zenith which, as opposed to the town Gopher Prairie, was a small city. The name he had settled on was George F. Babbitt.

The Sinclair Lewis once more basking in literary glory was

something of a new person. In the words of *The Bookman,*
Main Street had "flooded his world with gold," and if nothing
else, Lewis was forever free of financial care. Not unnatu-
rally, this had made his personality flower, faults and virtues
greatly magnified. Also, the man who from childhood had
been acutely aware of his ugliness suddenly found himself a
celebrity, peered at with interest, respect, and admiration.
Small wonder that Sinclair Lewis had reacted by becoming
immensely pleased—even delighted—with himself.

He still worked hard, perpetually jotting down facts and
ideas for future books, each item systematically filed in the
proper place. Lewis always had a compulsion, rather than a
desire, to write, and was driven to labor for long stretches,
even when it was not necessary. Under the pressures of fame
he had begun smoking cigarettes at a furious rate and consuming more liquor than formerly.

Lewis the celebrity seemed unable to remain still, leaping
from chair to chair or—when standing—pacing fitfully from
one end of the room to the other. He was completely unself-
conscious now—or was it totally self-centered? Depending
on his mood, or the amount of alcohol in him, he could be
charming, arrogant, or downright rude. "He is really not one
person, but four or five people of various temperaments, all
mixed together," thought his friend William Woodward.

With the mantle of fame tossed lightly over his bony
shoulders, Lewis had overnight become attractive to young
girls, a situation unthinkable a few years ago. Good fortune
had also produced in him an unexpected desire to doll up.
Previously an indifferent dresser, he now had spurts of adorn-
ing himself in the fancy suitings of the dude, with accessories
like spats, fancy waistcoats, canes, and sometimes a monocle.

His marriage, which appeared so ill-starred at the beginning, had astonishingly lasted nearly a decade. Yet there were
frictions in the household. One of Lewis' complaints was that
his wife never seemed to understand he was working while
looking out a window. Beautiful, stylish, extravagant Grace
Hegger Lewis annoyed her husband in other ways, but he still
depended on her. Lewis was an indifferent parent, fully

capable of jealousy over attention paid his young son. The English sculptress Clare Sheridan may have exposed fissures in the marriage when, after a tour of the country, she cited Lewis as "One of the few Americans I have met who is not submerged by domesticity, although he is married."

Still, the most obvious change in Sinclair Lewis was in his loquacity—"his ceaseless volubility," Mark Schorer calls it. Certainly he had always loved to talk, and grasped every opportunity to do so. But as a famous personality, he considered it his *right* to dominate conversations. Practically unstoppable, he leaped rapidly from subject to subject, building with relish toward his inimitable exhibitions of mimicry and verbal satire.

But the new expansiveness was not entirely his fault. Because of *Main Street*, he had been encouraged, even paid, to speak in public. Immediately after publication, he embarked on a lecture tour centering in the Midwest, but also including New York, Princeton, and Hamilton, Ontario. His topic was modern literature, and he extolled Dreiser, Hergesheimer, Sherwood Anderson, Zona Gale, and Cabell, while berating audiences for neglecting them in favor of refined English fictioneers.

As a lecturer Red Lewis was no howling success. Equipped with copious notes, he stepped onstage and began to talk. As long as he stuck to the notes, his talks were coherent and challenging. But he usually abandoned the notes to move erratically around the stage, his ideas as jumpy as his motions.

From a personal point of view, this lecture tour had a three-pronged purpose. First, it supplied him with some fast money, since the big *Main Street* royalties had yet to roll in; next, it helped promote the novel (Lewis, who had worked in the publicity departments of publishing houses, was very conscious of this); and last, it allowed him to gather material for *Babbitt*.

Using Cincinnati as home base, he utilized the days between lecture engagements to range the Middle West, filling both mind and notebooks with fresh observations. Soon his accumulated research material included maps of a small city drawn to scale, floor plans of urban homes, and notes on the characteristics and daily life of the genus businessman-booster. It added up to a small library of American urban life in the Midwest.

Accompanied by wife, child, mother-in-law, and bulging library, Lewis set sail for Europe on May 17, 1921, just a few weeks after the Scott Fitzgeralds. The last time Red Lewis crossed the ocean he had been a college boy tending cattle in the hold. Now he dined in style at the captain's table.

Like the Fitzgeralds, Lewis went first to London, but here any similarity ends. Unlike Scott and Zelda, Sinclair Lewis loved Europe. From now on, this man who by automobile travel and general restlessness had become so familiar with his own forty-eight states, enjoyed England and the Continent nearly as much. In time, Europe became as important as the United States to this most American of writers.

What the overseas world thought of Lewis is a different matter. One biographer says that after *Main Street* the novelist's life became one of "noisy desperation." England was the first area exposed to this phenomenon, and Lewis struck the literary world of London like a cyclone. Deep in him lay the conviction that American authors were as good (or better) than their English brethren any goshdamn day in the week, and he had no hesitation in expressing this view to Londoners. He further ingratiated himself by telling newfound friends, "England is the nicest part of America."

British authors responded to this Yankee invasion in varying ways. Lewis particularly desired to meet H. G. Wells, but on a first meeting, Wells found Lewis' raucous verbosity hard to take and carefully kept his distance—though it must be admitted that they became good friends later on. Arnold Bennett was pleasanter, perhaps because a man who stammered badly envied one who spoke with staggering speed. Rebecca West's reaction was typical: "After five solid hours I ceased to look on him as a human being; I could think of him only as a great natural force, like the aurora borealis."

Following a few strenuous weeks as literary lion of London, the author took his family to the English countryside, settling in a lovely Elizabethan cottage in Kent where he began to write *Babbitt*. Further stresses in his marriage became apparent as Lewis commenced a pattern of intensive periods of work, followed by solitary junkets on his own.

The first of these was to Paris, a city Lewis had not visited before. His days were dutifully devoted to sightseeing, but at night he anticipated a warm welcome from what he called "that Paris bunch" of expatriates. (This group had not yet attained the dimensions of the near future when it often seemed there were more American writers on the Left Bank than at home. Harold Stearns had just arrived as Lewis made his trip. Ernest Hemingway was still in Chicago.)

But Lewis found himself unpopular among the Paris bunch. In part this was because of his *Saturday Evening Post* background, but also because he had dedicated *Main Street* to Joseph Hergesheimer and James Branch Cabell. The Lost Battalion's dislike rose to annoyance as Lewis proved himself so immersed in the character of George F. Babbitt that after a number of drinks he began acting the part of Midwest booster. "Garçon, garçon," he bellowed at waiters, adding in a loud aside to those around him, "Let me tell you, they give us better service in Zenith." At other times he demanded of jejune expatriates, "Have you ever been in the Zenith Athletic Club? Say, there's a real swell place."

Lewis had just sold the movie rights to *Main Street* for forty thousand dollars, and he bought rounds of drinks with enough prodigality to ensure a measure of acceptance on the Left Bank. But his novels had not yet been published abroad, and he was still unknown to the French men of letters, a fact which rankled. In his cups, he like to rise to his feet shouting that he was the American Flaubert. Once as he did this, a Yankee voice shouted back, "Sit down! You're just a best seller!"

One more stint of hard work in England was followed by a second visit to Paris, this time with Grace. By now his reputation had caught up with him, and a few distinguished men tried to see him. But he was either sleeping off a night of drinking or sought to make them the butt of practical jokes. He met James Joyce, who failed to say a word—did Lewis give him a chance? A luncheon with Edna St. Vincent Millay, who had been sent abroad for a year by *Vanity Fair*, was equally unproductive.

Instead of returning to England, the Lewis ménage (Grace's mother had gone home) moved on to Italy, where Lewis wrote diligently in Rome and at Pallanza on Lake Maggiore. He still went off on his own trips—at least once in the company of a young blonde. Lewis was never a lecher on the scale of, say, Theodore Dreiser; rather, he seemed to relish the *admiration* of attractive women more than sexual conquest. But still he could not resist an occasional indulgence of his unexpected appeal to sweet young things. At the end of these infidelities, he returned to Grace and his son, and it is to be presumed that the couple made further efforts to save their floundering marriage.

As *Babbitt* neared completion, Lewis went alone to London, where he proudly accepted dinner invitations from Somerset Maugham and sought acceptance on a writer-to-writer basis from John Galsworthy, Lytton Strachey, Frank Swinnerton, W. L. George, and others. Grace rejoined him at the book's completion, and after a year abroad, the Lewises returned to await one more publication date.

They bought a Cadillac—a far cry from the Model T Ford of early marriage days—and settled down at Hartford, Connecticut. This allowed Lewis to go to New Haven for his fifteenth Yale reunion. As the most famous graduate of his class, he had the rare privilege of evening up scores with former classmates. Addressing the reunion dinner, he began, "When I was in college, you fellows didn't give a damn about me." Then he ticked off a list of episodes and social snubs, together with the names of those responsible. Fortunately, his hearers were so heavily insulated by before-dinner drinks that the speech seemed nostalgic rather than insulting.

Making frequent forays into Manhattan, Lewis reestablished himself on the domestic literary scene. If Mencken, Nathan, and others had forgotten the author's brashness, they were forcefully reminded of it. In that insensitive day, Americans laughed uproariously at the fractured English of various immigrant groups, with newspapers gaining circulation from ethnic comic strips like the Katzenjammer Kids, Alphonse and Gaston, Abie the Agent, and Ish Kabibble.

In line with this, Sinclair Lewis had perfected Irish-American, Swedish-American, German-American, Midwest, Down East, and Deep South dialects. George Jean Nathan pictures a night when the versatile monologist seized a literary get-together and held the floor with a mixture of dialects:

> *"Ladies and Chentlemens: It is gewiss a great pleasure, gottinhimmel, fur me to have been envited to shpeak to you dis eefining. In rising to address mit you, mit my impromptu shpeech in mine vest pocket, I am reminded uff der shtory uff der zwei Irishers, Pat und Mike, who vas riding on der choo-choo car. Pat und Mike, I forgot me to tell you, vas sailors in der Navy. It seems Pat had der unter berth und by und by he heard such a noise von der ober berth und he called oop asking warum? Und Mike he answered, 'Shure und begorra how can Oi ivver get a night's shlape at all, at all? Oi've been tryin' to get into this damn hammock ivver since eight bells!' Now, ladies und chentlemens, shtanding up here before you great folks, I feel me a whole lot like Mike und maybe after I've sprechen along fur a while, I may feel me so darn shmall I'll be able to crawl me into a choo-choo hammock mineself mit no trouble at all, at all."*

On this occasion the men present—Mencken, naturally, among them—got revenge by solemnly rising at the end to toast the skills of "Lewis Sinclair," "Sinclair Lewisohn," "Upton Sinclair," and "Heinrich Lewis." After suffering this, Lewis had the temerity to inquire whether the assembled guests had actually enjoyed his monologue. "The answer," Nathan writes, "was a volume of inelegant mouth noises."

Yet Lewis had the last chuckle; this same discourse, rendered into Midwest lingo, turned out to be one of the speeches delivered by George F. Babbitt before the Boosters Club of Zenith.

Lewis next visited Sauk Center, where his older brother had followed their father's footsteps by becoming a country doctor. Lewis was already mulling over the subject of his next novel and was torn between a medical-practitioner hero or a labor leader like Eugene V. Debs. In Chicago, he met Dr. Paul de Kruif, a young man with a Ph.D. in bacteriology. From him Lewis learned for the first time of doctors engaged in laboratory research, and they seemed to him like fearless explorers of the unknown. *Here's my next book,* he told himself.

On achieving his impressive degree, De Kruif had discovered in himself a desire to write. After contacting Theodore Dreiser for advice, De Kruif had gone ahead and finished a book called *Our Medicine Men,* which was soon to be published. Lewis decided to make full use of Dr. de Kruif's medical and writing know-how in the projected novel.

But in the meantime, there was *Babbitt.* . . .

None of the uncertainties surrounding the advent of *Main Street* attended the début of *Babbitt.* Where an advance printing of fifteen thousand copies had been deemed enough for the former, early runs of *Babbitt* totaled eighty thousand, with the expectation of others raising the number to 200,000 in a few months. Only hints of success preceded *Main Street's* publication; *Babbitt* had assurances. Mencken mailed his *Smart Set* review to Lewis ahead of time. One line read, "I know of no American novel that more accurately presents the real America."

Also stepping forward with words of praise were Ludwig Lewisohn, John Farrar, Zona Gale, Upton Sinclair, Owen Johnson, and the English novelist May Sinclair, who in the *New York Sunday Times* wrote, "In his hands *Babbitt* becomes stupendous and significant." In the *Post,* Carl Van Doren called the novel "a masterpiece of language, a lexicon, a grammar of commentary on the American tongue." Burton Rascoe's reaction was, "One of the finest social satires in the English language . . . a successful, amusing, ironic document." Yet to Lewis, the most gratifying aspect of *Babbitt* may have been the speedy way the title slid into the vernacular. From publication day on, the sole way of characterizing the genus businessman-booster was to say, "He's a Babbitt."

However, the chorus of praise greeting the novel was not without sour notes. The avant-garde magazine *Broom* awarded Lewis its booby prize as Babbitt of the Arts. Perceptive Mary Colum wrote that in Lewis' case, "significant material passes through a mind that is not significant; he labels the material instead of transforming it." Finally, the cultured tones of Edith Wharton arose to state that *Babbitt* depended too heavily on slang.

This was unfair of the aristocratic authoress, especially since the novel was dedicated to her. Georgie Babbitt's monologues and speeches, where most of the slang occurs, are highlights of the book, exposing the gusto and banality of the go-getter personality. To Babbitt, dollars are "good round plunks." To a fellow booster, encountered only a few hours before, George hollers, "How's the old horse thief?" The friend yells back, "All right, I guess; how're you, you poor shrimp?" Babbitt shouts, "I'm first rate, you second hand hunk o' cheese." Here, and in his later *Man Who Knew Coolidge*, Lewis' genius for reproducing language reaches a peak.

Mrs. Wharton would have done better to point out that George F. Babbitt was not a spontaneous character; rather, he appeared to be "managed" by an author who moved him from one revealing situation to another. In short, the new book was less a novel than a performance. Lacking plot or subplots, it examines under varying pressures George Babbitt, age forty-six, typical Midwest realtor, and unenthusiastic husband and father.

Discussing his book before publication, Lewis had explained Babbitt in these words:

> *He is the typical T.B.M.* [tired business man], *the man you hear drooling in the Pullman smoker; but having*

once seen him, I want to develop him so that he will seem not just typical but an individual. I want the novel to be the G.A.N. in so far as it crystalizes and makes real the Average Capable American. . . . He is all of us Americans at 46, prosperous but worried, wanting—passionately—to seize something more than motor cars and a house before it's too late.

If nothing else, this presaged his intense preoccupation with Babbitt's character. For if *Main Street* lacked strong central figures, Babbitt was too strong. Of him Lewis writes, "He serenely believed that the one purpose of the real estate business was to make money for George F. Babbitt." No less serenely, Lewis seemingly felt his novel offered only the opportunity to vivisect Babbitt. Some of Lewis' friends believed he saw his main character as what he himself might have become, had he remained in the Midwest and conformed to its mores. When this possibility was broached to Lewis, he snorted derisively.

As a college boy, Babbitt had aspired to be a lawyer-politician, but instead became a victim of the very syndrome exposed by Scott Fitzgerald's *This Side of Paradise.* When at last Georgie got up nerve to kiss his girl, she promptly considered herself engaged. Babbitt never could extricate himself from this sticky web. As a married man, he became a self-styled "whale of a realtor" and won presidency of the Zenith Boosters Club, part of a national organization promoting friendship among Regular Fellows. But even so the core of his existence was empty.

The reader is with Babbitt as he rises in the morning after a night of drinking and poker with fellow boosters, as he pontificates to his family over breakfast, as he drives to work and (strange to relate!) has difficulty parking before his office building, as he lunches at the exlusive Roughnecks' table at the Zenith Athletic Club, as he sells houses, lots, and even graves, as he delivers a cliché-ridden speech at the Get-Together Fest of the Zenith Real Estate Board in the Venetian Ballroom of the O'Hearn House, as he dallies with a

Bohemian group known as The Bunch who try to act like Scott Fitzgerald characters and burn the candle at both ends in the manner of Edna Millay.

Babbitt expounds his views on religion, the Republican Party (for him there is no other), labor unions, socialism, the rich and poor. He makes vague attempts at marital infidelity and suffers through the tragedy of a close friend. When his wife visits an ailing relative, he drinks heavily with The Bunch and is rather too neatly saved from toperism by her return. Wrongly suspected of radical ideas, he is once more rescued—by Zenith's innate neighborliness—as his wife is stricken with appendicitis.

He has a childish pride in Zenith and loves his Dutch colonial home. (He also dotes on comic strips and Mack Sennett bathing beauties.) But Babbitt is no happy fellow; at night he has a recurring dream of a dainty fairy princess. Next he begins to see real-life signs of her in a cute manicurist in his barber shop and in the flapper next door who elopes with his son. Still, his existence remains empty. "I've never done anything I wanted to do in my whole life," he complains to his son at the conclusion of a novel called by *The New Republic* "hideously true to the worst things in America."

Critics of the day rated *Babbitt* over *Main Street*. Comparing the two, Carl Van Doren said, "[Lewis'] seat is higher and his eyes see further." Ludwig Lewisohn asked, "Is *Babbitt* as good as *Main Street?* There need be no hesitation in answering: it is better." The *Daily News* of Greensboro, North Carolina, thought the book would make waves outside the literary world: "*Babbitt* will be reviled from one end of the country to the other. It will be hated, spat upon, and possibly burned by the common hangman. But it will be read."

In early hard-cover editions, *Babbitt* did not equal the splendid sales of *Main Street*. Cheaper editions and paperbacks over the years have pushed it ahead, however. One reason may have been *Babbitt's* lack of drama. Fiction readers like to identify with characters, and this was difficult with the people on the pages of *Babbitt*. It was far easier to aspire along with Carol Kennicott, shallow though her dreams might be.

Main Street dominated the best-seller list for an entire year, but Babbitt never achieved the same distinction. In 1923—its second year of life—*Babbitt* climbed to the number-four spot among nationwide sellers and hung there, behind Gertrude Atherton's *Black Oxen*, Arthur Train's *His Children's Children*, and *Enchanted April*, by the English author who signed herself "Elizabeth."

Still, *Babbitt* and *Main Street* were identical in that both failed to win a Pulitzer Prize. That year the award went to Willa Cather's *One of Ours*, possibly her least worthy book.

Few, if any, authors tried to emulate Sinclair Lewis. So potent was his formula of mimicry, slashing satire, and intensive research that others were frightened off his private preserve. Those who did seek to portray small-town life and types usually did so in quiet, subtle fashion.

Yet satire was possible in other fields, and one writer who attempted it valiantly was William Woodward, a close friend of Lewis. Had Woodward's novel *Bunk* been less diffuse, it might have become the *Brave New World* of the Twenties.

Woodward's own life was like a satirical novel of the era. Born in South Carolina, he was a youth of unusual intelligence who attracted the attention of schoolteachers and college professors. After working as a newspaperman, he became a well-paid expert in public relations and was hired as publicity director by the Wall Street Industrial Finance Corporation. Where most literary men appeared baffled by the intricacies of Wall Street, Woodward found them childishly simple. Soon he was executive vice-president of the corporation, with control over forty banks. Still, the work bored him, and in 1920 he resigned to devote full time to authorship.

Bunk deals with Michael Webb, like Woodward the possessor of outstanding intelligence. Scanning the U. S. A. of the time, Michael was appalled by the mediocrity around him. It seemed to him that the world has been undergoing a Second Rate Revolution from the beginning and now in the Twenties has achieved an Age of Authoritative Mediocrity. "The opportunities open to the second rate mind are greater than ever before in history, particularly in the United States," he concludes. "In this great and smiling land there is a place for everyone, and everyone should know his place and keep it."

He decides to write a book called *The Importance of Being Second Rate*, and sets about interviewing Second Raters. The research over, he commences to dictate to forty-two secretaries. The final work adds up to sixty thousand pages (not words!), which the publisher figures will fill eighty-six volumes. The mighty manuscript is returned to Michael with instructions to cut, but after three months of rereading he cannot find a single paragraph to sacrifice.

The publisher then hires a staff of confirmed pessimists to read the epic. They decide that only thirty-six pages possess real worth. A compromise is reached, and *The Importance of Being Second Rate* appears in book form. A failure at first, it becomes highly profitable after two promoters grab it and— in the best Twenties tradition—elevate it to success by organizing Second Rate Clubs around the country.

Michael expects to be named Chief Second Rater, but the promoters consider him a First Rater and toss him out of the movement. The post goes to one Timothy Bray, the first person to decide that the sword in *Jurgen* was really a penis and had launched the public outcry against the Cabell novel.

In a burst of inspiration, a disillusioned Webb recognizes the existence of Bunk in the world, and simultaneously perceives the need for debunking. "Bunk, my dear lady," he explains to an admirer, "is the diminutive, or pet name, for Buncombe." "Buncombe" derived from a Congressman from Buncombe County, North Carolina, who qualified his long-winded orations by saying, "Speaking only for Buncombe." The word had come to typify a combination of bombast and

phoniness, while frequent usage shortened it to Bunk. Debunking meant "taking the bunk out of things."

Michael Webb sets himself up as a professional debunker
—"a pricker of bubbles, a devastating intellect among contented morons." His first clients are novelists of repute who
aspire to sell popular stories to the big-money *Saturday Evening Post*. He "debunks" them by having girls read their
novels aloud in high-pitched, nasal voices. "At the end of a
paragraph, the girl stops and asks the patient what he meant
by the words she has just read," Michael explains. "Cures
have been affected in twenty-four hours."

Michael then takes over. "You literary fellows are always
thinking about Tolstoi and Anatole France," he lectures.
"You ought to study the advertising in the magazines just as
carefully as you would study a manual of literature. In America, the art of advertising has outgrown [that] of creative
writing. Advertising represents more closely the spirit of the
people than literature itself does."

So far, so good . . . But the author, having prepared an
elaborate structure of satire, more or less abandons it. If
bored by money making, Woodward nonetheless seemed to
share the contemporary love-hate emotion toward self-made
millionaires. Midway in the novel Michael accepts an invitation to visit the vast Westchester County estate of Richard
Ellerman, who has made $60 million in none-too-scrupulous
deals on Wall Street and elsewhere. On the estate is a carefully kept maze of hedges and walks, where guests often get
lost, sometimes forever. Ellerman's mind is described as
"single-track . . . blind to wide horizons and bent solely on
material acquisition." At challenging moments his philosophy
is

> *I am the man of business;*
> *I am the man that thinks;*
> *I am the doer; the go-getter.*

Part of Michael Webb's fascination with Ellerman is the
latter's son Bingo, a playboy repeatedly sued for breach of
promise by chorus girls. Says Michael: "My analysis shows

less than one percent of bunk in Bingo—the lowest percentage I've ever found in any person." But Bingo, of course, is brainless.

Supposedly at Ellerman's for pleasure, Michael can't quit debunking. One fellow guest is an eighth vice-president of Ellerman Enterprises who complains that words fail him at board meetings. "The way to do it," Michael tells him, "is to reject all sober sense. You are trying to think up something important to say. Well . . . the plain fact is that everything important was said before you were born, and now if you say the same thing again it makes people bored and moody." He advises the fellow to talk nonsense, and before long the eighth vice-president is on the way to becoming first.

It's an odd novel, which ends as Michael marries a simple girl and appears headed for the life of Second Rater. Altogether, the book is an admixture of modern fiction, and real and fanciful satire. Carl Van Doren thought it "satire seasoned with wisdom," and so it is. But the critic on *The Dial* showed more astuteness when he accused Woodward of hurling too many ideas in the air and lacking the writing skill to keep them aloft. Yet he concludes, "By comparison with the mass of stuff which litters the bookmarket, *Bunk* stands out like a woman in a red dress."

Not all the satire written in the 1920's was the masculine, hard-hitting variety. *Jennifer Lorn*, first novel by poetess Elinor Wylie, was a satire on the eighteenth-century novel. It is hard to find another book in all literature greeted with such unbridled rapture by critics and fellow craftsmen.

Elinor Wylie's first poetry appeared in 1912, and since that time her reputation had increased. In order to comprehend her work fully it was necessary to consider the author's passionate interest in Shelley—"a woman by an archangel attended," one critic called her. To Louis Untermeyer, "She possessed to the utmost degree the classic poetic temperament."

By common consent, Mrs. Wylie was also the most beautiful woman in the literary firmament—"beautiful but high strung, frail and . . . vain of her loveliness," a friend thought. Her smile was praised as "childishly lovely," her ethereal face haloed by a mop of "lion-colored hair." Her pale countenance and stately bearing made her appear "the queen of a white country." To Isabel Paterson she was

> reckoned a beauty, but that is not the word. She had many points of physical beauty: thick, springing chestnut hair, expressive eyes of that mixed green-brown-grey miscalled hazel, the classic length of limb from hip to knee, and delicate wrists and ankles. Her neck especially was lovely as a marble column. She dressed with taste and care, in the newest mode; and made it her own. But it was her carriage, her air, that produced the total effect.
> She had elegance. . . .

Yet these exceptional endowments were marred by a high, shrill voice and an intensely serious self-absorption that often made her humorless to the point of absurdity. Once, seeing a woman reading one of her novels, she walked over and said, "How I envy you reading that beautiful book." From anyone else this might be a self-deprecating joke, but Elinor Wylie meant it.

Elinor Wylie was no less intense about her hatred of popular magazines, especially the *Saturday Evening Post*. "I can't bear the look or the feel or the smell of it," she announced grandly. When she came to call, friends scurried to hide such magazines.

Elinor Wylie also stood out as the femme fatale of the book business, with a life resembling one of Joseph Hergesheimer's modern novels. Born on Philadelphia's Main Line, she was the daughter of a onetime Solicitor General of the United States. At twenty, she married Philip Hichborn, son of an admiral. Next she startled the world by eloping with Horace Wylie, a married man fifteen years her senior. After this, Hichborn killed himself.

The wealthy Wylie was forced to give his wife most of his fortune to obtain a divorce; until the final decree, he and

Elinor had to live abroad as Mr. and Mrs. Waring. Free to marry at last, they returned to Washington, D.C., where the lady added Sinclair Lewis to her platonic admirers. No doubt it was through Lewis that she met William Rose Benét, author and poet, who for a brief period had worked as an advertising copy writer and for Mennen's Talcum Powder concocted the deathless slogan, "The petal texture of a baby's skin". Mrs. Wylie and Benét were attracted to one another, and in 1921 she began divorce proceedings against Wylie in order to marry Benét.

Jennifer Lorn, her eagerly anticipated novel, recounted the adventures of young Sir Gerald Poynyard and his fragile bride Jennifer in the India of Warren Hastings. Jennifer is so surpassingly lovely that men cannot resist paying her lavish compliments—more or less as Elinor Wylie expected in real life. "Your wrists and ankles are the most delicate experiments in turned ivory that I have so far had the privilege of observing," says one distracted swain. "The Pope's smallest comfit-box is clumsy in comparison."

Jennifer Lorn was a sensation in top-echelon literary ranks. In Richmond-in-Virginia, Cabell was "electrified" by the book. Sinclair Lewis cabled the author from London, "At last a civilized American novel." Then he sat down to write:

> ⤳ *I wonder if there has ever been written a more distinguished first novel? . . . If the critics had any sense, if the analysts had any sense, they would see that you, both in your poetry and in* Jennifer, *together with Hergesheimer, Cabell, and Van Vechten, make a more important "news item" than all the bellowing of politics and business put together, because you four mean definitely that for the first time America has ceased to be a colony, has become a Power.*

To such effusions, Carl Van Vechten added his own. Having read *Jennifer Lorn* once, he could not trust his throbbing senses and "to find some slight flaw, some rift in artistry, some hesitation in the creator's precision, I went straight through the book again—in vain." With this, Carlo organized a torchlight procession of himself and friends that wound through the streets of Manhattan in honor of the perfect book. He next wrote Emily Clark in Richmond:

> ✒ *Have you read* Jennifer Lorn: *I consider it one of the masterpieces of all time. Indeed, I don't think I ever read any book I liked better . . . perhaps the most authentic book in seven million . . . a book in seven million.*

Even the professional critics joined in. Hard-to-please Isabel Paterson in the *Tribune* devoutly found *Jennifer* "a masterpiece." In the *World,* Maxwell Anderson wrote, "At times . . . it is deliriously impossible, at other times no more than barely incredible, and quite often only improbable."

So, obviously, was its effect on the literary world!

The Ever-Delayed Departure for Great Neck ......

Scott and Zelda Fitzgerald . . . .

Scott Fitzgerald did not fare too well with his second novel, *The Beautiful and Damned*. Published the same year as *Babbitt*, it proved disappointing to most critics, one having the effrontery to call the author "a doer of poor things well."

Scott had completed the first draft of this book before departing for Europe in the spring of 1921. Returning to these shores, he and Zelda had vowed, as prospective parents, to bypass the speakeasy circuit of New York in favor of life in a normal locality.

Accordingly they first tested Zelda's hometown of Montgomery, Alabama. It may have been congenial to her, but failed to satisfy Scott. Next they went to *his* birthplace, St. Paul, which seemed more like a metropolis.

Scott, of course, was a shining celebrity there, the latest instance of local boy making good. He set a commendable example at first by renting a downtown office and working long hours on his manuscript revision. Socially, he and Zelda were sought-after luminaries who brought the ambiance of wicked New York to country club dances and parties.

In October 1921, a daughter was born to the couple. Christened Frances Scott Key Fitzgerald, she thus became one of the rare girl children named after a father. Ever after, though, she was known as Scottie. Mencken saluted the event by wiring, "NAME HER CHARLOTTE AFTER CHARLES EVANS HUGHES," and the numerous other messages of congratulations indicated that the golden couple had not been forgotten by the tea dance, speakeasy, and literary sets of Manhattan.

Parenthood failed to subdue these two Jazz Age symbols. It was easy to find sitters to stay with Scottie, leaving Scott and Zelda free to cavort in the hip-flask tradition of contemporary sheik and sheba. "Three o'clock in the morning we've danced the whole night through," ran the dulcet lyric of a popular song, and the Fitzgeralds brought these mellow words to life. After completing *The Beautiful and Damned*, Scott turned to making fast bucks by short stories for the *Post* and other magazines. It was all very exciting, if a trifle empty, for the glamour of Manhattan had turned the pair into cosmopolitans far exceeding the cream of St. Paul.

In March 1922 they left Scottie in Minnesota to travel to New York for publication of *The Beautiful and Damned*. Staying at the Plaza, they turned the occasion into an endless party, with so much heavy drinking that Scott forgot to contact some of his best friends. Back in St. Paul, he attempted to make amends by confessing by letter, "I couldn't seem to get sober enough to tolerate being sober."

This problem suddenly seemed mild as reviews of the book floated in. An air of disappointment pervaded comments on *The Beautiful and Damned*, and no critic saw fit to call it superior to *This Side of Paradise*. Essentially Scott's second novel was a tragedy—and this may have been the trouble. Because of his own Jazz Age image, together with the blithe spirit of many of his short stories, readers and reviewers may have been led to expect a gin-scented romance—what one commentator called "young love in incandescence."

Still, there seemed to be something out of focus with *The Beautiful and Damned*, perhaps because the novel was half social satire and half a romance of newly married Anthony and Gloria Patch. Once again Scott had written a projecttion—"a pell mell," a review said—of his recent life, dreams, and giddy experiences. Anthony Patch, the hero, was a grandson of venerable Adam Patch (unfondly known to the world as Cross Patch), a multimillionaire on the order of John D. Rockefeller, Sr. Fitzgerald obviously envied the inherited-wealth status of his fictional alter-ego. Gloria is again the Plaza-oriented, quintessential flapper—"a girl of heavenly glamour," who spouts the heedless Jazz Age philosophy: "If I wanted anything, I'd take it; I can't be bothered resisting things I want." The novel also abounded in further dicta for the Younger Generation. One says, "A woman should be able to kiss a man beautifully and romantically without any desire to be his wife or mistress."

Scott had made full use of the sojourn in Westport during the summer of 1920. Details of discovering a house are included, along with the subsequent wild parties and Zelda's drunken dash along the railroad tracks. Tana, the Japanese houseman beloved by Nathan and Mencken, also crops up.

Tragedy's instrument is old Cross Patch, who one night pays an unheralded visit to the Westport cottage, finding the wildest of parties in progress. Gloria is performing a drunken swan dance to the music of a flute played by the faithful Tana, while Anthony is engaged in petting a girl guest. "A monstrous pall" settles over the jolly inebriates as Old Moneybags surveys the proceedings from a doorway. For reasons best known to himself, Scott puts this scene in the form of a playscript, with stage directions revealing that the maximillionaire has this day donated fifty thousand dollars to the cause of Prohibition. Wordlessly, Cross Patch turns on his heel and makes haste back to New York, determined to slice Anthony out of his will.

From here on the book offers a ghastly depiction of what the saner side of Scott feared might really happen to him. Anthony Patch begins to drink with dedication, slowly developing into a shattering case of cirrhosis-of-the-liver decay. In nasty fights with Gloria, he tries to destroy her gallant spirit, as Scott had possibly attempted at times with Zelda. Anthony winds up a sodden wreck in a rooming house on Claremont Avenue in the Bronx, exactly where Scott lived as a struggling copy writer. Then, in a surprise ending better suited to a magazine serial than a serious novel, Anthony breaks his grandfather's will (old Cross Patch had left the fortune to his butler). So at book's end Anthony is an embittered, alcoholic, semi-invalid—but a man worth a convenient $30 million.

It is hardly surprising that with satire fighting love story throughout a blurred book resulted. One casualty was the spontaniety, or immediacy, which had been the most winning feature of *This Side of Paradise*. Comments biographer Arthur Mizener: "Fitzgerald never made up his mind whether he wanted to stand apart from [his characters] and treat them satirically or to enter into their experience with sympathy and understanding." Said Carl Van Doren at the time, "He has trusted . . . his doctrine more than his gusto."

Even so, there is much to be said in favor of *The Beautiful and Damned*. It provides a far stronger narrative than *This Side of Paradise*, even if the author did still indulge himself by presenting scenes in play style and other oddities. Yet his characterizations were better, though some of the personages described most carefully appear only once. Edmund Wilson, Mencken, and Nathan were astute enough to see that Fitzgerald had attempted to write in a different vein, and credited him with near success. However, the approval of the last two may have been influenced by their appearance in the novel as thinly disguised characters. Nathan is flatteringly portrayed as Maury Noble, "a brilliantly meaningless figure in a meaningless world."

But for the most part *The Beautiful and Damned* was misunderstood, with the most savage fire coming from Burton Rascoe who, like others, supposed Anthony Patch to be an older Amory Blaine:

> ◈ *The charm of* This Side of Paradise *was precisely in its puerilities. There we had a young man setting down his adolescent notions about love, capitalism, and literature at the very time he was thinking them. Now that he is three years older we find that he has not matured at all and that he has taken himself seriously as a thinker. . . .*

No one of late years has appeared on the horizon with a happier verve than Fitzgerald or with a more promising narrative talent; and no one ever collapsed into the banal and commonplace as he has in this novel.

The critical reception was a shock to Scott—but, then, a prepublication condensation of the novel had appeared in *Metropolitan Magazine,* and he conveniently persuaded himself that the critics disparaging the book had read only this shorter version. Thus fortified, he began assembling a collection of his recent short stories to be published as *Tales of the Jazz Age.* This contained "Mayday" and "The Diamond as Big as the Ritz," two of his better magazine stories, yet he persisted in dismissing the whole as "A book for those who read as they run and run as they read." It was, he insisted, "aimed at the countless flappers and college kids who think I am a sort of oracle." At this same admiring group he aimed newspaper feature articles which asked questions like "What kind of wife will the girl make who has numerous petting parties?"

Summer in St. Paul, with its surrounding forests, hills, and lakes, was ever-pleasant, and the Fitzgeralds elected to remain there until late 1922. Meanwhile, Scott had started a play called *The Vegetable, or, From President to Postman,* a farcical satire in which a henpecked clerk is persuaded to run for the Presidency. In a second-act fantasy, he is elected; a third bumps him back to reality. After reading an early draft, Edmund Wilson declared, "no doubt, the best American comedy ever written." An ecstatic Scott began boasting about "my awfully funny play that is going to make me rich forever."

In October, the Fitzgeralds returned to a New York which had never ceased to cherish them. Indeed, the new celebrity curtain, painted by Reginald Marsh for the Greenwich Village Follies, included a sketch of Zelda leaping into a fountain. Ernest Boyd celebrated their reappearance by writing, "The wicked uncle, Success, has tried to lead these Babes in the Woods away and lose them, but they are always found sleeping peacefully in each other's arms."

To Boyd the Fitzgeralds seemed as fresh, eager, and glowing as ever. Yet Scott has written that he and Zelda had "unwillingly matured," and New York no longer seemed the same:

> We began doing the same things over again and not liking them as much. We had run through a lot, though we had retained an almost theatrical innocence by preferring the role of the observed to that of the observer.

John Dos Passos, who had been traveling abroad, now encountered Scott and Zelda for the first time. After knocking at their Plaza door one noontime, he thought there was "a golden innocence about them . . . they were both so hopelessly good-looking."

After the trio went downstairs for lunch with a main course of Bronx cocktails, the Fitzgeralds persuaded Dos Passos to accompany them on a house-hunting expedition to Great Neck, Long Island, then a literary-theatrical colony whose residents included Ring Lardner, Ed Wynn, George M. Cohan, and Florenz Ziegfeld. Piling into a rented chauffeur-driven touring car, they began a twenty-five mile ride which passed through the Corona garbage dumps to be made famous in *The Great Gatsby*. As the trip proceeded, Scott started to nip at a bottle of gin. Dos Passos also made rueful note that the pair supposedly high-spirited but never vulgar were rude to the Great Neck real-estate agent.

En route home, Scott continued his nipping, and Dos Passos became uncomfortably aware of Zelda, whose ideas of flirting were often disconcerting. In St. Paul the flapper wife had on occasion startled a dance partner by grinding her pelvis into his groin while saying, "My hips are going wild; you don't mind, do you?" Men got ideas from such actions and sometimes trouble ensued. A few of the things Zelda said and did this afternoon apparently caused Dos Passos to blink, but out of respect for Scott he paid no heed. Years later he put it this way, "Even the first day we knew each other, I had come up against that basic fissure in her mental processes that was to have such fatal consequences."

The Fitzgeralds' interest in suburban Long Island was dictated by financial problems, for even in St. Paul the two had managed to spend money faster than it arrived. After a few weeks in New York, their situation was critical. Earning twenty-five thousand dollars a year, Scott disposed of thirty-five thousand or more. He had been raised a Roman Catholic and, though no longer religious, retained a conscience that was deeply troubled by his drinking and extravagance. "I can't reduce our scale of living, and I can't stand the financial insecurity," he often complained. Again he said, "I can't live on less than thirty thousand dollars a year and to do it I have to write a lot of rotten stuff that bores me and makes me depressed."

Over the first four years of the Roaring Twenties, Scott Fitzgerald earned the fabulous sum of $113,000, chiefly from magazine stories but with assists from movie sales and book royalties. Despite unenthusiastic reviews, *The Beautiful and Damned* sold forty-three thousand copies and brought in about ten thousand dollars.

But it was never enough, and through Scott's conversation ran the doleful refrain "I'm so tired of the feeling that I'm living beyond my income." Edmund Wilson characterized his wanton extravagance as "an invincible compulsion to live like a millionaire." A particular brand of husbandly pride drove him to wish Zelda the best of everything, but whatever he missed, she tracked down on her own. One of their close friends jotted in his diary, "Fitz hard up, but Zelda nagging him for a $750 fur coat and can she nag!"

At the end of October, the move to a three hundred dollar-a-month home on Gateway Drive in Great Neck was supposedly an economy measure. Actually it proved the opposite, for it gave the profligate pair two locales to spend money. Among other things, they had bought a second-hand

Rolls Royce—"their cars were always romantic but second-hand," a writer has noted wryly. Almost every afternoon they grew restless in Great Neck and used the Rolls to reach the tea dances and speakeasies of Manhattan.

Here they moved gaily from the Palais Royal to the Plantation to the Rendezvous to Barney Gallant's. On drunken nights Scott was a lavish tipper who often gave headwaiter or waiter—or both—a tip equal to the amount of the entire check. Finally, long after midnight, the overstimulated pair began rounding up friends to take home in the Rolls for a continuance of the revelry. Ernest Boyd called this process the "ever-delayed departure for Great Neck."

On the rare nights when Scott and Zelda drove home alone, they might be found in the morning asleep on the front lawn or in the front seat of the car. Still, the wonder is that they reached Great Neck at all. Both were erratic drivers who were downright dangerous when soused. Scott once drove his dignified editor Maxwell Perkins off the road and into a pond, "because it seemed like fun." Zelda once shot across the Queensborough Bridge so fast that the police stopped her on suspicion of being Cecilia Cooney, the Bobbed-Haired Bandit, making a getaway from a stickup.

"For us the city was inevitably linked up with Bacchic diversions, mild or fantastic," Scott wrote later. The words were no less true of Great Neck, where the Fitzgeralds specialized in wild parties. Lasting a weekend or longer, these wingdings fulfilled a deep desire in Scott, who once fixed eyes on the middle distance and intoned:

> *Think of being able to give a stupendous house party that would go on for days and days, with everything that anybody could want to drink and a medical staff in attendance and the biggest jazz orchestras in the city alternating day and night! I must confess that I get a big kick out of these glittering things.*

Except for doctors in attendance and alternating jazz bands, the parties at the Fitzgeralds offered everything else, and soon it became fashionable to attend a Great Neck bash.

The roster at one included screen star Gloria Swanson (making the film *Zaza* nearby), Sherwood Anderson, John Dos Passos, Marc Connelly, Dorothy Parker, Neysa McMein, Rube Goldberg, and an assortment of speedy Ivy League marrieds, plus actors and showgirls from Broadway hits. Before his captive audience, Scott liked to render a patter song of his own composition entitled "Dog, Dog, Dog," which Burton Rascoe recalled as "pathetic." At one party he was upstaged by a mysterious gate crasher who sang the ditty "Who'll Bite Your Neck When My Teeth Are Gone?"

The Great Neck parties became endurance contests in the consumption of Prohibition booze, usually some variation on bathtub gin, whiskey tinted with creosote, or beer needled with ether. In a joke of the period, a bootlegger reassures his customer, "This stuff's right off the boat." Replies the customer, "Yeah, scraped off." At times even Scott and Zelda found the parties wearisome, Scott making sharp cracks about the premises becoming a roadhouse. At one point the couple posted facetious house rules reading, "Visitors are requested not to break down doors in search of liquor, even when authorized to do so by host and hostess"—"Week-end guests are respectfully notified that invitations to stay over Monday, issued by host and hostess during the small hours of Sunday morning, must not be taken seriously."

Most guests considered such things outrageously funny, but at least one saw the emptiness. Actress Laurette Taylor (whose arrangement with her husband let her attend parties alone) was a Great Neck guest to whom Scott paid lavish, if maudlin, attention. Miss Taylor arrived home in tears. When asked why, she said, "I have just seen the doom of youth. Do you understand? The doom of youth itself. A walking doom!"

Entries in Scott's diary indicated the consumption of alcohol: "A series of parties . . . Drunk . . . Still drunk . . . On the wagon." A friend to whom Scott boasted of going without a drink for eight days said, "He talks as if it were a century."

In the words of biographer Andrew Turnbull, Scott and Zelda "complemented each other like gin and vermouth in a martini, each making the other more powerful in their war with dullness and convention." He goes on, "They faced life not ignobly, but with a mad sort of daring, committed to doing as they pleased and never counting the cost." The two engaged in bitter quarrels during drinking bouts, but seldom over drinking itself; in this field, each bravely tried to out-guzzle the other. According to Scott, "Zelda and I sometimes engage in terrible four-day rows that always start with a drinking party, but we're still enormously in love and about the only truly happy married couple I know."

It would be five more years before Scott Fitzgerald became a true alcoholic, yet his footprints on the melancholy path were already visible. Up to this point he was a convivial imbiber who enjoyed drinking with a group. Now during the day he vanished for a quick snort; drinking, a friend thought, had become necessary, "like taking a pill." As always, over-indulgence turned Scott into an antic figure, whose cavort-ings, whims, jokes, sensitivities, and truculence often made for a difficult host. One observer thought liquor "turned him inside out; beyond a point, he became a person possessed."

Perhaps for this reason he developed a vast admiration for his Great Neck neighbor Ring Lardner, who remained courtly and dignified even when blotto. In fact, Lardner was the only real friend the Fitzgeralds seemed to make during their Long Island sojourn. Scott called him "six foot three inches of kindness," and on some nights the two sat drinking until sunrise. One such occasion took place while Joseph Conrad visited the Nelson Doubleday estate at nearby Oyster Bay. After disposing of a quantity of booze, Scott suggested that they go to Oyster Bay and perform a dance on the Dou-bleday lawn to show Conrad the immense admiration Ameri-can authors had for him. Somehow the two reached the grounds of the estate and began a tipsy fandango across the greensward. An unfeeling caretaker chased them off.

Of course, the real reasons for Scott's drinking lay hidden in the depths of his psyche. Sheiks and shebas of the Teeming Twenties drank from hip flasks to enhance life, to make it more exciting. On the surface this was obviously Scott's reason and Zelda's too. Yet Scott's consumption had a destructive quality hard to explain by Jazz Age pleasure patterns. The twenty-eight-year-old man was hurting himself and his precious talent and he was the first to know it. Friends excused him by saying he was shy—but aren't we all?—and needed liquor to fortify himself.

It is more possible that Scott wanted to be *liked*. In one of his short stories, he makes a character say, "I found that with a few drinks I got expansive and somehow had the ability to please people. . . . Then I began to take a whole lot of drinks to keep going and have everybody think I was wonderful."

This may be the definitive word.

Scott had been lazy in Great Neck. He once figured that since arriving in New York, he had written only one hundred words a day. His indolence was encouraged by *The Vegetable*, a play admired by those who read it. In the spring of 1923, the highly respected Broadway producer, Sam H. Harris, accepted it for fall production, and on the night of November 20, it began a tryout run in Atlantic City. The premiere of a Scott Fitzgerald play was so great an event that a trainload of celebrities journeyed to the tryout. Among them was Mayor John F. "Red Mike" Hylan of New York City, a man not known for cultural interests.

The distinguished audience found the first act just bearable. With the second, or fantasy act, *The Vegetable* collapsed. No one realized it better than Scott, who rushed backstage to beg Ernest Truex and others in the cast to forget the show and meet him at the nearest speakeasy. They refused, and he went alone. *The Vegetable* closed forever at the end of one week.

High hopes dashed, the Fitzgeralds returned to Great Neck, where Scott faced the brutal realization that he owed at least five thousand dollars, with nothing coming in. It was a moment of truth, and he rose to it nobly. Going on the wagon, he established a workroom over the garage, and set about writing himself out of debt. His soul, he said, "ached to write something *new*—something extraordinary and beautiful and simple and intricately patterned." Yet popular short stories brought in the money. Between late November and April 1924 he wrote eleven short stories, together with a few articles like "Does a Moment of Revolt Come Sometime to Every Married Man?"

On most days he worked twelve-hour stretches which wore him out physically and made him cough, itch, and suffer stomach pains. It also did much to induce the insomnia which plagued the rest of his years. "I really worked hard as hell," he said later, "but it was all trash, and it nearly broke my heart as well as my iron constitution."

In all, he earned seventeen thousand dollars and, with a few dollars ahead, was able to contemplate writing his extraordinary and intricate novel—as always, his mind ran along the lines of his and Zelda's recent past. But he still talked economy, and suddenly Zelda popped up with the notion of going to Europe and "living on nothing a year." It seemed brilliant to Scott—"I would take the Long Island atmosphere that I had familiarly breathed and materialize it beneath unfamiliar skies." The projected book was, of course, *The Great Gatsby*.

In May 1924, the Fitzgeralds—with Scottie—again boarded an ocean liner and sailed away from New York. It was a sad moment, for the golden couple never really returned to the city whose style, glitter, and spirit so intrigued them. In the future, Scott and Zelda would pass through New York and occasionally pause for a time. But never again would they be citizens of the metropolis with which they enjoyed the most conspicuous petting party of the Jazz Age.

Several times in the future Scott Fitzgerald described his emotions on thus quitting New York, but he never mentioned a subject which must have bothered him. In its broadest sense, this was that, with all his fame, he had failed to produce a top-selling book. In turn, this merged with an unhappy realization which may have bothered him more—that the Jazz Age had left him behind.

Since 1920, the year of *This Side of Paradise*, Scott had published four books—two novels, two short-story collections. In the first of these, promiscuous kissing had provided the sensation, and the same was true in the last—Fitzgerald still seemed to believe promiscuity began and ended right there. Yet the Jazz Age had changed since 1920, and other authors, more aware of the fact, were cashing in.

One was Dorothy Speare who, in *Dancing in the Dark* and *The Gay Year*, pictured noncollegians doing their damndest to act like collegians. Her flappers were bolder than Scott's, drawing caricatures on bare knees with lipstick, enjoying allnight petting parties, drunkenly fending off the advances of amorous men. This novelist was especially adept at the vivid slang of the moment, while Scott seemed oddly unaware of it. One of her shebas commended the sapience of a date by telling him, "You spit a bibful." Again, a girl expresses the world weariness of the young by saying, "Life is as flat as stale coffee grounds."

The works of Dorothy Speare were outdistanced in 1923 by *Flaming Youth*, a novel by a Warner Fabian who turned out to be the veteran Samuel Hopkins Adams. Here, at last, was the real thing, with brazen talk of going-all-the-way, pregnancy, abortion, and nude swimming parties. Essentially it is the saga of Pat Fentriss, a girl whose lessons in life came from two older sisters who shot craps with boy friends and guzzled from flasks. Eager to outdo her siblings, Pat yearns to be deflowered. After it happens on the living-room sofa, she leaps to her bare feet and cries, "I'm not sorry! I'm not! I'm not! I'm *glad!*" In both book and movie, *Flaming Youth* became one of the notable products of the Twenties. The author followed it with *Unforbidden Fruit*, which was even franker.

Whether Scott was annoyed by the attention given these books is not known. But he must have been galled by *The Plastic Age*, by Percy Marks. For even as Scott bade farewell to the New York skyline, this was the second most popular novel in the country, its author reaping rich cash rewards. Like *This Side of Paradise, The Plastic Age* was a college novel and for the most part a shallow imitation of Fitzgerald. One thing to be said about Scott was that he avoided clichés. Percy Marks employed them in abundance—the boy's nervous arrival at college, homesickness, hazing, fraternities, football games, the fond visits of parents.

But the enormous popularity of *The Plastic Age* was, in a sense, understandable. Professor Marks (who lost his teaching post at Brown because of the book) at least dared admit that petting parties, soul kissing, and the consumption of gin might kindle the sex urge in collegiate prom trotters. Indeed, the success of his book can be traced to two scenes which took place during fraternity dances.

Marks' freshman hero, Hugh Carver, is appalled as his frat brothers lurch drunkenly about, arms around short-skirted girls who either whisper, "Let's pet" or else drink themselves into laughing-crying jags which end as they throw up on the campus. When a chaperone asks well-behaved Hugh to fetch her coat, he goes to a room and finds a couple entangled on the bed. Disgusted, he grabs the coat and leaves.

A year later, matters have changed. Sophomore Hugh is as drunk as anyone as he dances pelvis-to-pelvis with a boozed-up sheba named Cynthia, who whispers in his ear, "Hugh, get me a drink, or I'll pass out." The two are part of a dance montage:

> ❧ *The couples pressed close together . . . swaying, barely moving in place—boom, boom, boom, boom—"Second-hand hats, second hand clothes—That's why they call me second-hand Rose. . . ." The saxophones sang the melody with passionate despair; the violins played tricks with a broken heart; the clarinets rose shrill in pain; the drums beat on—boom, boom, boom. . . . A boy and a girl sought a dark corner. He shielded her with his body while she took a drink from a flask. Then he turned his face to the corner and drank. A moment later they were back on the floor, holding each other tight, drunkenly swaying. . . . Finally the last strains, a wail of agony—"Ev-'ry one*

*knows that I'm just Sec-ond-hand Rose—from Sec-ond
Av-en-ue."*

As the music ends, Cynthia begs "Ta-take me somewhere,
Hugh." He knows exactly what she means, and leads her to
the first available room. This time he and Cynthia are
amorously entwined on the bed when the room's owner
barges in. He is not as tolerant as Hugh the year before.
Outraged, he yanks Cynthia to her feet and hustles her to a
sorority house. Then he returns to lecture a still-drunken
Hugh. . . .

. . . Yet maybe Scott Fitzgerald, transatlantic passenger, was looking ahead rather than back. One resolution
known to be on his mind was to hunt up and encourage the
young expatriate writer named Ernest Hemingway.

Probably Scott heard of Hemingway through Edmund
Wilson, for the latter was the first critic to write favorably of
Hemingway's prose (he did not think so highly of the poetry
about which the fledgling author was then so proud). In an
early review of Hemingway's short stories, Wilson was impressed by the author's descriptions of bullfights. He spoke of
the dry-point quality of Hemingway's words, and compared
them to Goya's lithographs.

However Scott had learned of Hemingway, he was by now
a fervent admirer—he had a "crush" on Hemingway's prose,
someone said. In Paris for nearly two and a half years, Hemingway had been urged by Ezra Pound, Gertrude Stein, and
others to quit his job as correspondent for the Toronto *Star*
and write full time. Yet no one saw his potential more clearly
than Fitzgerald, who among other things hoped to push
Hemingway toward his own publisher, Scribner's, and its
understanding editor Maxwell Perkins.

It is interesting to examine the position of these two men in
mid-1924. The twenty-five-year-old Hemingway was almost
penniless and known in the United States only to a few re-
patriated expatriates and a handful of readers of Left Bank

magazines. Twenty-eight-year-old Scott, on the other hand, had made over $100,000 from his writing and possessed a name familiar to every literate American and many not so literate. He was in a position to help Hemingway with advice and money, and he did both.

Yet over the years the see-saw of Fate would drastically reverse the balance of these two authors . . .

"When Does Louis Write?"

Algonquin Round Table .. Louis Bromfield

In the Twenties we had fun," Burton Rascoe once wrote. Seemingly it was the kind of fun that communicated, for many inhabitants of the country were convinced that the literary world of mid-Manhattan was a supremely lively spot and its denizens highly favored folk.

One reason for this widespread (and not altogether mistaken) belief was the amount of publicity given a group that convened six days a week for luncheon in the Algonquin Hotel, at 59 West 44th Street in New York. From the aloof pages of *Vanity Fair*, as well as the daily newspaper columns of F.P.A., Karl K. Kitchen in the *Sun*, S. Jay Kaufman in the *Telegram*, and—especially—the syndicated "New York Day by Day" of O. O. McIntyre, America had learned of the scintillant Round Table of the Algonquin.

To the 1920's, both early and late, the Round Table represented contemporary wit, usually expressed in the form of the wisecrack. Algonquin regulars liked to believe the word "wisecrack" originated at their Round Table, but actually it stemmed, as "wise crack," from a monologues of the homespun stage comedian Charles "Chic" Sale. The one-line wisecrack polished and perfected by Algonquin wits, was the form of humor most appreciated by Alexander Woollcott, drama critic of *The New York Times* and unchallenged doyen of the lunchtime group.

Woollcott was especially delighted when one person's wise-crack promptly got topped by someone else's. Yet, after all, the ideal wisecrack was the one impossible to surpass. One day at the Algonquin, playwright George S. Kaufman was asked to define satire. "Satire is something that closes on Saturday night," he quipped. Here was utter perfection, the swift retort impossible to improve. In New York, the true sophisticate became the person who by nightfall knew the best crack uttered that noon at the Round Table.

For nearly twenty years the Algonquin Hotel had been favored by stage and movie celebrities like the Barrymores, Douglas Fairbanks, Sr., Mary Pickford, Laurette Taylor, and Constance Collier. It gained literary flavor as Mencken picked it for his semimonthly visits to New York from Baltimore. Frank Case, manager of the hotel, was largely responsible for its unique popularity, since this gentlemanly boniface had a true fondness for artistic folk. Case, who became owner in 1927, could hold his own in any contest of wits. He comes down to us as the individual to say, "Time wounds all heels."

The several versions of the founding of the Round Table all involve fussy, caponish Alexander Woollcott. By the least complex, he once dined at the Algonquin and fell in love with its angel-food cake. Arranging a luncheon for himself, F.P.A., and Heywood Broun, both of whom worked downtown on the *Tribune*, he recalled the cake and picked the Algonquin as the place of meeting. The occasion proved so pleasant that he said, "Let's do this every day."

At first, Woollcott, Broun, Adams, and a few invited guests occupied a small table in the Pergola Room. As numbers grew, the luncheons were moved into the larger Rose Room, at a table near the door. Still the tribe increased, and Frank Case began reserving the round table in the center of the room for his pet patrons.

Originally members referred to the luncheons simply as Board Meetings. At that time the nation was in the throes of the Ouija Board craze. A waiter named Luigi was assigned to the table, and the wits then dubbed themselves the Luigi

Board. When a caricaturist was assigned to sketch the assembled group he titled his finished work "The Algonquin Round Table," providing the world with the term it liked. However, members themselves always preferred the Vicious Circle.

Regular members of the Vicious Circle—that is, those free to sit down when they felt like it, without invitation—included Woollcott, F.P.A., Heywood Broun, Marc Connelly, George S. Kaufman, Charles MacArthur, John V. A. Weaver, Laurence Stallings, Deems Taylor, Frank Sullivan, Russel Crouse, Donald Ogden Stewart, Brock and Murdock Pemberton, John Peter Toohey, and Harold Ross, the bristle-haired powerhouse who was editor of the *American Legion Magazine*, but would soon found *The New Yorker*.

On the distaff side sat Edna Ferber, Neysa McMein, Beatrice (Mrs. George S.) Kaufman, Jane Grant (Mrs. Ross), Alison Smith (Mrs. Crouse), Gertrude Atherton, and Alice Duer Miller, whose *Saturday Evening Post* fiction was deplored but whose aristocratic lineage and up-to-the-second smartness let her in. Youth and beauty were represented by Peggy Wood (Mrs. Weaver) and Tallulah Bankhead, then a glowingly lovely young girl with a throaty voice and partiality for gutter language. When the luncheons first began, Case heard complaints from other diners that Tallulah laughed too loudly over the sallies at the Luigi Board. But as the fame of the gatherings grew, her raucous guffaws seemed perfectly all right.

In early days, Robert Benchley, Robert E. Sherwood, and Dorothy Parker were most brilliant young Round Table talents. All three worked on the sophisticated *Vanity Fair* until the unhappy day when Mrs. Parker devoted one of her clever "I hate" verses to Billie Burke, actress wife of Follies producer Florenz Ziegfeld. Ziegfeld objected, and Mrs. Parker was fired. Sherwood and Benchley resigned in protest —a not inconsiderable gesture, since neither was established in the literary world. Sherwood quickly found a job on the humor magazine *Life*, leaving Mrs. Parker and Benchley to pool resources and hire a thirty-dollar-a-month office in the Metropolitan Opera Building, within easy walking distance of the Algonquin. Here they nursed vague notions of press agentry, but no one entered the office until Mrs. Parker lettered "Men's Room" on the door.

At first Franklin P. Adams dominated the Round Table as the oldest, best known, and highest paid of the founders. Yet slowly Woollcott became the mother hen of the Vicious Circle, packing it with congenial souls who relished his bitchy insults and gushing sentiment. Yet even Woollcott could be a victim of the table's verbal scatter shot. At one gathering he held diners enthralled by concocting a "dream" cast for *Macbeth*. Abruptly turning to Peggy Wood, a young beauty then best known for musical roles, he shot one of his celebrated barbs. "I don't think you'd be very good as Lady Macbeth, do you, Peggy?" he inquired acidly. "No, Alec," Miss Wood answered sweetly, "but I think *you* would."

Said one commentator, "It is no injustice to say the sophisticates of the Round Table are pleasurably aware of their sophistication." Another thought that members of the Vicious Circle "lived off each other's wits." United by tight bonds of common literary and entertainment standards, the group formed a close-knit mutual-admiration society, obviously delighted to be in each other's company. Illustrative of this was Heywood Broun's description of Woollcott as "the smartest of Alecs."

Members of the circle became so enamored of their joint talents that one Sunday night in 1922 the group hired a Broadway theater to present a full-scale revue titled *No, Sirree*. Written and performed entirely by themselves, this was called "An Anonymous Entertainment by the Vicious Circle of the Hotel Algonquin." Its purpose was to prove that Round Tablers could write the wittiest stuff in America, and members of a select audience loyally agreed.

During one Algonquin luncheon, Dorothy Parker rose from her chair at the Round Table to say, "Excuse me, everybody, I have to go to the bathroom." Then she bent low to confide, "I really have to make a phone call, but I'm too embarrassed to say so." During a discussion of college morals the same little lady said, "If all the girls who attended the

Yale Prom were laid end to end, I wouldn't be a bit surprised." Explaining his allergy to productive work, Robert Benchley cracked, "Anybody can do any amount of work, provided it isn't what he is supposed to be doing." One lunch hour the wits put heads together and created this bit of verse:

> *There are so many feather beds,*
> *So many little maidenheads,*
> *There's practically no excuse*
> *For sodomy or self-abuse.*

Honored guest one noon was Ring Lardner, just returned from Washington, where he had met Calvin Coolidge, the Chief Executive admiringly known as Silent Cal. "I told him my funniest story," Lardner reported, "and he laughed so hard you could hear a pin drop." One day Heywood Broun showed up soaked to the skin by a summer shower. He quickly ordered a warming glass of wine, but did not like what Luigi brought him. He gulped it down anyway, saying, "Oh, well, any port in a storm."

Again, Marc Connelly wore a new blue suit which attracted an unusual amount of lint. Brushing himself off, he muttered, "I'm going to have a suit made of lint and see if it picks up blue serge." Yet examples of Round Table wit invariably return to Dorothy Parker. Once she reported that the night before a man she detested asked her to dance. "Dance with you?" she said to him. "I'd rather be caught in a midnight fire at sea." Someone complimented beautiful Clare Boothe of *Vanity Fair* by saying, "She's kind to her inferiors." Mrs. Parker snapped, "Where does she find them?" Telling about renting a new apartment, she warned the others present not to be disappointed by its size. "It's just a little place to lay my hat and some of my friends," she explained.

These and other witticisms made the Round Table so famous that both New Yorkers and out-of-towners lunching at the hotel begged to be seated nearby. The Bohemian writers and poets of Greenwich Village and of the Paris Left Bank might dream of changing the world and creating new techniques in the arts. But those who lunched at the Round Table typified literary and cultural success to an admiring nation. Those permitted to pull up chairs at the celebrated table had either achieved commercial success, or were clearly pointed that way. Lloyd Morris set this matter in focus by asking rhetorically, "Is not the Round Table a kind of stock market, establishing the daily value of professional reputations?"

As time passed, a bit of the easy spontaneity departed Round Table sessions. Members of the oft-quoted group could not help realizing that any smart lunchtime remark would soon be known around town. Some sought to win this instant fame by dreaming up a smart crack ahead of time, then dropping it into the conversation at a strategic moment. "They hoarded their smarties" is the way one writer put it. One Round Tabler later confessed to waiting five full sessions before tossing his verbal firecracker.

In the years of the Round Table practically every well-known American and English writer sat there at least once. Guests had to be careful, for the Vicious Circle, in Edna Ferber's words, "could not stand bores, hypocrites, sentimentalists, or the socially pretentious." She continues, "They were ruthless toward charlatans, toward the pompous, and the mentally and artistically dishonest. Casual, incisive, they had a terrible integrity about their work and a boundless ambition."

In 1923–24, the group attained new prominence as Gertrude Atherton featured it in her top-selling novel *Black Oxen.* Mrs. Atherton labeled them The Sophisticates, and went on, "There was a great deal of scintillating talk in this group on the significant books and tendencies of the day. It was an excellent forcing house for ideas and vocabularies. They appraised, debated, rejected, and finally placed the seal of their own august approval on a favored few."

Mrs. Atherton may have given the Round Table the best of it, for usually it was an arena of opinion dominated by Woollcott, whose quixotic enthusiasms were often strenuous to follow. Members of the Vicious Circle had from the beginning imitated the smartest of Alecs in loathing O. O. McIntyre, a columnist conscienceless in stealing the quips of the table. McIntyre also gave his out-of-town readers a lurid, inaccurate picture of metropolitan life, which further infuriated The Sophisticates.

Hatred of McIntyre continued full blast until Woollcott learned that the columnist had said, "There are no illegitimate children—only illegitimate parents." Here was an epigram worthy of the Round Table itself, and apparently an original smartie to boot. Instantly Woollcott's contempt turned to admiration. From then on, no one at the Algonquin dared disparage Oscar Odd McIntyre.

Not all admired the Vicious Circle. Playwright-producer-songwriter-actor George M. Cohan dismissed it as "a Round Table with not a square man at it." H. L. Mencken avoided the Round Table during his monthly sojourns at the Algonquin. George Jean Nathan stayed away because of his intense dislike of Woollcott. Once Nathan stirred up a literary tempest by calling the overenthusiastic Woollcott "the Alka Seltzer of Times Square." Again, he said the *Times* critic acted "like a butterfly in heat."

Others accused the Round Table of literary logrolling and its members of shamelessly shouting the praises of fellow members' books and plays. One who especially downgraded the Table Round was a mighty mite named Anita Loos, whose phenomenal career as a writer of film scripts included salvaging the career of Douglas Fairbanks, Sr.

Miss Loos, a girl so tiny that friends called her Bug or Buggie, was daughter of the manager of a West Coast theatrical company. After viewing a few early movies, she began writing film scenarios at the precocious age of fourteen—or was it younger? The first one she mailed East—in those days movies were made on the sidewalks of New York—was entitled *The New York Hat*. It was promptly bought and made into a notable pioneering film with Mary Pickford, Lionel Barrymore, and Lillian and Dorothy Gish.

Like the mountain coming to Muhammad, the film industry moved to Miss Loos' doorstep in Hollywood. Soon the talented teenager was writing for none other than D. W. Griffith. The famed director had signed Douglas Fairbanks to play romantic leads, but his work seemed disappointing. Fairbanks was about to be fired when Miss Loos came up with a gymnastic-action script that shot him to stardom. When one of her scenarios was scheduled to be filmed in Manhattan, Fairbanks recommended the Algonquin.

When the Vicious Circle discovered the proximity of this brainiest of flappers, its members sought to annex her. Anita failed to respond. After one meeting, she decided, "They behaved with that overly casual air which is an attempt of the unsophisticated to appear at ease." The girl from Hollywood thought Woollcott's insults crude, Neysa McMein's sarcasms needlessly devastating, and Dorothy Parker "a lone wolverine." On the whole she found them suffering from group narcissism, an inability to appreciate the world beyond the Algonquin.

The universe of books also faulted the Vicious Circle. Nearly all members could be called authors in one way or another, yet their major concerns were usually plays or newspapers. Even Edna Ferber, a simon-pure fictioneer, had always wanted to write plays and even now had begun working with George S. Kaufman on such collaborations as *The Royal Family* and *Dinner at Eight*.

If the Round Table was aware of books, those it chose for joint approbation failed to satisfy the bookish. The Vicious Circle rhapsodized over *If Winter Comes* by England's A. S. M. Hutchinson, a book described as "a literary photograph of a lovable personality," and the collective praise of The Sophisticates helped boost it into a best seller. Yet men like Burton Rascoe were infuriated by this extolling of Hutchinson, for it seemed to set him above domestic writers like Dreiser, Lewis, Hergesheimer, and Hecht. "The continued plugging of A. S. M. Hutchinson," Rascoe wrote, "seemed to [expose] the very bankruptcy of all critical standards in their ranks."

Rascoe undertook to teach the Vicious Circle a lesson by

attacking another Hutchinson effort called *This Freedom.* "If it had not been a book by an author whom Broun, Adams, and Woollcott acclaimed as though he were a great artist," he later wrote, "I should have reviewed it along with other run-of-the-mill sentimental novels. Instead, I analyzed it at length, showing just wherein Harold Bell Wright was a more capable and distinctive novelist."

As a result, Hutchinson's publisher canceled all advertising in the *Tribune.* Rascoe still believed he had struck a mighty blow for literary freedom until he found himself out of a job when the *Tribune* and *Herald* merged to make the *Herald-Tribune.* In large part because of the Hutchinson matter, he was toppled from his eminence as book reviewer and lively chronicler of "The Bookman's Daybook."

A special twist of the knife came as he was succeeded by Stuart P. Sherman, a critic known to dislike Dreiser and other writers Rascoe favored. Yet after brief exposure to Manhattan, Sherman drastically altered his viewpoint and even approved the writers whom he had previously dismissed as "these young people." As for Rascoe, he visited the Left Bank, worked for a syndicate, then became editor of *The Bookman.*

The Algonquin was literary twenty-four hours a day," reads one tribute to the 44th Street premises. So great was its charisma that even those who disliked the Vicious Circle felt impelled to lunch there, no matter where they might sit. Thus, while the Round Table flourished, a group of purely literary folk met at another table which—to them, at least— was known as the Little Round Table.

Burton Rascoe was a stalwart of the Little Round Table. Other regulars were Christopher Morley, publisher Earle Balch, literary agent Paul Reynolds, and reviewer Harry Hansen. Yet by far the most colorful patron of Little Round Table—and, indeed, the man responsible for its existence— was twenty-six-year-old Louis Bromfield, the latest novelist to brighten the roster of the Literary Decade.

In artistic circles of the time, this newcomer had an amazing distinction: of all living writers, he was suddenly the one most to be envied. The Younger Generation might consider Scott Fitzgerald the luckiest author of the era, while the older might envy the turbulent genius of Sinclair Lewis. But Louis Bromfield, here was a fortunate fellow! If nothing else, he appeared to function completely without effort in the sweaty field of authorship. No one ever saw Bromfield huddled over a troublesome typewriter or heard him lament the lonely miseries of creativity. Instead, the cliché question among his friends was "When does Louis write?"

A rangy six-foot-two, Bromfield always appeared relaxed and easygoing. Careless of dress, he had the kind of homely-handsome features that are warming to look upon, and his friendly grin was attractive and disarming. The author had a wife he loved and who adored him in return. He seemed to like everyone; everyone liked him. More than any other writer of the Twenties he fitted the description in Joseph Moncure March's *Cocktail Party*:

> He had that air of poise without pose
> That only a well bred person shows.

Louis Bromfield also had such great appreciation of music that he was once employed by the *Musical Courier*. Yet of all the arts he most enjoyed ballet, and this tall, loose, untrained man was surprisingly capable of executing ballet steps himself. With all this went a deep religio-mystic streak which eventually emerged in *The Strange Case of Miss Annie Spragg*, generally considered his best work written during the Twenties.

Friends of Bromfield inevitably speculated about what made him tick so harmoniously, but got few answers. Born in 1896 in Mansfield, Ohio, he came of a line of Midwest pioneers. His parents were hard-working farm folk who—here, perhaps, lay a clue—were unusually energetic. Louis grew up with a deep love of the land, but also dreamed of some day writing novels. Farming seemed to win out as he enrolled in the Cornell University Agricultural School, but dissatisfaction soon drove him to New York for an arts course at Columbia. In World War I he became a pioneer in the American Field Service ambulance drivers with the French army. In time, he won the Croix de Guerre.

With him in the ambulance corps was a contemporary named Larry Barretto, whose background was much different from Bromfield's. His full name was Lawrence Brevoort Barretto, and he belonged to a not-too-wealthy branch of two of the oldest families on Manhattan. Barretto also yearned to write novels, and before the flickering campfires of war-torn France, the two boys talked hopefully of the day when each would be a recognized author. The time seemed remote, however, and on demobilization they secured prosaic literary jobs. Ties between them tightened as Bromfield wed Mary Appleton Wood of New York and Appleton Farms in Ipswich, Massachusetts. Barretto was introduced to Mary's cousin at the wedding and shortly thereafter, married her.

The two young men were writing books in their spare time, and it is said that Bromfield destroyed four manuscripts before completing one that seemed right. Larry Barretto, however, won recognition first; his novel *A Conqueror Passes* was published early in 1924. It dealt with the readjustment of a soldier to civilian life, a theme also utilized by Laurence Stallings in *Plumes* and William Faulkner in *Soldier's Pay*.

Louis Bromfield's *The Green Bay Tree* appeared a few weeks later. Though a proud farm boy in spirit, the writer had turned to the steel towns of Ohio as his setting for a book about the vicissitudes of the aristocratic Shane family, inhabitants of a feudal domain surrounded by belching steel furnaces. Bromfield's female characters were usually better than his males, and he hovered lovingly over Lily, the beautiful Shane who turned expatriate in Paris. His novel was strong on narrative, a fact noted by the reviewer who cited "its respect for the rich tradition of the Anglo Saxon novel . . . balanced by a fondness for experiment." Another enthused, "The sense of life is in this book." Yet the most glowing praise came from Stuart P. Sherman who found in Bromfield's prose "a glamorous forward movement which affected me like the cantabile style in music."

With such reviews, Louis Bromfield became an overnight celebrity—which failed to surprise those who already knew him. Louis' last job had been in the promotion department of the publishing firm of G. P. Putnam's Sons, where his assistant was a coldly beautiful girl named Frieda Inescourt, who pursued a stage career at night. In time, Frieda Inescourt became one of the leading actresses of the Twenties, undaunted by drama critic Percy Hammond's complaint of her iciness: "She has the sex, but not the appeal." Of her attractive boss at Putnam's, Miss Inescourt wrote:

> ⋐ *The starlight of destiny was in his slate-blue glance, and the thrust of his loose-knit body was unmistakably forward. He was sure of his direction; sure as few of us ever are in this muddled sphere. He knew what he was traveling away from and what he was traveling toward. . . . He was going places, but his lounging gait and a certain semi-insolent, sprawling ease in all circumstances suggested that he had no sense of being pressed for time.*

A few professed to detect ambition at the core of Louis Bromfield. "He didn't exactly hate publicity, and he knew how to get it," a friend pointed out. Yet this ambition was never objectionable; on him, you might say, it looked good. In the words of an interviewer:

> ⋐ *Success makes some men aloof, reserved and uncharming. Louis Bromfield, successful, is gregarious, expansive, and overflowing with good fellowship. His pleasure in success is not a miser's hoard to be enjoyed secretly, but a wealth to be shared in congenial company.*

But always the question remained, "When does Louis write?" To Frieda Inescourt, this was never a real baffler. She says:

> ⋐ *I am afraid there is nothing more mysterious about Louis . . . than the fact that he possesses an inexhaustible*

fund of native energy which enables him to live hard and play hard, and get his writing done in odd moments without fuss or fanfare or ostentatious insistence on seclusion.

In every way, the literary world found Bromfield stimulating to have around. After *The Green Bay Tree* he began a second novel, *Possession*. Yet few could believe it. The ebullient young man seemed to be spreading his charm everywhere but at the typewriter. Mornings were devoted to his wife and three young daughters. At noon he appeared at the Little Round Table of the Algonquin, then went to his publishers' or passed the afternoon with friends. In the early evening he and his wife went to a cocktail party, then to dinner, to a play or ballet, and finally a night club.

"He had an extraordinary way at cocktail parties," a friend remembers. "He seemed to be made for them." According to another, "He brought a festive air to any gathering, probably because he had such a damn good time himself."

In the course of a long career, Bromfield finally broke down and confessed to a reporter that he liked to work two hours a day, preferably from 9:30 to 11:30 in the morning. He was able to work so little because, even when gregarious, his mind was busy digesting his material. By the time he sat at the typewriter his ideas had more or less crystallized into what he wanted to write. He concluded, "The thing is, I don't fiddle around when I do write." His wife had this to say:

    ◄§ *His vision is first and last that of novelist, seeing things, people, and events in terms slightly outsize of reality, colored and expanded by what some may call imagination and some call genius. This quality gives both to his writing and to his talk . . . a tremendous intensity and excitement.*

Like Scott Fitzgerald, Bromfield was able to supplement his book income with short stories in popular magazines. This in turn allowed him to maintain two establishments, one at Cold Spring Harbor, Long Island, where the lover of the land spent time like a country squire with his family. The Bromfields also kept an apartment in Manhattan for the parties Louis loved.

The ones he gave were never drunken routs like those of Scott and Zelda, but stimulating gatherings featuring good talk and lively congeniality.

Bromfield was never a purely literary man; rather, he aspired to be a citizen of the world. His myriad interests included agriculture, economics, music, painting, politics, religion, ballet, theater, travel, movies, and books. At his parties he liked to gather around him "doers" in all these fields. "Dullness is an agony to him,"-his wife once wrote. Trapped by a bore, Bromfield became so upset that brown splotches appeared under his eyes. Socially, he himself was a highly entertaining talker, but never a wit.

For the added success of his cherished parties, Louis Bromfield tapped a unique source by employing a male secretary named George Hawkins, who became almost as famed in the literary community as his employer. Tough, masculine, foul-mouthed rather than profane, this diamond-in-the-rough contacted bootleggers and otherwise smoothed Bromfield's social and professional paths. What well-born Mary Appleton Wood Bromfield thought of George Hawkins remains an abiding mystery, but one who recalls them says, "I think Mary was always a bit put out by George."

Bromfield waited for the publication of his five-hundred-page *Possession*, then took his family and George Hawkins to France. Except for occasional trips back home, he remained there over the next fourteen years. Thus he was not in the United States when his *Early Autumn* won the Pulitzer Prize in 1927.

Overseas the Bromfield brood set up headquarters at a farm in Senlis, thirty miles from Paris. Here the farmer-author began introducing American vegetables to France and hybridizing dahlias. But Bromfield also loved sun, fun, frolic, sport, and city life, and for them all kept moving tirelessly around the Continent. A publicity release put out by his American publisher had him wintering in Switzerland, spending springtime in London, summering at his own villa at St.-Jean-de-Luz in the Basque country, and passing autumn in Senlis or Paris, where he maintained an apartment on the

Boulevard Flandrin. On this circuit, Bromfield skiied, golfed, swam, painted, drove sports cars, danced, gambled, read, attended bullfights—and wrote novels.

Obviously "expatriate" is too mild a word for Louis Bromfield. He became exactly what he aspired to be, a figure in the international whirl who today would figure among the Jet Set and the Beautiful People. He was on a first-name basis with Fitzgerald and Hemingway whom he occasionally met on the boulevards of Paris. But these two never entered his exalted orbit. Bromfield was introduced to Gertrude Stein, who immediately succumbed to his pervasive charm and became one of his closest friends, which may have made Hemingway jealous. For the most part, however, he moved among people who, like himself, thought every split second of life was for living.

When the Bromfields were in residence, the farm at Senlis became the in place to visit. Every Sunday morning top members of the Paris diplomatic, artistic, and expatriate sets got into cars or trains to head there. The unflagging hospitality of the house—supervised by Mary Bromfield and George Hawkins—took care of the hungry, the thirsty, and those who came only to spend time in the captivating company of Louis Bromfield, author. Usually so many showed up that the Bromfields could not recall their names. "Senlis," Mary Bromfield was once heard to murmur, "has become a trifle *too* popular."

Among those present on average Senlis Sundays were Gertrude Stein, Alice Toklas, the Maharani of Cooch Behar, and the Maharaja of Baroda. The last two eventually turned Bromfield's questing intellect toward India, about which he wrote *The Rains Came.* It proved to be his most popular novel, though not the best of his twenty-five books in as many years.

Battle of the Aesthetes

Edna Ferber . . Anne Parrish . . American Mercury

Despite emergence of the likes of Louis Bromfield, the year 1924 really belonged to Edna Ferber.

This energetic lady, small of body, large of head, ambitious of mind, was author of *So Big*, a novel which sold over 300,000 copies and won praise from all parts of the nation. In Manhattan, gentlemanly Charles Hanson Towne pontificated, "We need this sort of writing in America." In provincial Emporia, Kansas, William Allen White flattered the author as "a legitimate daughter of the Dickens dynasty."

A few reviewers were crass enough to note flaws and crudities in the book, but Miss Ferber (don't forget) was a member in top standing of the Algonquin Round Table. So any dispraise was drowned out by hoarse hosannas from the Vicious Circle.

Edna Ferber, book writer since 1912, was no dazzling newcomer. Nor did she write the type of fiction attractive to the civilized minority; hers was superior escape stuff aimed at heart rather than mind. More, her writing was frankly commercial, usually done with magazines in mind and book publication hoped for but no certainty. Yet in Edna Ferber's favor it can be said—if one tries—that she was never preoccupied by the very rich or very poor, but devoted her attention to middle-class working America.

Her main characters were additionally interesting because the author endowed them with the drive and determination she herself possessed. Offspring of an immigrant Jewish father and an American-born mother, Edna grew up in Appleton, Wisconsin, determined to better herself by writing—then just about the only colorful career open to females. After high school, she worked as a three-dollar-a-week reporter for the local newspaper, but fiery ambition propelled her to Chicago, a city she continued to appreciate through life. She went there to write whenever possible, in the belief that its lusty atmosphere added sinew to her prose.

Her first magazine story (for which she received $62.50) was called "The Homely Heroine," and in a way this title sums up her own dauntless career. But if Miss Ferber presented an unquenchable ego to the world, she underwent occasional moments of self-doubt. One came in 1912, after completing her first novel *Dawn O'Hara*. Convinced it was a failure, she actually threw out the manuscript. Her adoring mother retrieved it from the ash heap and insisted it be sent to a publisher, who accepted it. Until the appearance of *So Big*, the other novels in Edna Ferber's life were *Fanny Herself* and *The Girls*.

Miss Ferber concentrated on short stories and serials for slick-paper periodicals, doing so many that seven collections had already been published. The most popular dealt with the breezy activities of Emma McChesney, female traveling salesman, a rarity in those days as well as now. The Emma stories were written with so much ingenuity and pep that in 1920 the editor of *Cosmopolitan* handed Miss Ferber a blank check with his signature on it. As long as she stuck to Emma, she could write her own ticket.

Yet Miss Ferber was again experiencing the urge to write novels. "I knew exactly where I was going, though I was having a terrible time getting there," she later recalled. Spurning the check, she wrote *The Girls*, a moderate success. She had enjoyed doing it; indeed, Edna Ferber always renewed herself by work, which to her was "the finest freshener in the world." A practical mind told her to return to profitable

Emma McChesney, but instinct ruled otherwise. For years she had pondered a novel on "the triumph of failure." Now she started—"I wrote it against my will," she once reminisced. "I *had* to write it." In years to come Miss Ferber beguiled reviewers (and infuriated colleagues) by insisting that she wrote the last line of her books first, then went back and caught up with it. Presumably the new novel, *So Big*, was written in this turnabout fashion.

The title derived from a cute habit of the book's heroine, Selina De Jong, wife of a small-time truck farmer outside Chicago. Selina liked to ask her growing son, Dirk, "How big is my man?" Little Dirk then measured a tiny space between thumb and forefinger before answering, "So-o-o big!" Inevitably, So Big became his nickname.

Selina De Jong was the character Miss Ferber had in mind as the triumph of failure. A deep lover of life, Selina was no more than a cipher by worldly standards. Of her life, Miss Ferber said, "Nothing ever really happened in it. The high dramatic moment came when she drove to town with a load of cabbages, turnips, and beets."

Yet a practiced hand like Edna Ferber's could not write without drama, and in *So Big* it arrives belatedly as Dirk matures into a highly personable and coldly ambitious young man. Though he enjoys accomplishment, grown-up Dirk totally lacks his mother's love of living—herein lies the author's point. After abandoning architectural studies, Dirk becomes a get-rich-quick bond salesman, then a boy-wonder investment banker. He is adored by Paula, an already-married society girl. Because of her, Dirk is freely accepted by Chicago's opera-going and fox-hunting sets.

When Dirk meets the carefree girl artist, Dallas O'Mara, it seems time for him to fall for her and substitute love of life for joy in living. But things do not turn out that way. The book ends inconclusively—tragically?—as Dallas departs for Paris to study art. Dirk might have persuaded her to stay but fails to make the effort. Instead, he bids her farewell, then returns to his Paula-designed digs and hurls himself on the bed, presumably realizing the emptiness of material success.

The phone rings and he knows it is Paula. Does he answer? . . . The book, which ends on this uncertain note, is replete with unanswered questions. Selina, the hard-working farm mother, loves only life; the son for whom she sacrifices so much turns out to be a materialist. How did it happen? Which is the real success, which the failure?

The adventures of *So Big* from typewriter to bookstore help reveal the reason the thrill-happy public of the Twenties was fascinated by its authors.

On completing her book, Miss Ferber underwent another fit of self-doubt. "I thought that I had written not a best seller, but a worst seller," she confessed once. "Not that alone, I thought I had written a *non*-seller."

But if an Edna Ferber manuscript lacked hard-cover potential, it could always be sold as a magazine serial. In her despondency, her working title of *So Big* seemed unbearably cute. Changing the title to *Selina*, she disposed of it to the *Woman's Home Companion*. When publisher Russell Doubleday suggested putting the installments into book form, Miss Ferber was horrified. "I feel very strongly that (we) should not publish it as a novel," she wrote in heartfelt fashion. "It would hurt you as a publisher and me as a writer." But he persisted, and in the process restored the title *So Big*. "Occasionally," Miss Ferber said later, "someone comes along and commits a best seller in all innocence. Of such was I."

What did success do to Edna Ferber? As a hard-working magazine writer, she had lived almost entirely in hotels. Now she rented an apartment on Central Park West in New York and joyously faced a future with "no bellboys, no bogus palms, no uniforms, no hotel clerks, and no printed menus."

A more subtle female was Anne Parrish, who had already written the novel *Pocketful of Poses*. Now, a year after, she was represented by *Semi-Attached*. Born in Colorado Springs, this writer was in her midthirties and part of the talented family that included artist Maxfield Parrish. Her own brother, Dilwyn, was an artist with whom Anne collaborated on children's books. As the wife of a corporation executive, Miss Parrish lived in New York City and Englewood, New Jersey. Her witty and amusing books—or so they seemed at the time—posed a particularly difficult problem for Alexander Woollcott, who doted on Edna Ferber as a person but thought Anne Parrish wrote the way a clever woman should. He solved this matter by getting to know Miss Parrish as well as Miss Ferber and doting on both.

Pocketful of Poses told of a girl who playacted from childhood, with the result that by maturity affectation and untruthfulness are second (or first) nature to her. *Semi-Attached* provided a more provocative theme. The author, a Colorado girl herself, had apparently plucked an idea from Judge Ben B. Lindsey, a Denver judge appalled by gin marriages and the number of young couples who subsequently appeared before him in divorce court. The compassionate jurist began quietly advocating trial marriages wherein partners lived together without benefit of clergy for a test period. If things worked out, they then got married and produced children. Four years later, Judge Lindsey's book, *Companionate Marriage*, rocked the nation, but at the moment his theories were known to only a few.

Semi-Attached involves Francie Graythorn and Bimbo Bennet, who meet in Switzerland while traveling with respective mothers. Francie, just passed twenty, is no flapper. True, she has dutifully read *This Side of Paradise, Flaming Youth,* and other encyclopedias of the Jazz Age, but their content made little dent on her intellect. Described as "an exquisite child," Francie needs no further molding; she is one of nature's own, friendly as a puppy and delightfully casual in attire. Despite his snappy cognomen, Bimbo is the opposite. Serious and upstanding, he tumbles for frivolous Francie— Chapter Three begins, "Bim lost no time in falling in love . . ." Francie falls equally hard for him and marriage seems inevitable except that this girl-child is fiercely opposed to it as an institution. In childhood she had been awakened at night by her parents' loud domestic arguments, and to her wise eyes, marriage appears to have crushed the happiness of everyone known to her. When conventional Bimbo tries to persuade her that it's a necessary, sacred ritual, she bursts out, "For the State, it's most convenient, but for the individual soul—oh, dreadful. It's indecent!"

So the winsome child suggests that they prevaricate to family and friends, saying a proper marriage ceremony has taken place. They will live for three years in unwed bliss; at the end of that time the official knot can be tied if still desired. It is trial marriage with a vengeance, and Bimbo is so smitten that he agrees.

They set up as young marrieds on Peachtree Lane in the Connecticut town dominated by the social Bennet family. Bimbo commutes daily to Wall Street, and in the eyes of the town, sweet Francie is just another newlywed. As a housekeeper, however, she is in a class with Zelda Fitzgerald, which irritates Bim when he returns at night. She also wears a dress made of window curtains to a gala at his parents' home. Yet love never loses its delicious potency, and when Bimbo forgives her, Francie is "drenched in bliss, her whole body tingling, an exquisite fire running through her veins."

With Bimbo at work, the irrepressible girl spends time among other young wives whose code of conduct, as she interprets it, is

> You must have "pep."
> You must do and say what the rest of your "crowd" does and says.
> You must never, never, never let anyone think you are a "highbrow."

While abiding by these rules, Francie solaces herself in the realization that she is really a scarlet woman, living in sin. She also conjures up spicy visions of the way her in-laws and married friends would react if they only knew. What really keeps her in line, though, is love for Bimbo, which thrives although these two have nothing whatsoever in common.

A worldly woman named Sylvia tries to steal Bimbo away by appealing to his mind, but when traveling he still writes

Francie letters which begin "Dear Person" and end "Me." Francie dallies with a kindred soul named Tommy, who teaches her Mah-Jong and gives her a phonograph record of "Song of the Volga Boatman."

Francie banishes fey Tommy from her life, in the belief that Bimbo has done the same with sophisticated Sylvia. But on learning that the two still meet in New York for an occasional lunch, the kitten turns tiger. First she informs Bimbo's mother of their unmarried bliss; the result is so catastrophic that Francie flees to relatives. There she is inconsolable until Bimbo tracks her down. Then the girl begs, "Bim, marry me—keep me with you!" If this had been a contemporary film, it would end with the implausible assurance "They lived happily ever after."

Miss Parrish wrote her novel with a light, detached touch that caused one reviewer to see "a blithe wit that prevents satire from becoming cynicism." Another, however, discovered "cheap smartness." A third said, "light, bright, and neat." As for Miss Parrish, she was hard at work on *The Perennial Bachelor* which a year later won her the two thousand dollar Harper Award for Fiction and made her a front-rank novelist.

A male writer who brought joy to a considerable segment of the 1924 reading public was Robert Nathan, by now author of three novels. The thirty-year-old Nathan had quit an advertising job after publishing his first work—*Kindred*, in 1919—to lead the pleasant life of gentleman writer. His books were a happy mixture of fantasy, allegory, satire, whimsy, wit, and wisdom. Those who liked him usually did so aggressively. *Autumn*, his second novel, told of Mr. Jimoney, a Vermont schoolteacher, and his housekeeper, Mrs. Grumble. After Jimoney's age forces him to retire, the book becomes a bittersweet fable into which the author weaves not only tragedy "but a vital mixture of the compound elements —love, hate, greed—that make up the sum of human existence." One reviewer praised the prose as "cool and fresh, like dew," while another saw "light, roving, unboisterous humor." Few of Nathan's partisans bothered to acknowledge the caddish reviewer who thought the book "unconvincing, unartistic, and unreal as a dream."

Nathan's third novel, *The Puppet Master*, concerned a maker of puppets and his creations. With this fantasy-allegory, the chorus of praise rose higher; one critic found "delicate, fragrant loveliness . . . his touch light and exquisite . . . his wisdom deep and ageless." Numerous books and many years later, Robert Nathan lamented, "I am aware that many reviewers consider me a milk-toasty writer." But whatever his own feelings, few authors have had such garlands of adjectives draped around their necks.

Another novel that year was E. M. Forster's *Passage to India*, an English import and one of the few novels of the Twenties which reads as well today. It was the fifth novel by this most self-effacing of authors, and proved to be the last in his lifetime. "I have nothing more to say," he declared, and the world believed him. But after his death in 1970 another novel on the subject of homosexuality was discovered.

Those on the alert for the main literary event of 1924 had to look toward the magazines. And here, it is pleasant to report, the men known as the Katzenjammer Kids of Literature were the reason.

Since the beginning of the decade, and perhaps before, H. L. Mencken and George Jean Nathan had found coeditorship of *Smart Set* irksome. Mencken especially felt constricted by a fare of sophisticated fiction, light verse, and epigrams. Even the name *Smart Set* rubbed him the wrong way. Increasingly, he desired to break into the exciting sphere of journalistic nonfiction, landing his editorial blows on glass jaws like "Methodists, Baptists, and other vermin of God." His dream was to devote the pages of a magazine to exposures about his native land that no other periodical would print—to dig deep into what he called "the whole gaudy, glorious American scene."

At the core of this lay an urge to write about politics. Since his first book, *Ventures in Verse*, in 1903, Mencken had written a biography of Nietzsche and coauthored the potboiler *What You Ought to Know About Your Baby*; he had collaborated on four books with Nathan and brought out his first *American Language* in 1919; he had produced *A Book of Prefaces, A Book of Burlesques, Damn! A Book of Calumny,* and *In Defense of Women,* along with the first four volumes of his vigorous *Prejudices.*

Now politics tugged at his surging mind. In part, this could be attributed to two recent events in his life, one humorous: In the summer of 1923 the Seven Arts Club of Chicago had nominated Mencken for the Presidency of the United States in the election a year hence. In all history, no nation had been as susceptible to nonsensical stunts as America in the Terrific Twenties, and Mencken's mock-candidacy won reams of publicity. Accepting the honor with fitting solemnity, the candidate designated Nathan as his running mate. With this, the two hammered out a ludicrous platform of 122 planks. One promised "to support the spoils system and to see that the intelligent minority gets all the soft jobs." Another vowed to shave off the beard of Charles Evans Hughes.

Politics also sparked the incident that finally cut Mencken and Nathan loose from *Smart Set.* A cherished part of Heinie's public image was despising the President of the United States. Indeed, of all the Chief Executives who passed under his scrutiny, Mencken probably liked only Calvin Coolidge. Of Woodrow Wilson he believed, "no viler oaf ever sat upon the American throne." Naturally, he detested Warren G. Harding, that empty man of Roman-senator handsomeness who succeeded Wilson in the White House. In an era when Presidents composed their own speeches, Mencken wrote:

> ✎§ *President Harding writes the worst English I have ever encountered; it reminds me of a string of wet sponges; it is so bad that a sort of grandeur creeps into it. Almost I yearn for the sweeter song, the rubber stamp of more*

familiar design, the gentler and more seemly bosh of the late Woodrow.

When Harding died suddenly in the late summer of 1923, Mencken could not refrain from composing a sardonic obituary for *Smart Set*. As coeditors and stockholders in the magazine, however, he and Nathan were outranked by a publisher-owner who refused to tolerate the belittling of a President. Mencken's caustic obit was dropped, and to the dissatisfied editors this provided the final straw.

But what next? The obvious thing was to start their own magazine and around them stood ample proof that it could be done. Seldom in American history had so many new magazines sprung suddenly to life. *Readers' Digest* began publication in 1922 in a Greenwich Village stable; *Time* commenced in March 1923; the sophisticated *New Yorker* was percolating in the frenetic dome of Harold Ross of the Round Table; Henry Seidel Canby and co-workers on the book section of the New York *Post* were projecting *The Saturday Review of Literature*—the last three, incidentally, first emanated from a building at 25 West 45th Street already hallowed by *Smart Set* offices.

In addition to this activity uptown, a few young intellectuals who dwelled on the Left Bank as expatriates—Malcolm Cowley, Gorham Munson, Kenneth Burke, and Matthew Josephson were among them—had returned to Greenwich Village, bringing with them avant-garde publications like *Broom* and *Secession*.

It might be expected, therefore, that Mencken and Nathan would have few fears of a similar venture. Yet the two did nothing until the discovery that Alfred A. Knopf, the man who published their books, was nursing ideas of a magazine. In the honored tradition of *Harper's*, and *Scribner's*, the Knopf magazine would give prestige to his firm as well as bring fresh authors to his stable, since the writer of a good magazine story or article might be expected to be gestating a book.

Knopf's intention became known to Mencken and Nathan

just before the rupture of the Harding obituary. At first the three men talked of trying to buy *Smart Set,* then decided on a brand new publication. The editors quit *Smart Set* in October 1923, with *The New York Times* reporting their upcoming venture as "MAGAZINE TO CATER TO 'CIVILIZED MINORITY.' " The facile mind of George Jean Nathan produced the name *American Mercury,* which was considered both dignified and noncommittal, while Knopf brought in his firm's book designer and typographer, who devised a distinguished format with a cover of Paris green.

All this made *The American Mercury* the handsomest culture magazine available to the reading public—which caused Mencken to grouse about "Alfred's fancy whorehouse typography"—to him more suitable to book than magazine. Because of its unusual design, together with exceptional type and paper quality, the *Mercury* cost fifty cents a newsstand copy, with subscriptions five dollars a year. The rate for writers was two cents a word.

If the format of *The American Mercury* was impressive, the offices from which it emanated were not. Initial planning for the project had been done in small quarters on 42nd Street, but soon Knopf found space in his new publishing offices in the Heckscher Building at Fifth Avenue and 57th Street.

At *Smart Set,* the irrepressible editors had decorated the anteroom with colorful magazine covers, gaudy ads for patent medicines, and posters for Moxie and similar soft drinks. In his own office Mencken placed his favorite brass spittoon, imported from Baltimore, along with old-fashioned furniture reminiscent of Dutch Sadie's, a cherished Maryland house of ill fame. Visitors to the reception room were given a printed list of Suggestions for Behavior, which began "You are kindly requested not to expectorate out of the windows."

High jinks failed to fit the decor of *The American Mercury,* which boasted a reception room and offices so drab that Mencken called the place "the undertaking parlor." In addition to the two coeditors, the staff included an editorial secretary, plus ten men and women in advertising and circulation departments. To Mencken, this was the ideal number for an intellectual magazine, and he intended to resist any temptation to bloat the staff by hiring copy readers, proofreaders, and researchers and checkers. Besides, he and Nathan were highly trained magazine men, able and willing to perform any function necessary. Nathan might look like a glossy boulevardier, but he usually arrived at 9 A.M. to keep the office functioning while Mencken stayed in Baltimore. As for Heinie, he was not above grabbing *Mercury* copy to check facts at the public library, a chore other editors assigned to myrmidons.

Still, a couple of Mencken ukases survived the transition from *Smart Set* to *Mercury*. One decreed that no carbon copies be made of letters typed in the office, for carbons meant files and files took up precious space. The second specified that only in cases of dire emergency did anyone in the office speak a word to anyone else before the hour of 11 A.M.

Nearing the date January 1, 1924, the first issue of the green-covered, 128-page *Mercury* made its debut shortly before Christmas 1923. Its first page contained a statement of policy, which modestly began:

> ◄§ *The Editors have heard no Voice from the burning bush. They will not cry up and offer for sale any sovereign balm, whether political, economic, or esthetic, for all the sorrows of the world. The fact is, indeed, that they doubt any such sovereign balm exists, or that it will ever exist hereafter. The world, as they see it, is down with at least a score of painful diseases, all of them chronic and incurable; nevertheless, they cling to the notion that human existence remains predominantly charming. . . . They have no set program, either destructive or constructive. Sufficient unto each day will be the performance thereof. . . .*

The editors became more specific as they commenced listing enemies by name and nature. Included were the Ku Klux Klan, the Anti-Saloon League, William Jennings Bryan, Billy

Sunday, lodge joiners, Methodists, Socialists, censors, capitalists, Greenwich Village, pedants, Prohibition, the South, and Southern cooking.

The lead article in the first issue was a mild debunking of Abraham Lincoln. Next came an essay by Carl Van Doren praising the almost forgotten Stephen Crane, as "the first modern American author." The political career of Senator Hiram Johnson of California was scrutinized and found wanting; teaching of American history in schools was exposed by Harry Elmer Barnes as "the drool system of learning," a phrase almost certainly furnished by Mencken.

But by far the most controversial piece in the issue stemmed from the Katzenjammer Kids' hatred of Greenwich Village. Heinie and Georgie had by this time attained the plateau known as the middle generation and perhaps for this reason violently disliked young bohemian writers, especially those on the Left Bank or in Greenwich Village. Some of the Paris expatriates had returned home (usually to the Village) in varying stages of disillusionment, but Mencken and Nathan continued to disparage the avant garde, maintaining that no worthwhile intellectual life existed below their beloved Luchow's on Fourteenth Street. On one occasion Mencken advised a young writer, "Don't ever, if you can possibly help it, go below Fourteenth Street. The Village literati are scum."

Ernest Boyd, brown-bearded, elegant, and massively erudite, fully shared this view, and in the initial *Mercury* helpfully provided an article, "Aesthete: Model 1924," which attacked the idealistic youth of the Village, particularly those involved in magazines like *Broom* and *Secession*. Dipping pen in vitriol, the Irish-born essayist began:

> *His thirtieth birthday is still on the horizon, his literary baggage is small or non-existent—but he is already famous; at least so it seems to him when he gazes upon his own reflection in the eyes of his friends, and fingers appreciatively the luxurious pages of the magazine of which he is Editor-in-Chief, Editor, Managing Editor, Associate Editor, Contributing Editor, Bibliographical Editor, or Source Material Editor.*

Boyd even seemed to include the editors of native magazines like *The Bookman* and *Dial* as he disparaged the credentials of editors under thirty:

>⋍§ *Information is the one thing the Aesthete dreads. To be in the possession of solid knowledge and well digested facts, to have definite standards, background, and experience, is to place oneself outside the pale of true aestheticism.*

In patronizing fashion, the author urged the dreamy Aesthete to find honest literary employment, in which case there would be

>*pep in the swing of his fist upon the typewriter as he sits down to a regular and well-paid job.*

In addition to such downbeat articles, the *Mercury* of January 1, 1924, carried fiction by Ruth Suckow and poetry by Theodore Dreiser. Nathan began a regular column of drama criticism, and Mencken reviewed books with the help of James Branch Cabell and others. There were other monthly departments, among them Americana, then and forever the most amusing feature of the magazine. It reprinted, with comment by the editors, absurd excerpts from American publications. The first *Mercury* included these two:

>⋍§ ARIZONA *From a harangue delivered to the Chamber of Commerce of Tucson by the Hon. H. B. Titcomb: The person who objects to the ringing of cracked bells from a church-tower I do not believe is a good citizen of any community.*

>⋍§ KANSAS *Latest triumph of the Higher Patriotism in Kansas, as reported by E. W. Howe in his interesting Monthly: The attorney general of Kansas has ruled that if a child in school refuses to repeat the flag pledge, its parents may be arrested and fined. . . .*

None of those involved in launching the *Mercury* had hopes of large circulation. Like his two editors—who were again stockholders—publisher Knopf anticipated an eventual top sale of thirty thousand copies a month, after a slow start. Accordingly, he cautiously ordered a first printing of five thousand copies, part for subscribers, the rest for Manhattan newsstands. Thus the Christmas of everyone involved was brightened as New York newsstand copies vanished like snow atop subway gratings.

The reason was Boyd's "Aesthete: Model 1924," the effects of which could not have been greater had the author dropped a sizzling bomb at the corner of MacDougal and West Fourth Streets. Greenwich Villagers of all types decided Boyd had *them* in mind when writing his piece; if this decision was not reached on their own, friends easily persuaded them. Malcolm Cowley, e. e. cummings, Matthew Josephson, and Kenneth Burke were especially outraged. More conventional writers like Edmund Wilson, Gilbert Seldes, John Dos Passos, and John Farrar also felt indicted in Boyd's viperish prose.

As word of the article spread, Village aesthetes began to scour the city, buying available copies of the green-hued periodical. "I got it at once and raced through Boyd's piece," Gorham Munson recalled. Then, as if moved by herd instinct, a crowd of affronted Villagers converged on Boyd's Nineteenth Street apartment and proceeded to render his Christmas hellish by jamming his doorbell, making threatening phone calls, shouting insults through a megaphone, and attempting to toss stink bombs in his kitchen window.

The commotion could not be disregarded and, as the unlikely siege continued, newspapers sent reporters to cover what was dubbed the Battle of the Aesthetes. If nothing else, it assured a sellout for Volume 1 Number 1 of the *Mercury* when it appeared across the country.

When told for laughs, the Battle of the Aesthetes can be hilarious. For one thing, an indignant Gorham Munson composed a derogatory verse about the middle-aged Boyd:

This mind has ticked itself away,
Emotion too has had its day;
Yet do not think he is a ghost,
He sprouts a beard as brown as toast.

To Boyd, though, nothing was funny. Cowering in his home, he grew desperate (or foolish) enough to seek telephone solace from Mencken. Never one to skip a practical joke, Heinie gravely warned his embattled contributor of bodily danger from "hard-boiled, furious, blackjack-toting aesthetes." When a compassionate Burton Rascoe paid Boyd a visit, he found him "barricaded behind his books, subsisting on depleted rations, and grown wan under the assaults and harassments."

Largely because of Mencken's baleful advice, Boyd feared to leave his quarters during the holiday. Finally, as the aesthetes slowly began drifting away, he gathered courage to take a walk. During it, he spied Gilbert Seldes, who of all possible aesthetes had least reason to feel abused. Seldes habitually carried a cane, which he now raised in friendly greeting. Boyd interpreted this as a threat and made haste in the other direction. Anxious to explain there were no hard feelings, Seldes tried to catch up. According to Malcolm Cowley, whose account of the entire episode remains unsurpassed:

> *Mr. Boyd walked faster. Seldes shouted and quickened his pace. It is easy to image the spectacle of those two prominent critics, both of them sedentary and peaceful by disposition, one fleeing with terror dogging his footsteps, the other pursuing with an uplifted cane and the most amicable intentions.*

Yet in fairness, it must be noted that Madeleine Boyd, (a wife who always called her husband "Mr. B") has stoutly maintained that her spouse was less frightened than amused by the rumpus outside his windows. Indeed, it is hard to imagine any Irishman being as spineless as the aesthetes picture Mr. B. Of the overall implications of the imbroglio, John K. Hutchens has written, "The row was silly, but in fact it says something about the period that so trivial a piece of literary business was a matter of public interest."

The Battle of the Aesthetes is usually credited with giving *The American Mercury* the impetus to exceed the hoped-for circulation of thirty thousand and eventually rise close to an amazing eighty thousand. Yet it is altogether probable that the publication would have achieved success anyway. With or without the ludicrous Battle, there was a public avidly awaiting *The American Mercury*.

In the forefront of potential readers stood the youthful highbrows then characterized as Young Intellectuals, a not altogether flattering term shortened in the brisk manner of the era to Y.I.'s. Most Y.I.'s were college students, male and female, whose bibles had heretofore been *Smart Set* and *College Humor*, the latter a lively imitation *Smart Set* in which Lynn and Lois Montross wrote Fitzgerald-type fiction and the by-line of Katherine Brush was just beginning to appear.

Now Y.I.'s were demanding tougher fare. Seizing on the *Mercury*, they relegated *Smart Set* to near oblivion and *College Humor* to fun hours. Years later M. K. Singleton, biographer of Mencken and the *Mercury*, invoked a Flaming Youth comparison to say, "Students flaunted the Paris-green magazine as a sign of intellectual independence—a kind of mental hip flask."

Not every Mercury-oriented intellectual was on a college campus. Members of the civilized minority and others of mental thirst embraced the *Mercury* with such fervor that it became a prime mover-shaker in domestic cultural life. According to Irene and Allen Cleaton in *Books and Battles*, "The *Mercury*'s influence was perhaps unparalleled in American history." A contemporary rose to warn of a new religion called "Mercurianity, the bible of which is a green-covered magazine."

If nothing else, *The American Mercury* stands forth as a publication consistently able to provoke sermons and outraged newspaper editorials. The popular cleric Dr. S. Parkes Cadman made pioneer use of radio to urge "pastors and orators" to speak out against the *Mercury* and protect the nation from its insidious iconoclasm. A professor at the University of Chicago echoed him, saying, "The only thing that makes me fear is the number of our students who read *The American Mercury*. On the campus you see it under every arm; they absorb everything in it."

Controversy only increased circulation, and soon the magazine had received enough letters from millionaires, lumberjacks, and other assorted types to boast an unprecedented vertical appeal to the public. In California, a young widow advertising for a post as housekeeper specified, "*American Mercury* readers preferred."

As a result of all this, Elisabeth Cobb, daughter of humorist Irvin S., hymned the editors:

> *Mencken and Nathan and God;*
> *Yes, probably, possibly, God!*

F.P.A. chose Mencken alone:

> *I like Mr. Mencken*
> *His voice is so loud:*
> *He hates all the boobs*
> *And he rails at the crowd.*

The Baltimore Anti-Christ

H. L. Mencken . . Alfred A. Knopf . . . .

Few were aware that, as *The American Mercury* circulation climbed, another Battle of the Aesthetes was being waged behind its portals. Contestants were none other than Mencken and Nathan, the disparate duo who for nearly twenty years had seemed to the public as close (in Mencken's case) as beer and pretzels or (in Nathan's) champagne and caviar.

A few frictions already existed between these apparent soul brothers. Nathan had always nagged Mencken to dress better. Burton Rascoe, who thought a man like Heinie "rose above his tailor," says Nathan expected his coeditor to attire himself like a Broadway actor. For his part Mencken, who liked his women mature, deplored Nathan's unflagging interest in tender young things. Once he grumbled, "Chorgie is slipping —I saw him with a girl who must have been fourteen; the usual age of his dates is ten-and-a-half."

However, such complaints were minor compared to a deeper schism. As Mencken's own interests broadened, he expected those of his partner to do likewise. Specifically, he hoped Chorge would lift his eyes above the playhouses of New York, London, and Berlin to view all the world as a stage. Nathan never did, and Mencken thought less of him. For his part the blasé Nathan, interested only in the surface and color of life, disliked the reformer-messiah side of Mencken.

Such conflicts were further exacerbated by *The American Mercury* itself. In fact, the first issue of the magazine was a bit of a shock to all involved except Mencken. With the project in its planning stage, Mencken had written to Sinclair Lewis, Cabell, Dreiser, Fitzgerald, and other *Smart Set* stalwarts, requesting contributions for the new venture. The letters implied that the *Mercury* would be cultural in tone, and those who received them were surprised by the lack of culture in issue number one. Even Ernest Boyd, who did so much to make the first *Mercury* notorious, was miffed by contributions other than his own.

Theodore Dreiser was upset; Lewis and Fitzgerald nonplussed. It was obvious that Mencken planned to stress politics and similar rugged aspects of the American scene. In *Smart Set* days, Mencken had amused himself by answering the telephone with the words, "The great critic Henry Mencken speaking." At that time, the word "critic" plainly meant "literary"; now he visualized himself as a rambunctious critic-at-large.

The person most annoyed by the first *Mercury* was George Jean Nathan. More than anyone else, he had expected the magazine to stress the cultural and, as coeditor and stockholder, considered himself justified in protesting articles like a dissection of Senator Hiram Johnson. For the second issue, Nathan brought in Eugene O'Neill's play *All God's Chillun Got Wings*, which the playwright wrote largely for the magazine. Nathan was beside himself with pride; Mencken insultingly unimpressed.

In Nathan's eyes, his partner grew wilder and wilder as he talked of printing articles from jailbirds and bums, and contacted the Socialist gadfly Upton Sinclair for advice on offbeat subjects. With his Germanic stubbornness and wide range of interests, Mencken proved a formidable foe, and Nathan found his influence slipping. Mencken too felt the pressures. "I'm going nuts," he complained to the publisher.

By the end of the first year Alfred Knopf had to choose

between his two warring editors. It was not difficult; Mencken's policy had produced those unlikely circulation figures. Early in 1925, Nathan quit as coeditor, to become a contributing editor who would write play reviews and not much else. In a characteristic statement he elucidated his differences with Mencken:

> *The beauty of the world diverts me. The problems of the world are of utterly no interest to me. I have never voted; I shall never vote. An art gallery is more important to me than Vice President Dawes.*

Problems beget problems, and with this settled, Mencken found another on his lap. Who would run the *Mercury* office? Even as editor of the most talked-about magazine in the country, Mencken could not abide Manhattan and planned to pass much time in Baltimore. Indeed, he expected to spend less time than ever in New York, perhaps only three days a month.

Suddenly the luckiest young man in the United States became Charles Angoff, a red-haired, craggy-faced Harvard graduate performing literary odd jobs in Boston. On the wild chance of getting a job on the *Mercury*, he had written Mencken, enclosing samples of his work. To his astonishment the letter got an immediate answer, bidding him visit Mencken at the Algonquin as fast as possible.

The meeting brought a few jolts to the young man. These began as Mencken went into the bathroom and calmly urinated without closing the door; such things were not done in Harvard society. Next Mencken volunteered a nugget of wisdom: "Never make love to a girl in a hammock, it can break your back." Then he referred to President Coolidge as "a son of a bitch" and called Woodrow Wilson "the arch-bastard of them all." Angoff's mind reeled. Yet the biggest shock of all came when he heard himself offered the job of managing editor of the *Mercury*.

A week later Angoff deposited himself behind a desk in the magazine's editorial office. He had just been introduced to Knopf and Nathan, who retained a desk on the premises.

Mencken was stuffing a briefcase with manuscripts, preparatory to leaving for Baltimore. At the door he paused to address his fledgling employee: "I'll be gone for three weeks, maybe four. I may go over to Hergesheimer's place for a few days. Anyway, the place is yours, you're the field general from now on. 'Bye."

Henry Mencken's objections to New York were many, and he never wearied of inveighing against what he called "the glittering swinishness" of a metropolis which was too noisy, too crowded, and altogether too confusing for profitable cogitation. At the same time he was fascinated by the place and wrote, "I hymn the town without loving it. . . . A truly overwhelming opulence envelops the whole place, even the slums."

He extolled Baltimore where he lived—with his mother, until her death in 1925—in the house of his birth at 1524 Hollins Street. To justify this strong preference for his native city, he borrowed a word from President Harding. "It bulges with normalcy," he liked to say. To tiny Anita Loos, he offered a broader explanation: "What makes New York so dreadful is that most of its people have been forced to rid themselves of their oldest and most powerful instinct—the love of home."

Yet it is a measure of Mencken that, while passing most of his time on Hollins Street, his editorial thunderbolts always sounded as if they burst from the heart of Manhattan. Though often called the Sage of Baltimore, he seemed more like a genuine New Yorker—and never more so than now, as he became sole editor of the *Mercury* and stood ready to become a national figure rather than a literary one.

Mencken's work habits were also more like those of a perspiring Gothamite than a Southern gentleman. He not only carried full briefcases of manuscripts to and from New York, but received and returned bundles of others through the U. S. mail. The busy man also wrote his own books, kept the files necessary for upcoming editions of his magnum opus on the

American language, wrote editorials and articles for the Baltimore *Sun*papers, and nurtured his elaborate practical jokes, writing those endless nonsense letters which began "Dear Wolfgang" or "Dear Alphonse."

A few friends went so far as to believe Mencken spent more time than admitted in New York City, for Heinie was often to be seen dining at Luchow's, the Blue Ribbon, Zum Brauhaus, or the Hoboken *Bierstubes* for which he had a fondness. In such surroundings, he was ever a man's man with few close friends but a multitude of acquaintances whom he once classified as "pedants, scholars, boozers, preachers, teamsters, politicians, highbrows, lowbrows, and medium brows."

Women liked him, and he liked them right back. Some females pursued him unashamedly, perhaps because his twinkling blue eyes, apple cheeks, and little-boy looks aroused the maternal. Brainy women were stimulated by his talk, which was as full of gusto as his writing. A few women loved him. One was Anita Loos, who for long periods cared more for Mencken than for her lawful spouse.

Mencken's strong appeal to the fair sex may have been aided by the fact that he stood foursquare in opposition to holy wedlock. Once he said, "Marriage is a wonderful institution, but who wants to live in an institution?" Statements like this were an open challenge; the gal who trapped Henry Mencken into matrimony would be a rare woman indeed.

But Mencken was essentially a male animal. His favorite dinner partners were men who, like himself, drank six martinis and ten seidels of beer with a meal. "I'm as thirsty as a bishop," he liked to say, as the tray with the first libations approached. In masculine company his conversation, often ribald, was studded with verbal gymnastics and challenging insights.

Below Mencken's robust exterior lay a full sampling of the paradoxes indigenous to great men. The enormously zestful writer and talker was also a dedicated faultfinder and complainer whose dubious opinion of the universe seldom permitted the luxury of enthusiasm. It has often been noted that his writing was at its best when taking the world (or a book) apart, and that his prose inclined to be routine when handing out praise. Still, Mencken was able to complain endlessly about the miseries of life while simultaneously enjoying himself—the Sage of Baltimore was like a man devouring a large meal, griping aloud at every mouthful but inwardly savoring each swallow. "Never have I known a man who got such fun out of life," a friend has written.

His odd dichotomy could best be seen in his health, which was generally good. Yet no more determined—or articulate —hypochondriac ever existed. Wrote Nathan: "In the twenty years I have known him, I received thousands upon thousands of letters from him, and not a single one has failed affectingly to mention some hypothetical physical agony that was making life miserable for him." When unable to identify his aches and pains, Mencken thought up new ones. Once he claimed to suffer from "aggravated lapis-lazuli of the left ventricle, without peristalsis."

The fond way Mencken wrote of his ailments indicated his inner satisfaction:

> ⊸§ *I have a sore mouth, can't smoke, my hooves hurt. . . . Hay fever has begun to caress me. . . . I am suffering painfully from my perennial malaises. . . . It won't be long now! . . . Hay fever has me by the ear and I am making the usual rocky weather of it. . . . What a world! . . . My hemorrhoids have come back after twenty-one years. The opening gun in God's spring offensive against me! . . . I am full of aches and malaises. No doubt the final break-up is beginning.*

Mencken the editor manifested other quirks. He quickly okayed material that reflected his own style and fistfight approach, a trait exploited by some authors. When articles he bought did not sound enough like him, he added trademark words like "pap," "boob," "swine," and "wowser." One of his pet tricks was to place "Herr" or "Dr." before names—thus Dreiser might become Herr Dreiser or Dr. Dreiser. At other times he planted German words and phrases amidst an author's cherished prose. One contributor objected: "I saw my article appear in the *Mercury* with such words as 'privat-dozent,' 'geheimrat,' 'bierbruder,' and 'hasenpfeffer,' which mystified my friends because I don't know German."

At the same time, Mencken was one of the few editors in history who genuinely liked writers. Of course, he was part writer himself, but his ruminations on authorship were usually sparked by the tribulations of others. Once he leaned back in his editor's chair to philosophize, "Writers, I find, hate to write; it drives them to drink. Artists on the other hand, love their work; they love to draw, love to paint, can't get enough of it. I wonder why?"

Mencken's sensitivity to writers extended as far as the cruel rejection slip. As often as possible, he sent back contributions with short personal notes. "I like the way you write," he might say, or, "You seem to have considerable facility, and I like your ideas—but this won't do." However, his comments on manuscripts dispatched from Baltimore to 730 Fifth Avenue were seldom so gracious. On one he wrote, "This smells like Aimee Semple McPherson's pants."

Yet Mencken remained considerate of authors, and earned this tribute from Benjamin de Casseres:

> ►§ Anyone who has dealt with Mencken in his capacity as editor of the American Mercury knows that he has not only introduced a new kind of magazine, but a new kind of editor . . . who gives immediate attention to your manuscript, pays spot cash, encloses return stamped envelopes with the proofs, and gives you second serial rights without asking.

If Mencken pleased writers as a breed, he occasionally disappointed those personally close to him. Quite a few of his friends were upset by his inability to appreciate poetry. Said Burton Rascoe, "As a critic of poetry he is, I think, the worst in the world." Others came to believe Mencken appreciated only realistic writing and thought the best American prose appeared in newspapers. As time passed Mencken showed increasing reluctance to embrace writers discovered by others, preferring his own unearthing. Two of his favorite discoveries among *Mercury* contributors were novelist Ruth Suckow and Jim Tully, the picturesque hobo-lumberjack who wrote *Shanty Irish* and *Circus Parade*.

The man who had done so much to promote Dreiser, Sherwood Anderson, Hergesheimer, Cabell, and even Sinclair Lewis seemed unhappily fixated at the point of discovery, remaining oddly unaware of the aims and struggles of novelist friends. Once Sherwood Anderson complained, "Henry never sees the tears and the sighs and the choked feelings between the lines." Scott Fitzgerald once yelled at him, "Goddam it, you don't know what a writer goes through, and what he fumbles for, you don't know the *grace* he searches for." Infuriated at Mencken's reaction to *An American Tragedy*, Dreiser wrote, "As to your critical predilections, animosities, inhibitions . . . Tosh! Who reads you? Bums and loafers. Nogoods."

Nor was Mencken eager to find virtue in the young writers who followed the footsteps of those he helped launch. He and Charles Angoff argued heatedly over the merits of John Dos Passos' *Manhattan Transfer*, with Angoff in favor. In time, Mencken said of Hemingway, "The man can't write. He is just a bad boy who's probably afraid of the dark." He was equally negative about William Faulkner and Thomas Wolfe.

But if close friends were upset by Mencken's lack of insight, the Great American Public accepted him as a vital force. Van Wyck Brooks saw in him "a literary statesman whose strategy and decisions affected us all. He cleared away provincialism in the American atmosphere, and aroused interest in the American scene. He knew little of the past, to him the moment mattered."

As such, Mencken was vastly admired by those who approved the *Mercury* and resoundingly hated by those who didn't. The number of *Mercury* enemies was great; never in history, in all probability, has an editor attracted such full-throated opposition over so long a period. The first issue of the magazine provoked four hundred editorials around the country, most of them angry. The number of Sunday sermons aimed at the same target was uncountable.

Mencken covered the Scopes Monkey Trial of 1925 as a working reporter for the Baltimore *Sun*papers, and his irreverent news stories earned fresh fury from the Deep South, the Bible Belt, and the Midwest. One Methodist publication dubbed the *Mercury* The Greenbacked Monster. The Reverend Herbert Jump, a Mencken enemy who might have been named by the Sage himself, accused the magazine and its editor of blasphemy. A Texas paper named *The Gospel* fulminated: "If a buzzard laid an egg in a dung hill and the sun hatched a thing like Mencken, the buzzard would be justly ashamed of its offspring." The *Bulletin* of the Anti-Saloon League of Virginia called Mencken "the idol of the earthly, sensual, devilish elements of our country. . . . His initials are H. L., meaning the first and last letters of the word Hell." If admirers called him the Sage of Baltimore, detractors preferred the Baltimore Antichrist.

Mencken's finest tribute may have been the way his attackers sought to ape his style. The *Tampa Times* called him "a maggot, a buzzard, a ghoul of newmade graves." To the *Times* of Jackson, Mississippi, he was "a howling hyena," to the San Francisco *Chronicle* "a pole cat," to the Nashville *Tennessean* "a mangy ape," and to the Iowa *Legionnaire* "a mad mongrel." The organ of the Ku Klux Klan cited his "mad mouthings" and branded him "a moral pervert." A New Hampshire newspaper said, "If Mencken only ran about on all fours slavering his sort of hydrophobia, he would be shot by the first policeman on duty." The New Haven *Register* called him "an indecent buffoon wallowing in obscenity as he howls with glee." The Philadelphia *Inquirer* thought, "Society needs Mencken as nature needs mosquitoes."

Mencken's reaction to this deluge of abuse was rapturous. He put Sara Haardt, a favorite *Mercury* contributor who in time became Mrs. Mencken, to culling the choicer insults from the national press. Ultimately the best excerpts were published in a book called *Menckeniana: A Schimplexicon*. In his introduction Mencken wrote, "This collection is not exhaustive, but an effort has been made to keep it representative."

No less than his enemies, Mencken could hate. His fiercest wrath was reserved for censors and censorship. In New York City, John S. Sumner headed the Society for the Suppression of Vice. A man who branded daring writers "immoralists," Sumner had made 475 arrests for literary obscenity in the years between 1920 and 1925. Most cases had been tossed out by judges on the bench.

The situation was far different in Boston, a city Mencken curtly dismissed as "the anus of America." Here an unrelenting Watch and Ward Society, led by the Reverend Jason Franklin Chase, not only suppressed books but worked harmoniously with the local judiciary. Among the books Chase had banned were Ben Hecht's *Gargoyles*, Aldous Huxley's *Antic Hay*, Floyd Dell's *Janet March*, Sherwood Anderson's *Many Marriages*, and John Dos Passos' *Streets of Night*.

An early issue of the *Mercury* had derided the efforts of the Watch and Ward Society in the article "Keeping the Puritans Pure." So a resentful Chase was only too happy to pounce on the number containing Herbert Asbury's "Hatrack," the story of a small-town prostitute. A Harvard Square newsdealer was arrested for selling a copy, but Mencken decided that, if anyone got in trouble, it should be him. He arranged through intermediaries to sell a copy of the magazine to the Reverend Chase on Boston Common.

It was a gutsy decision, for the action carried the strong possibility of a two-year jail sentence. Nonetheless, Mencken traveled to Boston, proceeding first to the city morgue for the required formality of obtaining a peddler's license. During this session he was described by a reporter as "in good fighting trim and in high spirits."

With his license and three copies of the offending *Mercury* under an arm, Mencken strode briskly to the area of the Common known as Brimstone Corner because Henry Ward Beecher and others had spouted so much fire and brimstone there. A large crowd had gathered, and Mencken stood among them until Chase and a police captain appeared. "Please don't deport him," a Harvard student begged the cop. Chase handed Mencken fifty cents and in return received a copy of the *Mercury*. Here Mencken proved himself the consummate jester, for he took Chase's half dollar and, to be sure it was good, ostentatiously bit it. Chase then shouted, "I order this man's arrest," and the police captain stepped forward. Henry L. Mencken, Sage of Baltimore or Baltimore Antichrist, was in the clutches of the law.

Free on bail, he passed an unhappy afternoon and night, for Boston friends told him that conviction was inevitable. Yet fortune smiled on this impish disturber of the peace. By sheer accident his case came before one of the few broadminded jurists in Boston and His Honor decided that anyone who paid fifty cents for a magazine was not likely to be corrupted by it. "There is nothing in its appearance or makeup which would suggest that it is anything but a serious publication," he ruled.

So Mencken had bested a formidable opponent. At the same time, the editor-author-critic increased his stature as a page-one figure. Yielding to the friendly persuasions of Joseph Hergesheimer, he next paid a visit to Hollywood. This trip turned into another of the highly publicized junkets of the Twenties, with reporters along the way making note of every utterance.

The fun evaporated a trifle when Mencken reached the film capital and found an intellectual Sargasso Sea, one of the few localities in the country where no one seemed to read the *Mercury*. Yet the Sage had seen no more than three or four motion pictures in his life, so he was able to retain his composure as screen luminaries like Betty Compson and director James Cruze said to him, "I've never read your magazine."

With total absence of guile, Mencken then replied, "I've never seen one of your movies, either."

It is safe to say that publisher Alfred A. Knopf, who had anticipated a *Mercury* with literary overtones like *Harper's* or *Scribner's*, was among those disturbed by Mencken's brash product. He had visualized the magazine not only as a grooming ground for young writers, but as a place to advertise his Borzoi books for free and as a showcase for the shorter works of esteemed Knopf authors like Willa Cather. But a magazine with brawling Jim Tully a valued contributor was hardly a spot for Miss Cather who, among other things, had recently converted to Catholicism.

The high newsstand price of the *Mercury*, together with its intellectual overtones, kept it from becoming a money-making venture on the order of *The Saturday Evening Post*. But its circulation did allow it to operate at a profit. So, lacking substantial grounds for complaint, Knopf had to be content to use the magazine for promotion of his books.

He did this by tasteful advertisements and a chatty column called "Borzoi Broadsides." In one of these, he explained that the Borzoi or Russian wolfhound imprinted on the title page of each Knopf book "was devised originally as a trademark but has come to be regarded by thousands as the hallmark of a good book."

Knopf paid further tribute to his books. "A Borzoi on the library table, or on the bookshelf, is a mark of distinction always," he wrote. In one "Broadside," he led *Mercury* readers behind the scenes of his firm to tell of an author whose second Knopf novel turned out to be inferior to his first. Informed of this, "the author quietly destroyed the manuscript and went to work on an entirely new novel. . . . This one delighted Mr. Knopf." He described another Borzoi stalwart as "an absolutely first-class mind stocked with erudition and able to [write] clearly, elegantly, and with wit."

This comfy-cozy approach to the book-buying public was one more innovation on the part of a dashing young man who had founded his own publishing house at the age of twenty-two, and promptly set standards of quality and taste for the entire book trade. Of Knopf, the old-line publisher George H. Doran has written, "He not only made beautiful books, but told the public they were beautiful books and thereby stimulated the public to require a more graceful format."

Borzoi books were a curious projection of the publisher's own personality. For Knopf loved books as some men love women. "I love books physically," he admitted once, "and I want to make them beautifully." What has been called a Prussian thoroughness aided him. Borzoi books were the proud possessors of striking bindings, colorful jackets, top-quality paper, and a wide variety of type faces, some new to the book world.

Though Knopf personally rated as an expert in the field, he employed both a book designer and a typographical expert to buttress his own superb taste. When one author inquired about the format of his upcoming novel, Knopf purred a contented answer: "My designer favors Caledonia, and I concur. This type has the hard-working, feet-on-the-ground qualities of Scotch modern face, along with a definite liveliness and grace."

Making a speech to booksellers, he began, "I do no one a serious injustice when I say that American books are *not* beautiful." Then he went on:

> I have found the prevalent idea that a good-looking book must necessarily cost too much to manufacture wholly fallacious. Good-looking books do cost—the publisher's time and thought. And so I have experimented with boards printed up in brightly colored Continental design, with Italian hand-made papers, with French papers, with a Russian artist's idea for binding.

Alfred A. Knopf, son of prosperous parents, was born into comfort on Central Park West. Until college days at Columbia, he had planned to be a lawyer. Then he wrote John Galsworthy, in England, requesting information for a term paper. Galsworthy's reputation in the literary world was that of an frosty snob, but his reply to the Columbia student was warm and understanding. For the first time Knopf thought book publishing might be a congenial lifetime profession.

He started as an eight-dollar-a-week accountant in the office of Doubleday, Page & Company. Tall, reedy, spiritual-looking, and black haired, he radiated a vague aura of the East which some thought exotic and others oriental. To Carl Van Vechten he resembled "a Persian prince." Even as a beginner in business, he nursed strikingly individual ideas of dress. If Burton Rascoe got into trouble by wearing blue shirts to *McCall's*, the twenty-year-old Knopf kicked up a storm at Doubleday, Page (not to mention on the streets of midtown Manhattan) by shirts of shocking pink and vivid blue. He earned further notice by a widespread moustache which Mencken described as "so immensely black that it seemed beyond the poor talents of nature, and yet so slender, so struggling that it was palpably real."

Nevertheless, the bizarre youth forged ahead at Doubleday, Page, advancing from accounting to book promotion, doubling his meager pay in the process. Joseph Conrad had recently become a Doubleday author, following unhappy experiences with five other American firms. Young Knopf undertook to promote Conrad as a living immortal, doing this with a dedication that caused George Doran to write, "To Knopf more than anyone, Conrad owes his fame and popularity."

Knopf next joined the publishing house of Mitchell Kennerley, one of the few men in the trade who considered books to be things of beauty. After minimal time with his new boss, Knopf felt the same way. Then, in 1915, he summoned courage to leave and start his own firm. Joseph Hergesheimer, Kennerley's top author, accompanied him.

Because other established authors already had publishers, Knopf in early days depended heavily on translations from Europe. The first of these—in fact, the original Borzoi book —contained four plays by Emile Augier, with a preface by Eugène Brieux, translated by Barrett H. Clark. The book was bound in orange and blue and set in Cheltenham, a new, pleasant typeface. Another Knopf translation, a novel from the Polish, incurred the wrath of John S. Sumner and got itself suppressed.

Knopf's initial success was a new edition of the W. H. Hudson classic, *Green Mansions* in 1916. At the same time, he brought out Thomas Mann's *Royal Highness*. Then Joseph Hergesheimer crashed through with *Three Black Pennys*, and struggle ended. By 1920, the Knopf list featured Hergesheimer, Mencken, Nathan, Mann, Willa Cather, Knut Hamsun, Sigrid Undset, Carl Van Vechten, E. M. Forster, G. B.

Stern, and Clarence Day. Then and always, the Knopf list was distinguished in the areas of history, music, belles lettres, and European fiction.

Knopf's original office assistant was his fiancée, a girl named Blanche Wolf. As Mrs. Knopf, she became a full-time partner, widely respected for her intuition, aggressiveness, and shrewdness. Alfred and Blanche Knopf always saw themselves as editors as well as publishers, and personally brought in at least two thirds of the titles on any Borzoi list. Their distinctive taste, augmented by Alfred's passion for design, made the firm unique, with quality rather than quantity its preoccupation. "Flair is the word for Alfred," a rival has said. "He has a touch of the snob, a restricted-universe concept of publishing. His house represents the rare-vintage school of publishing." This was proved when the million-copy-seller Fannie Hurst cut loose from Doubleday to join Knopf. Her three Borzoi books did not sell as well, and she returned to her original publisher.

The career of Alfred and Blanche Knopf has extended productively into the 1970's, and through the years the publisher has won further admiration as a hedonist, gourmet, wine connoisseur, flower fancier, and conspicuous dresser. "He garbs himself as handsomely as he garbs his books," reads one meaningful tribute. With the passage of time, Knopf has turned into a formidable person, capable of demolishing an editor with the words "I don't know what you are trying to say, but even if I did know, I wouldn't be better off." To Geoffrey Hellman, who wrote a long Profile on him in *The New Yorker*, this later Knopf seemed "A man of commanding presence, compelling mustache, and a resolute, piratical mien."

In view of this, it is difficult to conceive of Charles Angoff finding Knopf "young and shy" on their first meeting in 1925. In fact, there are those who believe Alfred Knopf was *never* young or shy. Any diffidence in Knopf at that time is particularly hard to comprehend because it was a year of triumph, marking his tenth anniversary as a publisher. Among his recent successes had been Kahlil Gibran's *The Prophet*, a totally unexpected success which over the years had sold four million copies (more than any other Knopf book) and is still going strong. In 1925, *Publishers' Weekly*, the *Variety* of the book world, had recently run a deferential account of the Knopf prosperity, revealing expansion plans of the firm. One part of it was a town-house office in London.

To celebrate this tenth year, Knopf had brought out another handsome book, entitled *The Borzoi: 1925—Being a Sort of Record of Ten Years of Publishing*. Every Borzoi book ended with a colophon which gave details of the printing, and the final page of *The Borzoi: 1925* told where the book had been printed and that its superfine paper was India-tint stock, with halftones on ivory-cameo paper. For some reason, the colophon omits typeface.

On this India-tint paper various Knopf authors wrote about one another. George Jean Nathan devoted his talents to Joseph Hergesheimer, who in turn covered Mencken. Carl Van Doren wrote about Nathan, while Thomas Beer did Willa Cather, Francis Brett Young evaluated D. H. Lawrence, and so on.

Mencken was accorded the honor of writing about Alfred Knopf, and in so doing broadcast what the publishing business already knew—that for all his flamboyant attire, financial success, and devotion to his chosen work, Knopf did not appear a happy man. He was, in truth, a gloomy Gus, addicted to distressing remarks like "Life is full of constant, sordid surprises."

Many aspects of worldly existence disappointed Knopf, among them the weather, which in his opinion had been better during his youth. Like Mencken, Knopf was a complainer but minus the verbal gusto that vivified the lamentations of the Baltimore Antichrist. Mencken summed Knopf up when he wrote, "He is not a merry man; he's a sad man, not the kind who ever kicks up."

Peak of a Decade . . *Arrowsmith* .

Great Gatsby . . Manhattan Transfer . . Poetry .

In 1925, the Literary Decade reached its crest, to make what in all probability stands as the most notable twelve-month in American publishing history. Just look at a few of the titles published during that historic year:

Arrowsmith, by Sinclair Lewis

The Great Gatsby, by F. Scott Fitzgerald

An American Tragedy, by Theodore Dreiser

Dark Laughter, by Sherwood Anderson

Barren Ground, by Ellen Glasgow

The Professor's House, by Willa Cather

In Our Time, by Ernest Hemingway

The Constant Nymph, by Margaret Kennedy

Death in Venice, by Thomas Mann

The Matriarch, by G. B. Stern

The Perennial Bachelor, by Anne Parrish

When We Were Very Young, by A. A. Milne

Manhattan Transfer, by John Dos Passos

Beau Geste, by Percival Christopher Wren

John Keats, by Amy Lowell

Porgy, by DuBose Heyward

Those Barren Leaves, by Aldous Huxley

Wild Geese, by Martha Ostenso

Carry On, Jeeves, by P. G. Wodehouse

The Venetian Glass Nephew, by Elinor Wylie

Possession, by Louis Bromfield

The Crystal Cup, by Gertrude Atherton

The Thundering Herd, by Zane Grey

The Pilgrimage of Henry James, by Van Wyck Brooks

Brigham Young, by M. R. Werner

Mrs. Dalloway, by Virginia Woolf

Jefferson and Hamilton, by Claude G. Bowers

The Private Life of Helen of Troy, by John Erskine

Hail and Farewell, by George Moore

Thunder on the Left, by Christopher Morley

The Informer, by Liam O'Flaherty

Gentlemen Prefer Blondes, by Anita Loos

This galaxy of books and authors was only external evidence of a thriving industry. Inside the commercial book world conditions were better than ever; Americans purchased, read, discussed, and depended on books as never before. There even existed a snobbish, well-heeled segment of the public anxious to support the institution—or was it a racket?—of limited editions, which were unusually beautiful books printed for connoisseurs in runs of five hundred to several thousand. After this one printing the plates were destroyed, thus guaranteeing eternal exclusivity.

Sometimes limited editions were superhandsome volumes of authors dead and gone. More often, in the Twenties, they were superior copies of books available to the public at regular prices. Autographed by authors and superbly designed, they were printed in rare type on extrafine paper and numbered to indicate position in the edition. Usually limited editions were illustrated by artists like John Sloan, Rockwell

Kent, Miguel Covarrubias, or Alexander King. For example, with the Cabell vogue in full swing, the firm of Robert M. McBride was disposing of special editions of Cabell novels at fifteen to twenty dollars a copy. *Jurgen*, intricately and lecherously illustrated by Ralph Barton, was particularly favored by male collectors.

In a book-conscious world, these striking limited editions were naturally the most desirable to possess. Yet other readers just as assiduously collected first editions, placing orders with bookstores ahead of time to get the initial trade editions of authors like Joseph Hergesheimer. Publishers cooperated by running off special first editions and releasing them ahead of time.

One afternoon at baseball's Yankee Stadium the handsome pitcher Waite Hoyt raised eyes heavenward and murmured, "It's great to be young and a Yankee." The same could be said of the book game; indeed, inimitable Ezra Pound had just done so by writing, 'It is after all a grrrreat litttttttterary period." Never, it appeared, had there been so many writing talents in America, not even in the heyday of the New England Transcendentalists. According to the Cleatons in *Books and Battles*, "Books that seemed more vital than books were ever to seem again were issuing from the presses of publishers who competed with each other for the productions of young men and women who had never had their names on title pages before."

Nor had the craft of authorship ever offered such stunning financial rewards. "Starvation was not fashionable among literary people," says one observer. "In the Twenties a successful writer's bank account was as cheerfully full of figures as a successful businessman's."

This was not always true. Ben Hecht was an established author who complained of good reviews and poor sales, inveighing against "that moody tyrant, the public." But there is no denying that in many instances the writing profession eminently fulfilled the American dream of overnight success. In the old days a novelist was expected to serve an apprenticeship on newspapers and magazines. Now inexperienced young men like Fitzgerald and Bromfield scaled the heights with first novels. "The public was ready for them, and they weren't forced to waste years," thinks Malcolm Cowley.

To literary folk of the day went the added pleasure of functioning in the liveliest sector of the arts. No less an authority than Ernest Boyd had risen to state flatly that in the first five years of the decade American literature grew up. This could not be said of the fellow cultures of music, painting, the dance, or any other art form except possibly the motion picture.

Authors had not only toppled Victorianism and puritanism at the start of the 1920's, but were presently in the forefront of the fight against a standardization of domestic life which inevitably followed stock-market prosperity. Anathema to most writers were such excrescences as advertising slogans, Detroit assembly lines, chain stores, babbittry, bunk, and Prohibition. United in scorn for what would one day be called Middle America, they sought to broaden contemporary minds by deliberately inserting bold ideas and scenes of sexual freedom in their works, then girding to fight the resulting attempts at censorship. Extolling city life, they mocked the hinterlands—why else did the nascent *New Yorker* take such pride in not appealing to "the old lady from Dubuque"? Fighting bigotry, authors of the day abided by the credo "Anyone who doesn't regard tolerance as one of the supreme virtues is to us intolerant."

This heady climate not only assured writers of an audience, but provided a fount of material as well. It was the moment in history when cautious Calvin Coolidge, a President who took after-lunch naps at his White House desk, stated, "The business of America is business." Scott Fitzgerald, on the other hand, found life in America "damn dumb and stupid and healthy." Authors could take aim at the Coolidge materialism, reflected in a soaring stock market, or at the nationwide smugness cited by Fitzgerald.

Between the two lay a multiplicity of topical subjects: a country where the buying of stocks at 10 percent margin turned plumbers into millionaires; a stepped-up Jazz Age with the middle-aged performing a Charleston as frantic as that of the young; continuing frustrations of small-town life; pressures of the city; the ever-grinding heel of big business; the raw excitements of rum-running and bootlegging; speakeasy fun; and changes in sexual morality. With so many targets a writer could hardly miss a mark. "If his disillusionment was bitter," writes John Hutchens, "it was, so to speak, a creative disillusionment."

Of all the population, writers also seemed to derive the most from the turbulence of the Twenties. According to the Cleatons, authors

> drank more than other citizens, showing the same eagerness to get happily and quickly plastered as members of the newspaper profession, to which most of them once belonged. When free love rose to an honorable estate they were among the first to savor its advantages and disillusionments. As speech grew franker, they conversed more freely and knowingly than other persons on hitherto unmentionable subjects, employing hitherto unmentionable words. They knew better and dirtier stories, their parties were more hilarious—in all things they were more extravagant in an extravagant era.

If the public admired authors, the authors responded by admiring the public. Even acerbic F.P.A. felt impelled to write, "The average American is above-average." While cultivating an attitude of so's-your-old-man sophistication, the public of the Twenties became excited easily. "It was one of their more endearing, if occasionally exasperating, charms," said Hutchens. Not only did the folk of the time become aroused about books, but often about the ideas imbedded in books. According to historian Mark Sullivan, "Ideas in books spread out during the 1920's to a larger proportion of the population than in any other country or time."

In the bubbling words of the Cleatons, the literary life was "whirling, lively, and new-seeming; idols were shot down daily; values turned somersaults." Authors went on lecture tours, and publishers arranged ambitious displays in book and department stores. People were reaching out for books in sufficient numbers to make reading an indoor sport. In a touch Sinclair Lewis might have invented, a Midwest laundry adorned its trucks with the sign, "I send my things to the Ideal Laundry—it leaves me more time for reading."

At the same time publishers, magazine editors, and literary critics enjoyed themselves almost as much as authors. Publishers still sat confidently in offices, secure in the knowledge that authors bearing manuscripts would appear in the anteroom. The middleman profession of literary agent, or author's representative, was comparatively new, and agents still hesitated to insert themselves aggressively between publisher and author. Among these pioneer literary agents were Carl Brandt, Ann Watkins, Harold Ober, Paul Reynolds, Leland Hayward, Madeleine Boyd, David Lloyd of the Paget Agency, and Alan Collins of Curtis Brown, Ltd. So book publication remained a relaxed profession easily molded into a man's own image. He could depend on solid, respectable authors, in the manner of George H. Doran, or woo book buyers with highbrow writers and exceptional bindings like Alfred Knopf, or depend on the bravura decisions, scattershot advances, and splashy promotions which were the trademark of Horace Liveright.

Magazines of the moment featured book departments and stellar book reviewers—how many average Americans awaited the monthly edicts of William Lyon Phelps in *Scribner's?* *Harper's*, *Scribner's*, and the *Atlantic* carried the short stories of important authors, and sometimes serialized their novels. *The American Mercury* might brag about raucous Jim Tully, but *Scribner's* had Ring Lardner, Laurence Stallings, Fitzgerald, and Hemingway. *The Century Magazine* favored Elinor Wylie, Sherwood Anderson, and T. S. Stribling, while *Harper's Bazaar* boasted Stephen Vincent Benét and Anita Loos.

College Humor pointed with pride to newly discovered Katherine Brush, and *Vanity Fair* printed Corey Ford's hilarious parodies of famous writers. In the midst of all this, the pristine *New Yorker* had begun to alter the pattern of the country's humor and sophistication. Until now our American sophisticate had been the one who read and relished H. L. Mencken. But *The New Yorker's* aloof, top-hatted Eustace Tilley, scrutinizing a butterfly through his monocle, shortly induced a different highbrow image. So began an era whose theme song, says John K. Hutchens, was "the gorgeous melancholy of Gershwin's 'Rhapsody in Blue,' whose journal was *The New Yorker*."

On big-city newspapers a roster of literary critics was as necessary as a stable of sports writers. Among New York's book-page stalwarts were Ben Ray Redman, Gorham Munson, Mary Colum, Lewis Gannett, Harry Hansen, Lewis Galantière, Clifton Fadiman, Gilbert Seldes, and John Cournos.

Years later Munson peered back and declared that book criticism of the era had "an enthusiastic muddle." Yet enthusiasm was never a crime in those days, and as a result adjectives of praise sliced through the atmosphere like hummingbirds in flight. Critics hailed pretentious books as magnificent, epoch-making, epic, impressive, thought-provoking, deep, profound, or monumental. Less ambitious efforts were intense, moving, graphic, realistic, stirring, or emotional. Lightsome efforts were sparkling, bright, merry, mirth-provoking, side-splitting, hilarious, gloom-dispelling, or hammock-reading. Adventure tomes were daring, thrilling, spine-tingling, thrill-inducing.

Critics who reviewed numerous books had difficulty maintaining originality, and one endeavored to outdo himself by employing these words of praise: "So engrossed was I that I forgot the proximity of a hot stove near which I had huddled —imagine my surprise when I found a hole burned in my pants." This tribute won added fame when a composing room foul-up placed a woman's name under it.

However, a few rasping voices were heard to complain that book reviewers of the day were often irresponsible, indulging in logrolling for friends and the throat-cutting of enemies. Such disparate authors as Floyd Dell and Louis

Bromfield declared that favoritism and vanity played so great a part in criticism that it was all but impossible to get a fair review in the United States of America. Dell thought critics were too often swayed by personality. If the author was a nice guy known to the critic, or shared friends with him, his work was likely to get a good reception. Mencken once wrote to novelist Carl Van Vechten that Ernest Boyd "had a hell of a time" thinking of something nice to say about Carlo's *Blind Bow Boy*, but that the critic had finally managed it. Of course, if the reviewer disliked an author and his pals, a *bad* review was in order.

Writing from France, Bromfield claimed to know of a critic who in a single year discovered nine "best" novels and three "best" biographies. He went on:

> ◄§ There is a rather tragic game in America called Discovering a New Genius and most "critics" play it. The young fellow gets no honest criticism when he needs it most . . . and the literary path of America is strewn with the blanching bones of young prodigies who on the publication of a single autobiographical novel have been hailed as literary messiahs.

But such querulous objections were brushed aside as book reviewers, full time or part time, cheerfully went about their stimulating work.

Authors whose books were evaluated by the reviewers of the Teeming Twenties lie today in a grab bag of the names of the remembered, the half-remembered, and the forgotten. In these early years of the decade, America's determined readers had a chance to become familiar with such domestic and foreign authors as Lewis Mumford, Clarence Day, Hendrik Willem Van Loon, Aldous Huxley, Homer Croy, Donn Byrne, Floyd Dell, Cosmo Hamilton, Enid Bagnold, Temple Bailey, Stephen Vincent Benét, E. F. Benson, Edgar Rice Burroughs, Lytton Strachey, Faith Baldwin, Coningsby Dawson, A. P. Herbert, Arthur Somers Roche, Grant Overton,

Walter B. Pitkin, Berta Ruck, Evelyn Scott, Elsie Singmaster, James Truslow Adams, Ruth Suckow, Margaret Culkin Banning, Storm Jameson, Stark Young, Ben Ames Williams, Sheila Kaye-Smith, Naomi Royde-Smith, and Thorne Smith.

William McFee, Rafael Sabatini, Leonard Merrick, Arthur Train, Carolyn Wells, John Buchan, Hall Caine, Somerset Maugham, E. M. Delafield, Hervey Allen, Norman Angell, Roger W. Babson, Paul Morand, André Maurois, E. Barrington, William Beebe, Rex Beach, Harvey Fergusson, Frances Parkinson Keyes, Rose Macauley, Margaret Kennedy, Pamela Frankau, Francis Brett Young, Stefan Zweig, Mazo de la Roche, Harold Nicolson, Gilbert Frankau, V. Sackville West, Paul de Kruif, John Macy, Lord Dunsany, John Drinkwater, G. B. Stern, Grace Zaring Stone, H. M. Tomlinson, Warwick Deeping, Robert Graves, Katherine Mayo, Charles G. Norris, Rebecca West, Michael Arlen, Larry Barretto, P. G. Wodehouse, Edmund Lester Pearson, and William Bolitho.

Glenway Wescott, T. S. Stribling, Jim Tully, Alice Duer Miller, Kathleen Norris, Irvin S. Cobb, Fannie Hurst, Ring Lardner, Cyril Hume, Gertrude Atherton, James Boyd, Dorothy Canfield, Upton Sinclair, Thomas Mann, Julia Peterkin, Barry Benefield, Martha Ostenso, M. R. Werner, Will Durant, Stark Young, Percival Christopher Wren, Emerson Hough, DuBose Heyward, Claude G. Bowers, John Erskine, Hermann Keyserling, Knut Hamsun, Oswald Spengler, James Joyce, Maxwell Bodenheim. Thyra Samter Winslow, Konrad Bercovici, Dawn Powell, Kathleen Norris, and Lowell Thomas.

From this feast of reading material, Americans had discovered they were not a very well-educated people. Rigid school curricula had so far stressed the dates and events of world history, providing little of the flesh, blood, guts, and gristle. The remarkable success of H. G. Wells's *Outline of History* in the first four years of the decade highlighted the public's interest in the color and sweep of the past. In the wake of this publishers brought out histories of art, literature, and philosophy.

With cynicism and disillusionment rampant, readers were

especially anxious to view notable personalities as vulnerable human beings. The first realistic biography of the decade was Lytton Strachey's *Queen Victoria*, a 1922 import which pictured Britain's dumpy, long-lived monarch complete with flaws and foibles. This and other probing books became particularly indigenous to the 1920's. Such books debunked, sometimes with a certain amount of fondness, more often with hatchet .in hand. M. R. Werner's biography of P. T. Barnum may have been America's first debunking biography; it gave a friendly portrait of Barnum while debunking the trickery of his trade. The same author followed with a not-so-gentle treatment of Brigham Young. John Erskine's *Private Life of Helen of Troy* was a suave mélange of fiction and fact which modernized the Spartan queen and turned her into a bit of a flapper. The giant success of this book led the author to modernize Sir Galahad, then Adam and Eve. A critic called them "pert debunkings."

But for the most part, the trend was a serious one. William Woodward himself entered the field with an irreverent *Meet General Grant*. Abraham Lincoln, paragon of Presidents, was whittled down to size by Edgar Lee Masters, while Rupert Hughes tried to make a mere man of George Washington. Debunking even went beyond personalities, with Thomas Beer exposing the Gay Nineties in *The Mauve Decade*. It can also be said that novelists deflated World War I. John Dos Passos' *Three Soldiers* had begun the process, of course, by exposing the so-called Great War as modern hell, and Ernest Hemingway was about to sound the keynote of the fictional war on war by writing, "You did not know what it was all about. You never had the time to learn. They threw you in and told you the rules, and the first time they caught you off base, they killed you." But not until the close of the decade did the Twenties find its finest antiwar book in Germany's *All Quiet on the Western Front*.

America's top novelists scaled heights in the peak year of 1925. Sinclair Lewis was represented by *Arrowsmith*, in many ways his best novel. With it, the reading public discovered that this purveyor of slashing satire possessed a heart. In a story of the worldly pressures besetting the young bacteriologist, Dr. Martin Arrowsmith, Lewis found an outlet for the idealistic streak so often inherent in writer-reformers.

Despite his high-sounding name, Dr. Arrowsmith was a gawky, uncouth, genius type, not only like Lewis in looks but in a ferocious desire to know everything possible about a subject before him. In the author's now-tender hands, he became an appealing character, as did Leora Tozer, the student nurse Dr. Martin meets on her knees scrubbing a floor in the Zenith (yes!) hospital. So *Arrowsmith* emerged as the first Sinclair Lewis book of the decade to appear without an accompanying uproar. Everyone liked it except a few nit-picking medicos.

While writing and researching *Arrowsmith*, Lewis had kept up his tireless pace, moving from the United States to the West Indies, to South America, to London. At his side was Dr. Paul de Kruif, who provided the medico-scientific data required and interpreted it too. De Kruif got along amazingly well with the nettlesome author, and the two remained close friends until the end, when De Kruif expressed the belief that his name ought to appear on the title page as coauthor. Lewis erupted in fury, and friendship ceased.

Obviously, Sinclair Lewis had not changed. In London, foreign correspondent George Slocombe made note of his "extraordinary energy of speech, a very great diversity of ideas, a certain air of frenzy in his look, speech, and gait." A more telling tale came as historian Philip Guedalla encountered George Jean Nathan on his annual play-viewing trip abroad. Said Guedalla to Nathan: "You are an American, and I have a message for you. If your country does not recall Sinclair Lewis at once, there will be war between England and the United States."

Besides revealing a tender side of Red Lewis, *Arrowsmith* opened vistas for other working writers. Until this moment few, if any, had sensed the dramatic forces at work behind the facades of hospitals, scholarly institutions, or big businesses. In *Arrowsmith*, drama derived from assaults on the fine-honed integrity of Dr. Martin, whose dedication to bacteriology was intensified by the example of his superior, Dr. Max Gottlieb, brilliant immunologist and pure scientist.

Sparkling Leora Tozer stands out as the only really bright spot in Dr. Martin's no-play existence. Lewis, whose own marriage had grown increasingly rocky, put his top efforts into Leora, making her a humid mixture of every man's dream of maiden-wife-mistress. When friends accused him of being in love with his own creation, Lewis answered ruefully, "She's the woman I always wanted to marry—but then nobody ever marries the right woman!"

If men loved Leora, women didn't. One wrote indignantly to Heywood Broun, who had drooled over the girl in his "It Seems to Me" column in the New York *World.* Leora was not a flesh-and-blood creature, the woman declared, but instead a man's idea of a woman. She was "as unintelligent as a cat . . . she sleeps around . . . cannot even cook . . . is a slattern."

In the book Dr. Martin marries Leora, and life broadens for both as he is lured to the esteemed McGurk Institute in New York. With its funds and excellent facilities, Dr. Martin soon isolates a germ killer which he names Phage. The publicity-conscious institute is delighted, and prepares a high-gear publicity campaign to promote Phage to world fame. Dr. Martin objects on grounds that his findings have not been fully verified. While he verifies, a Frenchman also discovers Phage.

Angered at Arrowsmith, the institute nonetheless gives him a second chance, leading a medical team to fight bubonic plague in the West Indies. Again he hesitates to use Phage, thus antagonizing both institute and native government. Leora dies of the plague, and as Martin reels from this shock, the publicity-hungry institute issues a report which greatly exaggerates the good effects of his work.

Such events prove thoroughly unnerving to a man whose true habitat is the lonely laboratory. Rather unconvincingly, he marries a wealthy woman who tries to turn him into a fashionable scientist. Failing, she gets a divorce. Dr. Martin Arrowsmith finally retreats to a self-contrived laboratory in the Vermont woods, determined to pursue research on his own terms. Somewhat like Selina De Jong in *So Big*, he is a failure in the eyes of the world. But again the tantalizing query: Has he actually succeeded?

For F. Scott Fitzgerald, dwelling in Paris and on the Riviera, this was *The Great Gatsby* year. As such, it should have been the best of his lifetime, for *Gatsby* is considered his finest novel and possibly the outstanding work of fiction written during the Literary Decade. Scott had again dipped into his recent past—and come up with a work with a Long Island setting, wild parties galore, and heavy accent on wealth. Jimmy Gatz, born poor but a dynamo of ambition, acquires a gentlemanly sheen at an officers' training camp of World War I. In the process, he falls madly in love with glamour debutante Daisy Fay, a girl with "a voice full of money." Sent overseas to fight, Jimmy returns to find Daisy the wife of super-rich Tom Buchanan.

Getting Daisy back becomes an obsession, and he decides the only way to do it is to make his own pile. Now calling himself Jay Gatsby, he joins forces with the underworld overlord Wolfsheim and derives enough rapid profit from bootlegging and its offshoots to buy an estate in West Egg, a mythical locality on the North Shore of Long Island, across the bay from the Buchanans. Wolfsheim, incidentally, is a sinister character (Gatsby is, too) who bears a resemblance to the real-life gambler Arnold Rothstein, a much-whispered-about figure in Manhattan hotspots. If nothing else, this proved that Scott Fitzgerald had not completely wasted his countless speakeasy nights.

In the manner of the Fitzgeralds, Gatsby gives fabulous, talked-about parties, mainly in the hope of blasting the Buchanan marriage apart. But if Daisy is fascinated by Jay Gatsby, the girl with dollars in her vocal cords never lets herself forget that he is only a token gentleman. Her husband Tom represents the real thing, even if he is currently bedding down with a garage mechanic's pretty wife. When Daisy accidentally kills the wife by running over her with a car, well-bred Tom lets the mechanic believe that Gatsby drove the murder vehicle. The mechanic kills Gatsby in his own swimming pool.

Scott knew he had written his best book to date, and once more allowed himself dreams of financial success. Reviews in America bolstered these hopes. Gilbert Seldes in *The Dial* saw "every part functioning in the combined organism. I cannot find in the earlier Fitzgerald the artistic integrity and the passionate feeling this book possesses." Carl Van Vechten, usually addicted to esoteric expression, was content to be colloquial: "This is a fine yarn, exhilaratingly spun." William Rose Benét in *The Saturday Review of Literature* was succinct: "We like the book!" Isabel Paterson disapproved—"a tale of the season only," she sniffed. Another reviewer found "melodrama, detective story, and fantastic satire, with his usual Jazz Age extravaganza . . . a graceful, finished tale."

The cable from Maxwell Perkins reporting favorable reviews closed with the words "SALES SITUATION DOUBTFUL." Sales continued poor, and once again Fitzgerald was doomed to disappointment. In all, *Gatsby* sold about twenty-five thousand copies over the spring and summer of 1925, then seemed to expire forever. Extra money arrived from a Broadway play adaptation, then a sale to Hollywood. Scott, again deprived of the status of best seller, took familiar refuge in drink. His steps on the doleful road to alcoholism became more visible as he let his life to slip into "1000 parties and no work." His next novel would not appear for nine long years.

If Scott Fitzgerald lost the accolade of best-sellerdom, it came almost miraculously to Sherwood Anderson. This fifty-year-old author had so far been a double-edged influence on his day. His easy, colloquial style in novels and short stories, together with a relentless probing of sexual impulses, put him on a pioneering level with Dreiser and Lewis. His personal life had left an equal imprint on the time. At age forty Sherwood Anderson had walked out on family and well-paying business to devote full time to writing. This drastic act was oft cited by others with artistic aspirations who sought to break established ties and find true selves.

Anderson's previous nine books, beginning with *Windy McPherson's Son*, had earned him the respect and even devotion of colleagues, but no great popularity. But his tenth, *Dark Laughter*, the story of a jaded, work-and-wife-weary reporter who escapes to vagabond along the Ohio and Mississippi, reversed the pattern. The 1925 public loved it, while the intelligentsia cringed.

Especially annoying to highbrows was a chorus of Negro servants chuckling its disapproval of the conventions and stupidities of masters—hence the title, *Dark Laughter*. On the Left Bank, Ernest Hemingway erupted in fury because his onetime mentor (Anderson, of course, had steered him to Paris) had turned out such a shoddy job of work. He was far from alone in this feeling. Scott Fitzgerald called *Dark Laughter* "cheap, faked, obscurantic, and awful."

This was also a major year for twenty-nine-year-old John Dos Passos, whose *Manhattan Transfer* employed a fiction technique new to his own work and to the world as well. Juggling a hundred or so noninterlocking characters, he used the mosaic of New York City as backdrop, vividly catching atmosphere, sounds, colors, rhythms, smells, and souls of the megalopolis. In 200,000 words he jumped abruptly from one scene and character to another, disregarding the transitional sentences hitherto sacred.

Interesting in retrospect are the adjectives applied to his innovative approach: "architectonic," "panoramic," "kaleidoscopic," "fragmented," and "neorealistic." In *The New York Times*, Lloyd Morris declared it could only stem from *Ulysses*, while another reviewer thought, "If novel it be, it is a novel with a rhythm, not a plot." The highest possible tribute came from the critic who called *Manhattan Transfer* "the Rhapsody in Blue of current fiction."

Only Sinclair Lewis, in *The Saturday Review of Literature*, appeared to realize that Dos Passos had used the technique of the cinema, with the abrupt transitions, or cuts, of the motion picture camera, along with flashbacks and prose close-ups. Having made this astute observation, Lewis—who never stinted in praise of brother writers—saluted "A novel of the very first importance . . . the dawn of a whole new school of writing. Just to rub it in, I consider *Manhattan Transfer* as more important in every way than anything by Gertrude Stein, or Marcel Proust, or even the great white boar, Mr. Joyce's *Ulysses.*"

At age forty-five, Carl Van Vechten could still be counted among "young" writers, his avant-garde enthusiasms usually landing him in new cultural terrains. Having just mastered the energetic intricacies of the Charleston, pinguid, white-haired Carlo turned his questing mind toward Negro culture, which few had yet bothered to notice. Enchanted by Harlem, he was busily calling attention to black literary talents like Paul Lawrence Dunbar, Countee Cullen, and James Weldon Johnson, as well as the torrid area's blues singers, tap dancers, songwriters, and night spots.

Inscrutable Carlo had kept on writing bizarre novels dealing with his particular netherworld of sophistication. Possibly his were the most erotic books of the time. But as handsomely designed Borzoi products dealing mainly with chichi homosexuality (and containing stylistic gimmicks like conversation with no quotation marks), the daring novels appeared immune from prosecution by antivice forces. This same amalgam of features, it might be added, seemed to keep them from popular acclaim.

Van Vechten's *Blind Bow Boy*, published in 1923, hangs on the perverse notion of a father seeking the most dissolute tutor possible for his son. It is populated by weirdo characters like Campaspe Lorillard, Zimbule O'Grady, and the Duke of Middlebottom, who says, "I have no friends; only people that amuse me, and people I sleep with." Engraved on his personal stationery is the motto "A thing of beauty is a boy forever." Campaspe Lorillard "does not know vices, she invents them." Another character "had Zimbule's name tattooed on his person so cunningly that it can only be deciphered under certain conditions."

The *Blind Bow Boy* was followed by *Firecrackers*, least

memorable of Van Vechten works. Still, it gained a certain distinction when *The Literary Review* assigned it for criticism to Albert Payson Terhune, rugged author of *Lad: A Dog* and similar outdoorsy tomes. Terhune found the ineffable novel "inconsequential, decadent mirth . . . in a sleezy, shimmering pattern."

Carl Van Vechten, incidentally, stands shoulder to shoulder with Sinclair Lewis and Scott Fitzgerald in his ability to pick excellent book titles. Indeed, it is hard to imagine the novels of any of these writers—during the Twenties, at least —with different names. Van Vechten's later novels were *Nigger Heaven, The Tattooed Countess, Spider Boy,* and *Parties.*

By mid-decade those elder statesmen of current writing— Joseph Hergesheimer and James Branch Cabell—showed signs of running down. Hergesheimer had failed to duplicate the impact of *Cytherea,* first novel to show the bored middle-aged emulating the jazz-mad young. Though he followed with *The Bright Shawl* and *Balisand,* the owl-eyed novelist was perhaps spreading himself too thin. Ever a major contributor to *The Saturday Evening Post,* he kept on collecting his antiques and glassware, wrote scenarios in Hollywood, and lectured before women's clubs, his pet subject being the Feminine Nuisance in Literature.

Once he and Mencken were invited to address an audience—not to debate, the announcement said, but to speak *together.* The two jokers did just this, walking side by side to the center of the platform, simultaneously jabbering out their own separate talks. Eventually Hergesheimer was capsuled by Clifton Fadiman as "the [John Singer] Sargent of the American novel." But if his overall career proved disappointing, Joe Hergesheimer the man appeared to be having an immensely good time in the Twenties.

Cabell, too, seemed happy for an exceedingly sensitive soul. Those privileged to visit him in Richmond-in-Virginia reported him gleefully mixing a self-contrived cocktail named the Ravished Virgin. Since *Jurgen,* he had published *The High Place: A Comedy of Disenchantment,* and *Skeins and Prayer Books.* These ended the lengthy saga of Dom Miguel and family which the author viewed as "an epos of humanity, a cycle of man." Reviewers considered both books superior to *Jurgen*, but the public had wearied of Cabell, with one review of *The High Place* beginning, "Too much of this!" Since *Jurgen*, books like *Flaming Youth* had been more explicit about sex, while the Virginia aristocrat's intricate prose proved increasingly irksome to follow in a rapidly whirling world.

Beauteous Elinor Wylie had just published her second novel, *The Venetian Glass Nephew*. Like Ben Hecht, this ethereal authoress was living proof that not all writers enjoyed the prosperity of the Twenties. From New Canaan, Connecticut, where she wrote her poetry and prose while serving as stepmother to the three children of William Rose Benét, she desperately informed Van Vechten, "I find I have unexpectedly to pay the interest, as well as the paying off, on the mortgage. There is a difference, though it takes an expert to understand." Faithful Carlo came to her rescue by persuading *The Century Magazine* to run her novel serially, with payment in advance.

The Venetian Glass Nephew was hailed as "lovely fantasy, with subtle and pervasive irony, elegance, and a style faultlessly particularized." Inevitably, Van Vechten reviewed it, discovering "aesthetic sustenance . . . its fragrant charm has an air of perdurability, as such things go." The fantasy novel dealt with Peter Innocent Bon, Venetian cardinal of 1782, who prayed for a nephew, since his holy vows precluded a son. Three Venetian scoundrels, one of them Giacomo Casanova, manufacture him a nephew of glass.

If Elinor Wylie was highly regarded as a novelist, she rated higher as a poet. This further highlights the literary plenitude of the era, for while books of prose tumbled off presses in unprecedented numbers America also enjoyed a Golden Age of Poetry. For the first time since Longfellow's *Hiawatha*, poetry books were big sellers, while the judges of the Pulitzer Prize for Poetry, established in 1922, wrestled energetically to choose annual winners among a glorious array of selections. Before 1926, they met this challenge by awarding the prize twice to Edwin Arlington Robinson, and once apiece to Edna St. Vincent Millay and Robert Frost. To young, irreverent Edna, the honor was "my thousand bucks."

In the inimitable parlance of the Twenties, old John Butler Yeats had "said a mouthful" when he opined that the poetic fiddles were tuning up all over the land. The poets he had in mind were the "solid" types—Robinson, Amy Lowell, Robert Frost, Carl Sandburg, Edgar Lee Masters, and perhaps Edna Millay. But at the same time, not-so-solid innovators were tuning up. At first they were Gertrude Stein, Ezra Pound, and T. S. Eliot, determined expatriates all, who nonetheless wrote on American themes. At first Miss Stein was considered a joke, while Eliot appealed to very few. Ezra Pound's *Lustra*, however, burst with pyrotechnic effect in 1917.

After the war, e. e. cummings, still more innovative, began to appear. Edna St. Vincent Millay in *A Few Figs from Thistles* boasted of burning her candle at both ends, and thus joined Scott Fitzgerald in giving the Younger Generation its defiant philosophy. In 1921 Elinor Wylie began a period of fecundity during which she wrote poetry and novels at a rate that may have hastened her death at forty-three seven years later.

So the stage was set for a decade when America's poetry was probably the best in the world. According to historian Mark Sullivan, "The fact is that during the period following the war the poetry [of] Americans was more important than that by poets of any country." One result was that poets were treated like celebrities. "I like to entertain ideas," Robert Frost told an interviewer; then he paused to muse, "I like that word 'entertain.' " Edwin Arlington Robinson, shyest of men, spent his winters in a New York hideaway where one reporter needled him by saying readers thought his poetry obscure. "Why cannot people read one word after another!" the poet demanded.

Around Robinson, Sandburg, Frost, and other titans

whirled a dazzling array of talents almost too numerous to mention—Conrad Aiken, Robinson Jeffers, Archibald Mac-Leish, Joseph Auslander, Louis Untermeyer, Alfred Kreymborg, Leonora Speyer, Stephen Vincent Benét, Witter Bynner, William Rose Benét, Hart Crane, Babette Deutsch, Padraic Colum, Sara Teasdale, Wallace Stevens, Maxwell Bodenheim, Genevieve Taggard, H. D. (Hilda Doolittle), Arthur Davison Ficke, and William Carlos Williams. In addition there were Negro talents like Countee Cullen, James Weldon Johnson, and Langston Hughes. Those who admired the poetry of the East found riches in Kahlil Gibran and Rabindranath Tagore.

Superior poetry begets—or should beget—good light verse, and in the Twenties this became abundantly true. Dorothy Parker was the light versifier most in tune with the time, her lines purveying the sadness which afflicted the lost folk (single women, particularly) in an era when there was too much to drink, too little true love, and lots of easygoing sex.

One critic compared the mood of Edna St. Vincent Millay's figs-from-thistles verses to the ecstatic emotions of a young girl at her first party—she was "too busy dancing her stockings through to notice the fetid air and jaded nerves around her." Dorothy Parker was just the opposite—she noted the bad air and jangled nerves, evoking them in rueful lines characterized as "exquisitely bitter" with tricky O. Henry finishes. Even so, her most famous verse of the Twenties was the innocuous

> *Men seldom make passes*
> *At girls who wear glasses.*

Dorothy Rothschild Parker lived a life much like the emotionally violated women of her poems and stories. According to Lillian Hellman, "Her taste in men was . . . bad, even for a writer lady." At least two top writers of the day were infatuated by tiny, witty Dotty, a flapperish thirty-two in 1925. But she had a compulsive drive toward less worthy males who treated her badly, at times brutally. Still, she retained faith in true love, or at least in its substitute, Sex. One day *The New Yorker* sent her a hurry-up appeal for the book column she wrote over the by-line "Constant Reader." Her reply became a classic—"Too fucking busy, and vice-versa." Years later she expressed her disillusionment with sex by saying, "The fucking you get isn't worth the fucking you get."

Dorothy Parker was surrounded by other light-versifiers, among them F.P.A., Christopher Morley, Arthur Guiterman, and Newman Levy, to name only a few. Especially cherished (and at the time considered a rival of Mrs. Parker) was Samuel Hoffenstein, whose popular volume was *Poems in Praise of Practically Nothing*. Described by Ben Hecht as "a man full of eerie problems," Hoffenstein limned the female form:

> *Nothing from a straight line swerves*
> *So sharply as a woman's curves.*
> *And having swerved no might nor main*
> *Can ever put them straight again.*

In both serious and light verse, the Twenties were a period of experimentation, ranging from the lower-case eccentricities of e. e. cummings to the bright vers libre of Don Marquis with his *archy and mehitabel*. Marquis himself saluted the wide variety of contemporary verse by writing:

> *There's a grand poetical "boom" they say,*
> *(Climb on it, chime on it, brothers of mine!)*
> *'Twixt the dawn and the dusk of each lyrical day*
> *There's another school started, and all of them pay.*

There was even a middle distance between heavy verse and light. Especially at home here was John V. A. Weaver, husband of Peggy Wood, who followed Carl Sandburg's advice about slang by writing poems in homey vernacular. His *In American* was seen as "cleverly constructed lyrics in the common, loosely phrased language of the streets." His second volume, *More in American*, exposed "the strange futility of urban existence."

Another in-between poet of the Twenties was Joseph Moncure March, who wrote two terse, pungent short-stories-in-verse titled "The Set-Up" and "The Wild Party." The heroine of the latter was introduced in this manner:

> *Queenie was a blonde, and her age*
> > *stood still,*
> *And she danced twice a day in*
> > *vaudeville . . .*
>
> *What hips—*
> *What shoulders—*
> *What a back she had!*
> *Her legs were built to drive men*
> > *mad. . .**

Yet in this blaze of noon in American poetry, the honor of being the most popular poet in the nation belonged to one Edgar A. Guest, a man whose volumes of verse sold millions where others sold thousands—or, in the case of Stephen Vincent Benét's still-to-come *John Brown's Body*, hundreds of thousands.

Edgar A. Guest was the combined Zane Grey-Harold Bell Wright of the poetry world, or was it the Kathleen Norris-Fannie Hurst? At any rate, the man whose admirers fondly called him Eddie was known to people on Main Streets who had never heard of Frost, Sandburg, or Ezra Pound. And why not? For Eddie Guest was the man who wrote, along with so much else:

> *It takes a heap o'livin'*
> *To make a house a home.*

* Reprinted by permission of the publisher The Bond Wheelwright Company, Freeport, Maine, from *The Wild Party/The Set Up/A Certain Wildness*, by Joseph Moncure March, copyright 1968.

Those Dreiserian Waves

Theodore Dreiser . . Horace Liveright . . . .

With all the glories of 1925, though, the most gratifying event of the year may have been the success, after publication on December 10, of Theodore Dreiser's *An American Tragedy.* Dreiser's early novels had cleared the literary highway for other writers; now, at long last, a Dreiser novel opened fresh vistas for Dreiser himself, repaying him in part for twenty-five years of harsh reviews and personal abuse from press and public.

Dreiser's last novel had been *The "Genius,"* published in 1915 and promptly vilified. John S. Sumner had moved forward to threaten the publisher with legal action, at which the book was withdrawn. While *The "Genius"* lay in limbo, Dreiser devoted himself to intermittent labors on *The Bulwark* (a novel begun in 1912 and not completed until 1944) along with *A Book About Myself,* the second volume of a soul-searching autobiography.

At the same time he produced short stories, plays, poems, magazine articles, personality sketches, play and music reviews, and even fashion notes, thus proving himself, as George Jean Nathan points out, one of the most versatile writers who ever lived. Not many of these pieces were done on assignment, and William Lengel, his literary agent, tirelessly circulated them around the literary marketplace, finding few takers. At times Theodore Dreiser was down to his last ten dollars, but when the pendulum of fortune swung back, he purchased silk shirts.

Before 1920, Dreiser's books had been published by a number of firms, among them Harper's. Then Horace Liveright set to work and laboriously accumulated the rights to all Dreiser works for his firm, Boni and Liveright. Among these was *The "Genius,"* and Liveright, together with Mencken and others, was now attempting to persuade John S. Sumner to agree to republication after removal of a few objectional paragraphs. Liveright had also advanced considerable amounts of money to his monolithic author and naturally hoped that, in return, Dreiser would provide a new novel, either *The Bulwark* or something else.

Having reached age fifty in 1921, Dreiser stood forth as a lumbering man with a florid face, protuding teeth, lopsided head, and a cast in one eye. "Pachydermic, yet sensitive," John Dos Passos thought him. Over the years since *Sister Carrie*, his self-absorption had grown to near megalomania. "I doubt that I have ever been in love with anyone, or anything, save life itself," he remarked once. Friends might be inclined to differ and say he was deeply in love with himself.

Dreiser considered any good fortune long overdue and flatly refused to jubilate about it. He thought himself the greatest novelist in the world, bar none, and had long urged Mencken to suggest him for the Nobel Prize, which he spelled "Noble" until corrected. Needless to say, he resented the triumphs of others, and his lip curled visibly at mention of Sinclair Lewis.

During Dreiser's bleak years he had lived in various unprepossessing Greenwich Village apartments, where he liked to draw the draperies and console himself by playing melancholy Russian music on the phonograph. To those who noticed him on Village streets he seemed more curiosity than celebrity. Edgar Lee Masters saw him as

> *Soul enrapt, demi-urge*
> *Walking the earth,*
> *Seeking life . . .*

Mencken was Dreiser's closest literary friend and admirer, at times showing it in odd ways. Though he and Nathan despised the area below Fourteenth Street, they nonetheless sought to brighten Dreiser's dark days by making the long trip downtown to stuff his mailbox with anonymous letters and silly brochures which to them were hilarious. One was a photograph of Czar Nicholas with the inscription "To Theodore, with a kiss on the cheek." Dreiser was unamused by this and other jokes, and no doubt because of this Nathan accused him of "obstinate moodiness," and went on to delineate him as

> *fundamentally a lugubrious fellow. Despite his fitful excursions into swollen humor, his nature is cast o'er with melancholy and even his occasional search for diversion of one kind or another has implicit in it a tendency toward and taste for the glum, the depressing, and the morbid.*

Such a Dreiser was acutely visible on a night in 1923 when the morose author made a surprise decision to host a party. To it he invited Mencken and Nathan, Ernest Boyd, Sherwood Anderson, Carl Van Vechten, and others well established in the literary world. He also included Village cronies not so well established, to create a somewhat hostile group whose members did not know each other well, or care to. To make matters worse there was nothing to drink (though most of his guests were known to be hearty guzzlers) and no females to brighten the atmosphere. Dreiser's front room was large, and he had placed all the chairs around the walls, as if at a dance.

The host did nothing to cheer his own gala, but sat gloomily indulging a favorite habit of folding and refolding his handkerchief. The party remained dead until the door burst open to admit Scott Fitzgerald who was, in the words of Llewelyn Powys, "a little the worse for drink." Under one arm Scott carried a gift bottle of champagne. Scott had never met Dreiser and peered drunkenly around until his eyes focused. Then he lurched forward, presented his gift, and said, "Mr. Dreiser, I get a big kick out of your books."

The other guests eagerly eyed the champagne. Dreiser accepted the bottle unenthusiastically and, lumbering out to the kitchen, stored it in the icebox. Then he returned to sit dourly in his chair. Says W. A. Swanberg, "The party was long remembered as fascinating for its very dullness."

When examined closely, however, Theodore Dreiser's turgid life seemed to include compensations not fully appreciated by him.

For one thing, he had total freedom to write, and Dreiser was one of those rare types who actually enjoyed the creative process, looking forward to the beginning of each day's labor rather then the end. To Nathan he confessed, "I am a writer; I am wretched when I don't write. If I don't produce three thousand words a day, I'm unhappy." Nor was Dreiser interested mainly in financial rewards. "I really don't want or need much money," he said once, "though under the existing order of things you can be sure I want and get every dollar that is coming to me."

Another compensation in Dreiser's life was women—or perhaps the proper term is girls. Or is it sex? For this lumbering man had so powerful an urge to possess attractive young females that he seemed to exude a venereal vitality which rendered seduction easy. W. A. Swanberg calls this magnetism "powerful Dreiserian waves" and speaks of "an interminable daisy chain of conquests." Mencken was not so charitably inclined and once snorted, "He is doing very little writing, but devotes himself to the stud." Dreiser, of course, was immensely proud of his prowess as a hulking Casanova. Encountering Floyd Dell for the first time, he gloated, "You know, Dell, I took a girl away from you once."

The Dreiser technique of seduction was never rough, blunt, or lecherous—a surprising state of affairs in view of his heavy personality. Rather, this unlikely virtuoso of the boudoir overwhelmed his victims with kindness, understanding, clumsy flattery, and even baby talk. At the same time, the venereal vitality subtly informed the girl that, despite his sweet words, Dreiser really lusted for her body. A surprising number of girls and women succumbed to these mingled blandishments, with one he loved and left wiring him, "I NEVER KNEW SUFFERING COULD BE SO TERRIBLE. AM NUMB WITH GRIEF AND ANGUISH. CAN'T GO ON WITHOUT SOME WORD FROM YOU."

Usually the girls who became entangled in Dreiser's web were brainy. Often they first wrote him from college, praising his novels, at which he began a careful letter campaign calculated to bring them to New York. Other conquests were bright Village girls eager to meet a person of his importance. On discovering that Dreiser considered himself a monumental genius, girls seemed to turn to putty in his hands.

If one he seduced could use the typewriter, Dreiser immediately put her to work typing up his pages of longhand manuscript. Those who showed critical judgment were used for criticizing, editing, and cutting his work. Always Theodore Dreiser seemed surrounded by a willing harem, its attractive members functioning as typists and literary aides. Not all were his bed companions, but whenever possible Dreiser paid for literary services in the coin of love. More, he blatantly used the lives and personalities of his harem in novels, short stories, and finally the book *A Gallery of Women.*

In the early 1920's, Dreiser's number-one girl was Helen Richardson, a young second cousin who had knocked on his door to meet her celebrated relative. Within days—or was it hours?—the two were in bed. Helen was "tall, shapely, sinuous, sensual—a smiling face framed by a mass of gold chestnut hair." Her beauty stunned Village Don Juans like John Cowper Powys and Harry Kemp, who heartily envied friend Dreiser.

Though increasingly aware of his infidelities—she once had cause to be jealous of a fifteen-year-old girl—Helen remained at his side, operating as secretary-typist and sharing his slumbers as often as possible. Soon the two traveled to Hollywood, where Helen's beauty and talent won her roles in films, once with sheik Rudolph Valentino. Had it not been for Dreiser's constant demands on her, as well as his towering jealousies (even while unfaithful himself), Helen might have become a movie star. But she chose to stay with the turbulent man who in his few cheery moods addressed her as "Dearest Deario."

Dreiser enjoyed juggling literary projects as well as love affairs. In Hollywood, he was supposed to be concentrating on *The Bulwark*, but really was not. Meanwhile, *The "Genius"* was republished after elision of only four paragraphs. No longer as sensational as it had seemed, the novel enjoyed a reasonably good sale. Boni and Liveright also brought out *The Color of a Great City*, a collection of Dreiser's pieces about New York, a metropolis he truly loved. "Everything happens here," he liked to say.

Yet Liveright really wanted a brand new novel and expected Dreiser to finish *The Bulwark*. Instead, the moody giant abruptly dropped it to begin a project that had long percolated in his mind. Ever a believer in the human moth entrapped by the flame of life, he considered the act of murder the ultimate betrayal by hostile fates. Into a murder tale he could likewise weave his favorite indictments of society as the cause of man's miseries.

For years he had kept clippings of crimes and trials which might be the basis of such a novel. Now he chose the 1906 case of Chester Gillette who in upstate New York was found guilty of murdering the pregnant factory girl Grace Brown, largely because she stood in the way of his social aspirations. Changing the name Chester Gillette to Clyde Griffiths, Dreiser began to plot *An American Tragedy*.

Mencken and others had warned him that his long absence in California was bad for his professional reputation; he was almost a forgotten man in New York. So with Helen he returned to the Village, where work on the new book began in earnest. Helen did most of the typing, while only the most intelligent among his trusted female helpers were allowed to criticize, edit, and slice. Dreiser visited the scene of the crime; he sniffed the dank air of Sing Sing's death house; he talked about homicidal motivations with psychoanalyst A. A. Brill; he rented an office next to a lawyer friend so as to get instant advice on courtroom procedures.

Withal, the words came slowly. "For some reason this

book is harder than anything I ever wrote," he complained. "I might as well be chipping it out of solid rock." After re- writing some chapters six or seven times, he broke down and wept at the lack of progress. At other times he philosophized, "You can't write any faster than you can write."

It has been estimated that Dreiser wrote over one million words for *An American Tragedy*, with more than half cut out by one or another of his female aides. The final manuscript came to over 400,000 words. Liveright editor T. R. Smith and his assistant Manuel Komroff trimmed out 50,000 more. Perhaps because these cuts were made by males, Dreiser ob- jected and restored half of them. The final version stood at 385,000 words, still too many for a single volume. Having scheduled the novel for early in the year, Boni and Liveright had moved publication ahead month by month. Now the firm decided to publish the book in two volumes, at a cost of five dollars for both. A limited, signed edition sold for $12.50.

Dreiser refused to remain in New York for the December 10 publication of his mammoth novel. Not only did he fear the critics—had they not parboiled him in the past?—but he was uneasy about the Society for the Suppression of Vice. On December 8, he and Helen left by car for Florida. Dreiser loved auto touring, and beautiful Helen was an excellent driver. The only upsets on their journeys came when Dreiser eluded her to communicate by phone or telegram with girls left behind.

En route the two paused in Baltimore to visit Mencken. It was a rainy day, and Dreiser left Helen in the car while he went inside to hobnob with his true friend. When Mencken learned of Helen's presence, he rushed outside, apologizing profusely. Mencken's mother was fatally ill upstairs (she died the next day) but Dreiser never inquired about her, though quite aware of her condition. Altogether it was a strange visit.

The travelers reached Florida, then at the height of its land boom, and did their best to relax, though Dreiser's continuing efforts to contact girls produced tensions. Then, after a few days of sunshine, Dreiser's life was transmogrified by a tele- gram from T. R. Smith which read, "REVIEWS AMAZING,

ENTHUSIASTIC, DIGNIFIED. YOUR POSITION RECOGNIZED. SALES EXCELLENT."

Now Dreiser dared return to a Manhattan which practically lay prostrate at his feet. Joseph Wood Krutch called *An American Tragedy* "the greatest novel of our generation," and others echoed his praise. During the two weeks after publication the book sold fourteen thousand copies, an enormous sale for a Dreiser book, especially an expensive double-decker, and sales momentum continued. Not a word had been heard from John S. Sumner and his legion of right-eousness. Indeed, the only sour notes came from Mencken, who called *An American Tragedy* "a shapeless and forbidding monster . . . a heaping cartload of raw materials for a novel, with rubbish of all sorts intermixed . . . a vast, sloppy, chaotic thing of 385,000 words, at least 250,000 of them unnecessary."

And so ended a friendship of eighteen years. . . .

The huge success of *An American Tragedy* also focused the literary spotlight on publisher Horace Liveright, who had so long coddled Dreiser, advancing him at least twenty-five thousand dollars against hoped-for royalties, while simultaneously displaying remarkable tolerance for the titan's aberrations, procrastinations, and prevarications.

In return, Dreiser gave his devoted publisher only contempt. Ever since the unhappy experience with Nelson Doubleday in 1900, Dreiser had loathed publishers, accusing them of falsifying his royalty statements, shirking the promotion of his works, and in other ways betraying his genius. This accumulated resentment had been dumped on Liveright's head.

"If you would just have a little more confidence in me," Liveright wrote once, "you would save your soul a lot of bitterness and make it much more fun for me to continue to put my best efforts . . . into your books." Dreiser replied by calling him a bandit, and meaning it.

The fact that Liveright took this abuse—almost willingly, it seemed—exacerbated Dreiser further. Yet in one letter to

Dreiser, Liveright found courage to write, "Stick to me, kid, and you'll wear diamonds." These snappy words, so redolent of the era, sounded like the Horace Liveright familiar to Publishers' Row and the bright lights of Broadway. For the intense man who acted like a mouse with Dreiser was a lion elsewhere. More than anyone else in the literary business, Horace Liveright symbolized the *roar* in the Roaring Twenties. You might call him the Jimmy Walker of the publishing game.

Just turning forty at the time, the good-looking Liveright wore his hair brushed severely back so that a taut countenance looked skeletal or, to some, machiavellian. In contrast, his smile is recalled as "sparkling" and "beautiful." Tall and razor thin, he weighed in at about 140 pounds, but his frail body was crammed with jittery energy. His was the driven personality of the plunger, an admixture of gambler, opportunist, and showman. It was said Liveright never had time to read manuscripts, although he did love to interview authors, especially the young feminine variety who seemed to abound at the time.

Yet if measured literary judgment was not his strong point, Liveright did have intuitive triumphs. One came as he flipped quickly through the pages of a bulky manuscript from Judge Ben B. Lindsey of Denver. Lindsey covered many topics in addition to his startling conception of trial marriage, which was discussed vaguely on the typed pages as "a companionate kind of marriage." Liveright's quick eye lighted on this phrase, and his mind transposed it to "companionate marriage." After the judge had revised his work to stress trial marriages, the book titled *The Companionate Marriage* became an outstanding seller.

Despite the name Boni and Liveright, Horace Liveright was the sole member of the firm, for the gentle, erudite Boni brothers, who began publishing in Greenwich Village, had found their high-pressure partner impossible to endure. A coin had been flipped in the air. Liveright won the toss, and gained control of a company that eventually became Horace Liveright, Inc.

No less than the decade he typified, Liveright was a bravura personality. Born in the grimy coal regions of Pennsylvania, he was a school dropout who matured with a taste for the finer things in life and a rare worship for authors. Anyone who could write, well or badly, seemed a hero to him. "No writer ever admired himself as much as Horace admired him," wrote Ben Hecht.

As a result, the Boni and Liveright anteroom was usually jammed with clamorous authors the publisher was only too willing to see. Hendrik Willem Van Loon once took him to task for this, saying, "You don't run your business right, Horace. A publisher should have dignity. Instead your office is full of ragbag creatures." Liveright forebore to mention that Van Loon had been one of the ragbag creatures until Liveright got him to write *The Story of Mankind*.

Above all, Liveright was a splashy merchandiser of books, willing to splurge on advertising campaigns, publish controversial or shocking works, and take a chance on new authors. He firmly believed in paying writers well, and those with promising ideas seldom left his premises without a contract and a first check. Using his skills as a promoter, he talked established writers into accepting Liveright contracts. One was Edna St. Vincent Millay who agreed to do a novel named *Hardigut*, projected as "amusing, satiric, ugly, beautiful, poetic . . . unmistakable allegory." Miss Millay never got around to finishing it.

Sometimes Liveright actually forced money on authors. At one point, he learned that Sherwood Anderson was living in Greenwich Village contentedly writing a novel. At this, Liveright began sending him seventy-five dollars a week. With this princely sum to depend on, Anderson found himself unable to write. Rushing uptown to Liveright's office, he begged, "Horace, Horace, please stop those checks! *Give me back my poverty!*"

Like Dreiser, Liveright was a tireless seducer. But if Dreiser could be called a Casanova—as he could—Liveright was a Don Juan, subject to the annoying inhibitions that can afflict the Juanist. Married and the father of two, he lived in fear that his wife would learn of his infidelities; he was also concerned about his father-in-law, to whom he usually owed money. Liveright also had a mistress, and worried about *her* finding out, too. These and other problems rendered him subject to occasional embarrassing impotence at peak moments. Yet he persevered. In the tradition of the famed theatrical producer David Belasco, Liveright had a hidden bedchamber next to his office. When he pushed a button, a section of bookcase swung open to reveal a frilly boudoir.

Such features rendered Boni and Liveright the least formal publishing house in Manhattan. Bennett Cerf, who worked there, called it "a madhouse," while others preferred "the asylum." Office informality often had sexual overtones, and few female employees walked the hallways without having their fannies pinched at least once. Nor were attempted seduction of girls from outside the office frowned upon. Ironically, the firm's colophon, or printed trademark, a hangover from the sedate Boni brothers, was a cowled monk seated at a Renaissance writing desk. Walter Gilmer, Liveright's biographer, calls the colophon "the most misleading trademark that ever existed in the book trade."

The firm's office occupied a onetime brownstone dwelling at 61 West 48th Street, just off Fifth Avenue. On one side lay the hallowed Gotham Book Mart, on the other a speakeasy. The atmosphere within was that of a gentleman's club, or a pleasant residence, with editors like T. R. Smith and Manuel Komroff occupying offices resembling comfortable parlors. Atop the building was a roof garden, complete with pergola, where the staff was allowed to relax. Liveright himself attempted to do justice to his bizarre personality by a richly decorated Italianate office impressive to most visitors. Ben Hecht, though, called it "a foolish-looking Florentine chamber."

In addition to Dreiser, Liveright at one time or another published the works of Sigmund Freud (*A General Introduction to Psychoanalysis*), George Moore, Sherwood Anderson, T. S. Eliot, Ezra Pound, Lewis Mumford, Ben Hecht,

Emil Ludwig, Max Eastman, Dorothy Parker, Edgar Lee
Masters, Robinson Jeffers, Ernest Boyd, François Mauriac,
Hendrik Willem Van Loon, Heywood Broun, Gertrude
Atherton, William Faulkner, Conrad Aiken, e. e. cummings,
Bertrand Russell, Maxwell Bodenheim, Alfred Kreymborg,
Liam O'Flaherty, Rose Macaulay, and others.

Yet the true name of the game at Boni and Liveright was
the discovery of fresh talent. Editors like Bennett Cerf, Lillian Hellman, Beatrice Kaufman, Julian Messner, Donald
Friede, Louis Kronenberger, and Saxe Commins diligently
read manuscripts in the hope of uncovering genius. It was
said that Liveright's typists, telephone operators, and stock-
room boys also took time out to read manuscripts.

Recently the staff had been impressed by a thin volume of
short stories by a Paris-based author named Ernest Hemingway. This had been transported from the Left Bank by Harold Loeb, editor of *Broom*, whose novel *Doodab* was soon to
be published by Liveright. John Dos Passos also played a part
in alerting the firm to Hemingway's existence.

In addition to the printed volume, Hemingway had en-
closed a sampling of other short stories, some written for
Ford Madox Ford's *transatlantic review*. According to Loeb's
account, he visited the office one day to find Beatrice Kaufman in the process of rejecting the Hemingway material. He
begged her to reconsider, or at least show the stories to someone else. Next, he heard that Liveright had sent a cable of
acceptance to Hemingway, agreeing to publish the stories
under the title *In Our Time*.

Here, of course, lay the difference between Liveright and
other publishers—he cabled, they wrote. Maxwell Perkins of
Scribner's had just heeded Scott Fitzgerald's advice and written Hemingway a letter expressing interest in becoming his
publisher. But Liveright's cable reached Paris first, and Hemingway became a Boni and Liveright author.

Liveright's titles for the fall season of 1925 have been
called "the most incredible list ever issued by a publishing
house." Led by *An American Tragedy*, they included Sherwood Anderson's *Dark Laughter*, Gertrude Atherton's *Crystal Cup* (her first since *Black Oxen*), and the American edi-

tion of Roger Martin Du Gard's *The Thibaults*, which later won him the Nobel Prize. In addition, there were novels by Heywood Broun, Paul Morand, and Konrad Bercovici, along with a limited edition of *Droll Stories* illustrated by Ralph Barton and the first American publication of Scott Moncrieff's translation of Stendhal. With this went *In Our Time*, the Hemingway short stories—and a few months later, *Soldier's Pay* by William Faulkner. Easy to overlook in such a galaxy was *Gentlemen Prefer Blondes*, by Anita Loos, destined to be a top seller of the decade.

In nonfiction, the Liveright list boasted books by Hendrik Van Loon, explorer Sven Hedin, Dr. Morris Fishbein, and Judge Ben Lindsey. Other authors represented by new or revised editions were George Moore, Eugene O'Neill, Lewis Mumford, Harry Kemp, Anna Louise Strong, Sigmund Spaeth, T. S. Eliot, Edgar Lee Masters, and Ezra Pound, whose *Personae* was also upcoming. Finally, a thick volume of poetry entitled *Roan Stallion, Tamar, and Other Poems*, the first major publication by Robinson Jeffers.

Yet in this spectacular season, the dollars-and-cents profit to the firm of Boni and Liveright amounted to a mere $8,609.12. In part, this was attributable to office inefficiency, for coordination between departments was so hopeless that books were often marketed at a loss. This was especially true of the runaway seller *Gentlemen Prefer Blondes*, which because of its Ralph Barton illustrations should have been sold at two dollars per copy. Because it was a small book, editors set the price at $1.50.

However, the main reason for the firm's lack of prosperity was Liveright's own profligacy. Not content with the perennial risks of book publishing, he had begun dabbling in Broadway play production, an even riskier game. (Some thought he took this step because the girls of the theater were prettier and more willing than those in publishing.) At the same time he played the stock market with zestful abandon. Though operating on stock tips from the millionaire philanthropist Otto Kahn and others, Horace Liveright always seemed to lose money.

Most of all, though, Liveright spent money on parties. According to Anita Loos, "The first business of his day was to arrange the night's fun." Usually his parties were given at the town-house office, though occasionally in his New York apartment or suburban home. Lillian Hellman has rated these Liveright parties as "A" and "B." Because of Prohibition, the "A" variety were called tea parties by Burton Rascoe, F.P.A., and other columnists who mentioned them in print. Yet there was less tea served than liquor. Still, the "A" parties were for the most part decorous affairs, serving the commendable purpose of honoring authors and visiting celebrities.

The "B" parties were something else. A few authors might be present for celebrity value, but other guests were men of wealth, bank presidents, and stock brokers from whom the host hoped to obtain stock-market tips. Also there were girls from the theater and fringes of the book, magazine, and newspaper worlds. Miss Hellman called them "semi-ins," and their unabashed purpose was to accommodate sexually the men of finance, either in Liveright's hidden boudoir, the roof garden, or on the upholstered office furniture. The world has a word for Horace Liveright's "B" parties, and that word is "orgy."

Before others, the publisher tried valiantly to convey the impression of the bold, nerveless big-time operator so beloved in the Twenties. Yet a perverse Fate had failed to endow Liveright properly for this role. Somehow his character had flaws; possibly he lacked true inner confidence. Ben Hecht hinted at this when he called him "an ego with no tune of his own." Padraic Colum merely says, "You didn't quite trust him."

One thing missing in Liveright was a sense of perspective. The several fields in which he operated required full concentration from anyone involved. For instance, he played the stock market on a scale that should have taken all his time; yet it did not, and inevitably he went broke in the 1929 crash. This was equally true of Broadway, where he produced *Dracula*, starring Bela Lugosi, and the first modern-dress *Hamlet*.

Liveright's compulsion to spread himself thin was no less apparent in his love life. The tireless satyr demanded of life a wife, mistress, and succession of round-heel conquests. The existence of his wife sometimes inhibited him, but when the first Mrs. Liveright got a divorce, he married again and still retained a mistress. Phases of flamboyant Liveright were utilized by Ben Hecht for the character Jo Boshere in his novel, *A Jew in Love*, while Tony Mallare, played by Noel Coward in the 1935 Hecht-MacArthur movie *The Scoundrel*, was wholly Horace.

Liveright's desperations were all too visible at Boni and Liveright, a firm always in dire need of money. The publisher's endless ingenuity is seen in one solution to this problem: he made a policy of hiring well-to-do young men who invested money in the firm. Among them was Bennett Cerf, who since college had been laboring half-heartedly on Wall Street. Cerf listened entranced to tales recounted by his friend Richard Simon, a Liveright employee until he quit to become a partner in the firm of Simon and Schuster. Cerf applied for his job and by investing ten thousand dollars (a sum which soon rose to forty thousand) became one of the company's three vice-presidents.

In early days Liveright and the Boni brothers had conceived the idea of the Modern Library, a series of cheap reprints of European classics. Over the years, the Modern Library had been the financial backbone of the house, bringing in steady, sizable amounts from sales of 300,000 copies a year. Yet so great was Liveright's need for cash in 1925—his father-in-law was pressing hard—that he agreed to sell the Modern Library to Cerf, who planned to brighten its format. Cerf managed to accumulate $250,000, and the sale was consummated on his twenty-seventh birthday. Random House, it might be mentioned, was founded as an offshoot of the Modern Library, solely to publish limited editions of "random" classics.

Liveright quickly went through the money acquired by this astonishing sale and dug up another vice-president in the person of Donald Friede, a twenty-four-year-old with a background similar to Cerf's. Friede had been unobtrusively learning the publishing business as an assistant in the production department. Overnight, he bought half interest in the firm and leapfrogged to first vice-president.

It's hardly surprising that Liveright's besetting problems turned him into a heavy drinker, and that sometimes he was found drunk at his desk. Yet he contrived to function and to impress the world with an extravagant personality.

This was especially true after the triumph of *An American Tragedy*. The publisher's abiding faith in Dreiser had been among his most daring gambles, and it had paid off. Only Dreiser remained unimpressed; in fact, the book's success only seemed to increase his contempt for Liveright. Shortly after publication day, the euphoric publisher summoned playwright Patrick Kearney and authorized him to turn the jumbo novel into a play. It opened on Broadway with Liveright as producer, and proved a fair success. Even this failed to kindle Dreiser's gratitude.

Neither Dreiser nor Liveright believed *An American Tragedy* had a chance of a movie sale. Yet as word of the impending play spread, Paramount Pictures expressed interest. Liveright felt his play project had sparked this, intimating to Dreiser that he, Liveright, should get a good-sized part of any Hollywood loot. Dreiser brushed the idea aside with scorn. Liveright, he said, was entitled to no more than the 10 percent fee he would pay a literary agent.

Dreiser further let it be known that he planned to demand $100,000 for the film rights, an unprecedented amount in those days. Liveright infuriated him by recommending that he ask only thirty-five thousand dollars. Dreiser concluded from this that his publisher was angling for a secret payoff from Paramount.

Such was the storm-signal atmosphere as matters rolled toward an incident famed in publishing annals. . . .

In mid-March 1926, Dreiser and Liveright were to lunch with Paramount executives at the Ritz-Carlton in New York. Possibly the two downed a few drinks in Liveright's office beforehand, as well as several others on arrival at the Ritz. On the way to luncheon Liveright had made it clear that he expected Dreiser to "take care of him." Dreiser nodded cryptically, but Liveright somehow got the idea that the author would give him any money over sixty thousand dollars.

At lunch, Dreiser expressed a desire to do his own bargaining, and asked Liveright to leave the table. Liveright reluctantly did so, returning to discover that ninety thousand dollars seemed to be the sum agreed on. With this, he intimated he expected thirty thousand as per agreement. "You will get your ten percent," Dreiser told him angrily. Then he went on to state, before witnesses, that he was under no obligation to "take care of" Horace Liveright.

For once Liveright became furious with Dreiser, the formidable man to whom he had so often turned the other cheek. "You're a liar," he snapped at the novelist.

Dreiser's face suffused with blood. Lumbering to his feet, he seized the cup of hot coffee before him and tossed its contents straight into his publisher's face.

Readers Prefer Green Hats
—and Blondes . . *Michael Arlen* . .
Bruce Barton . . *Anita Loos* . . . .

W hatever goes up has got to come down," runs the time-honored saying. And even amidst the rich abundance of the year 1925, there were signs that—inevitably—the literary tide had commenced to recede.

It is hard to blame writers for this, though some have tried. According to Peter Munro Jack, authors of the day

> *were all too easily and lavishly praised as wonder boys and girls, and the critical and social background gave them no incentive to match their peculiar state of mind against the general state of the world. . . . They really did not develop at all, and a great deal of genuine talent was blanketed in a cozy bed of adolescent complacency, with the critics crooning it to sleep.*

Yet authors are traditionally hypersensitive to the pressures of any era—as are publishers to a lesser extent. Now the writers and other citizens of the United States of the 1920's were subject to a fresh set of forces. Even with postwar disillusionments and Jazz Age frenzy, the first five years of the decade had been a time of development and mental challenge, with (if nothing else) the population tossing off Victorian bonds and inhibitions, to live a life of unprecedented freedom and stimulus.

Suddenly this pattern seemed out of style, as the public took the step from a constructive life of development to a plateau that craved sensation. The country had indeed achieved what a prescient Scott Fitzgerald had forecast as "the grandest, gaudiest spree in history." Or, as he said on another occasion, "The Jazz Age had a wild youth and a heady middle age."

Surfeited with cynicism, paper profits, and bootleg gin, citizens of the nation had propelled themselves into Scott's heady middle age. Known as the Era of Wonderful Nonsense, this unbelievable period embraced flagpole sitters, dance marathons, Peaches and Daddy Browning, endurance air flights, home brew, big butter-and-egg men, the Charleston, makin' whoopee, raccoon coats for college boys, flapping galoshes for girls, yellow slickers for both, the Varsity Drag, popular songs like "Sleepy Time Gal," "The Prisoner's Song," "Yes, We Have No Bananas," "Vo-Do-Dee-O-Do," and "Doo-Wacka-Doo," sugar daddies, gold diggers, Eskimo Pies, nightclub shouts of "Hello, Sucker," and marriages, murders, and funerals seemingly cut to order for the big-city tabloids which set the frenetic pace of the time.

Scott Fitzgerald, who probably pondered the Twenties more than anyone else, put it this way: "The Younger Generation corrupted its elders and eventually overreached itself less through lack of morals than from lack of taste." In this perfervid atmosphere, the book industry was, to use Malcolm Cowley's words, "booming like General Motors." Nearly twice as many books were published as in 1920, and alert minds had begun dreaming up ways of capitalizing on their popularity.

One sharp mentality belonged to Harry Scherman, thirty-eight, who had once worked with Albert and Charles Boni on something called the Little Leather Library. Scherman believed the public was confused by the number of books hurtling from the nation's presses. He was equally aware that numerous Americans anxious to read the latest books did not live near the bookstores of big cities and towns, the only places where new books could be bought.

Until now, Pulitzer Prize selections had served as books of the year, with the public rushing to secure them once winners were announced. Harry Scherman had in mind a committee of judges similar to those of the Pulitzer board which would pick outstanding books on a weekly or monthly basis. But how to reach those untapped millions who did not live near bookstores? The answer might be sending books by mail. . . .

Already indicative of fresh trends were the enormously successful stunt books, typified by the Crossword Puzzle books published in 1924 by Simon and Schuster. Crosswords with thirty-two interlocking words had been a feature of the New York *World* since 1913, but the puzzles had been sloppy and haphazard. Then Margaret Farrar, wife of John Farrar of *The Bookman*, had been called in by the *World* to improve its puzzles. The brand-new firm of Simon and Schuster, desperate for books, asked Mrs. Farrar to supervise preparation of a book of best puzzles. The fledgling firm was so uncertain of the project's dignity that the first crosswords were ostensibly published by the "Plaza Publishing Company." The project seemed so meretricious that F.P.A. refused to write an introduction to the book.

Yet the Crossword craze swept the country, leading to other mind-teasing books like *What's the Answer?*, *Guess Again*, and *What's Your Average?* On the French Riviera, Scott Fitzgerald perused a letter from home which informed him of the soaring success of such books. To him they indicated "a wide-spread neurosis, gently signaled, like a nervous beating of the feet."

The process of change—or was it cheapening?—could be seen in the continuing turmoil in the sphere of sex literature. Possibly book readers of 1925 were as eager to read so-called pornography as were their children and grandchildren nearly half a century later when at last the dam broke. But so many preventive laws stood on the legal ledgers of the 1920's that publishers could easily be intimidated and books banned.

Not only laws but men stood in opposition. So respected a figure as Professor Bliss Perry of Harvard was capable of saying, "The American public is facing a clear and present danger through unclean books." Senator Reed Smoot of Utah saw fit to inform members of the U. S. Senate that ten minutes of skimming through James Joyce's *Ulysses* were

> *enough to indicate that it is written by a man with a diseased mind and soul so black that he would even obscure the darkness of Hell. Nobody would write a book like that unless his heart was just as rotten and as black as it could possibly be.*

Overseas George Bernard Shaw followed the American censorship hassle with sardonic interest. He labeled it all "comstockery," after Anthony Comstock, who had preceded Sumner as head of New York's Society for the Suppression of Vice. Sumner himself was quiescent for the moment, but Boston continued its active book banning. Late in 1926, *An American Tragedy* was suppressed there as "manifestly corrupting to the morals of the young." Since Mencken had got away with vending a copy of *The American Mercury* on Boston Common, Donald Friede of Boni and Liveright felt emboldened to sell a copy of Dreiser's novel to a detective on the identical spot. He was taken before a hostile judge and forced to stand trial, with Clarence Darrow one of his lawyers.

The Boston prosecutor concentrated on Dreiser's brothel scene, where a young whore begins to disrobe before Clyde. "Would you like your fifteen-year-old daughter to read that?" he demanded of the jury. Darrow rose to observe that a two-volume, nine-hundred-page, five-dollar novel was not meant for fifteen year olds. "But *supposing* she got hold of it?" the unfriendly judge interposed. Found guilty, Friede was sentenced to three months in jail or a fine of three hundred dollars. He paid the fine.

Until these strict morality laws were erased from the books, writers and publishers would be unable to dabble deep in sexual waters. Even so, novelists of the day did fairly well. Many of them had ceased to scrutinize the American scene in favor of probing human character, often following the murky paths charted by Sigmund Freud and Havelock Ellis.

One sexual trailblazer was an English import titled *The Green Hat*, a novel so exceedingly successful that it outsold literary landmarks like *Arrowsmith* and *Gatsby*. The dapper author of *The Green Hat* might have stepped from the pages of his own novel. Michael Arlen was the well-chosen pen name of Dikran Kouyoumdjian, age thirty, of Armenian parentage but England educated, already the author of published novels and short stories. Small and well-proportioned, Arlen dressed impeccably in Continental fashion. "His ties and socks are a gracefully subdued symphony," reads one description. "With evening dress he wears a gardenia, together with one black pearl stud and one white." It was further noted that the phenomenal success of *The Green Hat* here and abroad allowed him to possess a Rolls Royce six inches longer than most.

During visits to New York, Arlen was considered an exciting embellishment to the local literary scene. Yet his hand-kissing charm and symphonic attire annoyed a certain type of female. Arlen was pursued across the Atlantic by a devastating crack by Rebecca West, who called him "every other inch a gentleman." In New York he had a celebrated encounter with Edna Ferber, who baited him by saying, "Mr. Arlen, you look almost like a woman." With a gallant bow he replied, "Miss Ferber, so do you!"

Males seemed to take him in stride however. "I like Mike," drawled the Southern humorist Irvin S. Cobb. "He's the only Armenian I ever met who never tried to sell me a rug."

In *The Green Hat*, the suave Arlen titivated readers with the saga of Iris Storm, a girl who has come down in literary history as Iris March. But the latter was her maiden name; her second and last husband was Storm, and in the novel she is most often Iris Storm. Iris' first spouse was the golden youth "Boy" Fenwick, who jumped from the window of a Deauville hotel suite on their wedding night.

Michael Arlen was a master of the teaser situation which, he kept assuring readers, would eventually be resolved. Not until the final pages of the novel is it revealed that Boy Fenwick had syphilis, but was so madly in love with tawny, nineteen-year-old Iris that he married her anyway. Overcome by shame or maddened by paresis, he took his life before touching her.

Iris reacts to this incredible situation by resolving to save Boy's reputation in the eyes of the world. "He died for purity," she announces cryptically, thus encouraging the belief that Boy had found her to be a nonvirgin and had erased himself because of her impurity. Further, Iris sets out to "prove" her impurity by propelling herself into nymphomania as fast as possible. Friends cut her dead, the world calls her a tramp, but Iris wears her promiscuity gallantly. "I have given myself, in disdain, in desire, with disgust, with delight," she brags. "I thought I would destroy myself with love's delight."

From childhood Iris has adored Napier "Naps" Herenden, whose haughty, titled father did not consider her a worthy match for his beloved son. Never has promiscuous Iris said, "I love you" to husband or lover. The sacred words are reserved for Naps alone.

After the death of her second, or soldier, husband in Ireland, Iris reappears in London. She is twenty-nine, shingle-bobbed in the best style of the chic, emancipated woman. The narrator of the novel lives in a town-house apartment under her twin brother, who is a near-hopeless alcoholic. Driving a yellow Hispano-Suiza and wearing a green hat, Iris visits the brother, to find him in a stupor. The narrator meets her on the stairs and invites her into his apartment, where the two converse until dawn. Then wanton Iris slips between the sheets of his bed and he follows. "She was a woman until she touched you," he reveals. "Then she became woman, and you water. Touching her, you touched all desire."

Arising from their bout of love, the narrator, several years younger than Iris Storm, is madly in love. "We have begun at the wrong end," he says plaintively, "but can't we work back?" To Iris, though, he is just a male, another one-night stand; besides, she craves friendship more than love. She tells him about the curse of nymphomania, calling it "the Beast." She goes on, "My shame must not shame you. . . . I am the meanest of all, she who destroys her body because she must, she who hates the thing she is, she who loathes the thing she does. . . ."

Still, the smitten narrator keeps bumping into Iris Storm as the novel penetrates the exclusive Mayfair set populated by the likes of Lady Pynte, Angela Ammon, Venice Pollen, Trehawke Tush, Hugh Cypress, and Colonel Victor Duck, "who has taken to caddishness like a drug, and goes on taking increasing doses."

Napier Herenden is included, of course; he is on the verge of marrying the wealthy child Venice Pollen. Naps does not know that Iris is in London until a few nights before the wedding when his snappy roadster passes her sleek yellow Hispano. There is a wild screaming of brakes as the two recognize one another. Even so, the marriage to Venice takes place on schedule.

The locale shifts to *haut monde* Paris where our narrator —like Arlen an author—spots the distinctive Hispano standing forlorn and idle. He tracks Iris to a hospital-convent, where she lies near death from septic poisoning. Can this be caused by childbirth, miscarriage, or abortion? Once again the author, master of sly suspense, refuses to tell. Finally it turns out to be a miscarriage of Napier's child, conceived on the eve of his wedding. A surprise visit from Naps saves her life, and soon Iris Storm is back in London, as dashing as ever while mingling with the Bright Young People soon to be immortalized by Evelyn Waugh. "Are you happy?" the narrator asks her. "Unbearably," she responds.

Iris is so utterly ravishing that Napier resolves to leave his child bride and run away with her. Yet Iris holds back because she too is fond of Venice. Still, illicit love conquers all, and secret plans for an elopement commence. Before leaving, Iris visits Napier's stern father for a final showdown. Naps and Venice also turn up, as does the narrator. In a supercharged scene, Iris at last reveals the secret of Boy Fenwick's suicide. Purged by this confession, she nobly whispers to

Naps that Venice is pregnant (not true) and dashes to her Hispano. Driving crazily off, she crashes into a big tree. On this fatal night, as on the first, she wears a green hat.

Numerous factors contributed to the fame and fortune of *The Green Hat*, which as a play brought stardom to Katharine Cornell and then served as a film vehicle for Greta Garbo. The book is written in cozy, whispery fashion, as if the urbane author adored every word. It also took readers inside a dazzling Mayfair set which few Americans knew existed. There are occasional flashes of wit, as when one man offers to lend money to another. "That's setting friendship to music," quips the recipient. Yet there are sentences rivaling Hergesheimer's in clumsiness—"I couldn't, you can see, not do anything just then."

Few reviewers dared stress the sex content of *The Green Hat*. In *The Bookman*, John Farrar said, "It puzzles, it dazzles, it is embroidered with gaiety of color and of phrase." Of course, *The Green Hat* was not a very sexy novel by later standards. One reviewer called Iris Storm "the first horizontal heroine," yet she is actually pictured in that position only once. For the most part, her promiscuity is a matter of gossip, a juicy topic of conversation for friend and foe.

Yet this sexuality was more than enough for the time. Most shocking was the fact that it involved a female, rather than the traditional male. There was also homosexuality (Iris' weak brother), abortion (as a possibility for Iris' illness), and the final fillip of Boy Fenwick's venereal disease. Given all this, word of mouth took over where critics feared to speak, and turned *The Green Hat* into the shocker of mid-decade.

Examples of lowered standards could also be found in nonfiction, where Bruce Barton's *The Man Nobody Knows* stood out as the most popular book of the Calvin Coolidge era.

This was perhaps fitting, since Coolidge as President had said, "The business of America is business." On his part,

Bruce Barton set out to portray Jesus Christ as a kind of super-Babbitt, nothing less than the Father of Modern Business. Author Barton was the handsome, dynamic head of the advertising agency Batton and Barton, which later became Batton, Barton, Durstine, and Osborn (a name said by comedian Fred Allen to sound like a trunk falling downstairs).

Like Michael Arlen, Barton acted as narrator of his book, presenting himself as an anonymous advertising hotshot who in Sunday School days decided Jesus Christ was a weakling and sissy. This remained his opinion until, amidst the turmoil of an advertising campaign, he suddenly thought, "Only strong, magnetic men can inspire great enthusiasm and build great organizations. Yet Jesus built the greatest organization of all. It is extraordinary!"

With this, he sets out to prove that Jesus Christ was really a booster, go-getter and—if you will—big butter-and-egg man. His chapters examine the Son of God as "The Executive," "The Outdoor Man," "The Sociable Man," "His Method," "His Advertisements," "The Founder of Modern Business," and "The Master." Jesus, he concludes, was tops in all these fields. Rather than a sissy he was—why, proof lies in the Bible!—a hard-working carpenter who not only developed great physical strength at his job but drove the money changers from the temple by a display of muscle flexing.

According to Barton, Jesus was no sensitive loner, but an outgoing greeter whose powers as an after-dinner speaker and general exhorter rivaled those of George F. Babbitt. Highly annoying to the author is the widely held belief that Jesus lacked a sense of humor. "Listen, hear his laugh," he begs readers, and goes on to castigate a Roman governor for allegedly calling Jesus "a humorless kill joy."

Barton most admires Jesus' executive ability. "He picked twelve men from the bottom ranks and forged them into an organization that conquered the world," he enthuses. Elaborating on this, the dedicated author shows Jesus not only as a vigorous backslapper and million-laughs guy, but as a master organizer who fully recognizes the potential of advertising and is no small shakes as a grabber of personal publicity. Businessman readers found in Barton's Jesus the fellow they'd most enjoy sitting next to on a train or meeting in a country-club bar; to old ladies he was the young man they'd most like to help them across the street.

Through all this, author Barton markets the inimitable business philosophy of the Twenties as skillfully as the ad world promoted Listerine and Lucky Strikes. Hopping from biblical to modern times, he uses inspirational anecdotes from the lives of Abraham Lincoln, David Lloyd George, and J. P. Morgan. Going from past to present, he cleverly ties the business beliefs of the go-getter to the biblical era:

> *It was very late in the afternoon. . . .*
>
> *If you would like to learn the measure of a man that is the time of day to watch him. We are all half an inch taller in the morning than at night; it is fairly easy to take a large view of things when the mind is rested and the nerves are calm. But the day is a steady drain of small annoyances, and the difference in the size of men becomes hourly more apparent. The little man loses his temper; the big man takes a firmer hold.*
>
> *It was very late in the afternoon in Galilee. . . .*

The vibrant author's master stroke comes as he invents a newspaper called the Capernaum *News* and proves the modernity of Jesus' acts by presenting them in terms of modern headlines:

> PROMINENT TAX COLLECTOR JOINS
> NAZARETH FORCES
> MATTHEW ABANDONS BUSINESS TO PROMOTE
> NEW CULT
> GIVES LARGE LUNCHEON

In case after case, Jesus is measured by up-to-date standards and found a winner. Even his miracles are turned into modern lingo:

PALSIED MAN HEALED
Jesus of Nazareth Claims Right to
Forgive Sins
Prominent Scribes Object
"Blasphemous," Says Leading Citizen
"But I Can Walk Anyway," Healed Man Retorts

"Nowhere," concludes Bruce Barton happily, "is there such a startling example of executive success."

Several rare distinctions adhere to *Gentlemen Prefer Blondes* by Anita Loos, the surprise seller of the final days of 1925. This slight, breezy book ran into forty-five American editions, got translated into thirteen languages, and has been presented to an eager public in play, movie, and musical-comedy form.

Gentlemen Prefer Blondes was so completely of the Jazz Age that probably no previous generation in history could have comprehended it. Yet the world was ripe for the semi-literate diary of wide-eyed Lorelei Lee, dizzy blonde, ex-chorus girl, and present gold digger. To fetching Lorelei "Fate kept on happening." She considered diamonds a girl's best friend, and by her moronic wisdom endeared herself to the reading public.

Hardly less than Iris Storm in *The Green Hat*, Lorelei was a horizontal heroine. True, there are no bed scenes in her book, but Lorelei is unmistakably a kept woman, her fancy upkeep underwritten by Moe Eisman, the Button King. In the book, Moe's expenditures are mostly for travel, since Lorelei persuades him to send her and the brunette Dorothy on a European tour. In Vienna, while visiting "the Central of Europe," she consults Dr. Freud who advises her to cultivate a few inhibitions. When a Frenchman amorously smooches her hand, she thinks, "kissing your hand may make you feel very good, but a diamond bracelet lasts forever."

The story behind *Gentlemen Prefer Blondes* is every bit as captivating as her goofy saga itself. Lorelei was conceived when Anita Loos (Mrs. John Emerson) thought herself in love with H. L. Mencken. One night George Jean Nathan joined the couple, bringing with him a bee's-knees chorus girl—"a witless blonde," Anita thought her. Still, Mencken was fascinated by the girl, not only teasing her into making inane remarks, but his gonads obviously stimulated by her snappy person. As a gamine-type brunette, Anita was every bit as cute as the dumbbell blonde, and felt much annoyed to find Mencken so obviously attracted to the other girl. Why, she asked herself, do gentlemen generally prefer blondes?

The question returned to haunt her a few days later when she and her husband boarded the Twentieth Century Limited for Hollywood. A fellow passenger was the empty-headed blonde, headed west for a screen test. For five days, males on the train (including John Emerson) paid fervent court to the dazzling dumbbell. To relieve her seething feelings, Anita grabbed a pad and pencil to jot down an acidulous personality sketch of her rival.

Back in New York, she showed her word portrait to Mencken, who chided her, "Do you realize, young lady, that you've made fun of sex, which has never before been done in this grand and glorious nation of ours?" Nonetheless, he encouraged her to expand the sketch.

Miss Loos then went abroad, and kept working away at the diary of a traveling gold digger. Henry Sell of *Harper's Bazaar* read her finished manuscript and agreed to publish it in six installments. Ralph Barton was called in to illustrate the series, and sales of the women's magazine skyrocketed as men bought it for Lorelei's stupid-smart wisecracks. T. R. Smith of Boni and Liveright visualized the *Harper's Bazaar* installments in book form, but saw them only as a gag publication for Christmas. If nothing else, the little book would give Liveright editors a unique present to bestow on friends.

Smith ordered a small printing, parceling out the copies to interested co-workers. The rest he had placed on the Christmas counters of bookshops, whence they seemed to vanish in seconds, while the Liveright switchboard buzzed with requests for more. Smith quickly concluded he had a seller, and ordered an edition which did not reach bookstores until after the holidays. Yet for a long time to come, *Gentlemen Prefer Blondes* sold as if Christmas came every day of the year.

While such books kept the reading public occupied, other changes were taking place within the book world.

One was recognition of the existence of ghost writing. Up to now the trick of having a book written to order for a famous person had been accomplished in relative secrecy. Yet as sporting figures like Babe Ruth, actors like Charlie Chaplin, Douglas Fairbanks, and Marie Dressler, and captains of industry, aviators, and Channel swimmers stepped forth as proud authors of books, a public already cynical began to suspect a helping professional hand. Often, the whispers ran, the help was so great that the alleged author never got to read his book until publication day. Even *The New York Times* took a position against ghost writing, defining it as "the practice whereby celebrities who lack the gift for writing may tell their life stories."

One reason for public's wising up was *The Saturday Evening Post*, in which many ghosted books appeared serially. Most of these were written in the glossy, superprofessional style of the *Post*, usually by the skilful technician Wesley Winans Stout. Bowing to widespread suspicions, the *Post* and other magazines occasionally acknowledged the hand of the ghost writer, listing his name with "As told to" in front of it. But the public of the late Twenties remained on the alert for ghost-written books, and with the best of reasons.

Book clubs had also appeared, following Harry Scherman's decision that one book a month would best satisfy his public. The pioneering Book of the Month Club was the result, promoted by the slogan "Handed to You by the Postman, the Book You Intend to Read." Scherman's board of judges included Henry Seidel Canby, Heywood Broun, Christopher Morley, Dorothy Canfield Fisher, and William Allen White.

Their first selection was Sylvia Townsend Warner's novel *Lolly Willowes*, mailed out in April 1926 to 4,740 readers. By the end of the year, membership had increased tenfold. Any good idea deserves its imitator, and within a year the rival Literary Guild had come to life. Its impressive judges were Carl Van Doren, Joseph Wood Krutch, Elinor Wylie, Zona Gale, and Hendrik Willem Van Loon.

Reaction to book clubs was mixed. Naturally, bookstores disliked them, since books at reduced prices mailed directly to readers cut into their business. Then, the authors who railed against standardization in American life saw it being applied to the field of books. Many who lived and labored in the cultural cosmos began to feel that the happiest feature of the early decade had been that readers spontaneously picked their own reading matter.

Advocates of book clubs retaliated by pointing out that more people than ever would now read worthwhile books—a promise fulfilled by the excellent early selections of the two clubs, among them Woodward's *Meet General Grant*, Walter Lippmann's *A Preface to Morals*, Carl Sandburg's *Abraham Lincoln: The Prairie Years*, Francis Hackett's *Henry the Eighth*, Shaw's *Intelligent Woman's Guild to Socialism*, O. E. Rölvaag's *Giants of the Earth*, Stephen Vincent Benét's *John Brown's Body*, Thornton Wilder's *Bridge of San Luis Rey*, and Erich Maria Remarque's *All Quiet on the Western Front*. While scrambling for position in beginning years, selections of the Book of the Month and the Literary Guild were of a quality seldom matched later on.

Still, discriminating publishers like Alfred Knopf continued to believe book clubs debased the taste of readers and established the wrong standards for authors. Informed by Harry Scherman that one of his books had been chosen Book of the Month, Knopf calmly replied, "Well, Harry, please congratulate your staff on having had the taste to make the choice." In other firms, however, a book-club selection usually set off an office celebration, for it brought prosperity and publicity to author and publisher.

Celebrations of another sort were suddenly a prominent part of the scene, as literary cocktail parties reached a peak. For by mid-decade the easy availability of hooch, plus widespread flaunting of the Prohibition law, had made open cocktail parties commonplace.

Possibly the first literary cocktail party in New York, or anywhere, took place early in the decade at the West 95th Street home of Alfred and Blanche Knopf. The Knopfs were in the habit of giving Friday evening soirees at which staple refreshments were sandwiches and fruit punch. Guests did not find this punch stimulating, and one night Thomas Beer and Carl Van Vechten dumped a bottle of gin into the bowl. With this the proceedings livened visibly, but the host was not amused. Choosing to disregard the obvious, he left others to exploit the time-honored affinity between authors and alcohol.

Horace Liveright's "A" parties were usually given in honor of a writer, preferably the lucky fellow with a book published that day. It made both sides happy, for Liveright loved his parties, while authors were flattered by festivities in their honor. Lillian Hellman calls Liveright "the first publisher to understand that writers care less for dollars than for attention."

People didn't "give" parties in the halcyon Twenties—they "threw" or "tossed" them. The fact that Liveright tossed parties for his authors was not lost on talents under contract to other firms, who demanded equal honor from their own publishers. Usually the resulting parties were given in the offices of the firm, with a bar set up in the reception room. Then the fun fanned out into offices, stock rooms, and even closets. Next morning the staff had to retrieve the glasses, and often bodies, left over from the night before.

Among those attending the average literary cocktail party would be the author being honored, his family, relatives, and friends, together with members of the Manhattan literary set who enjoyed the bibulous affairs. It was always a mark of distinction to have Elinor Wylie present, and this lovely lady appeared at more parties than might be expected in view of her considerable output. Among males, brown-bearded, brown-garbed Ernest Boyd was a top favorite, his elegance and wit assuring him a perpetual cluster of admirers. At one party Boyd detected the tones of wisecracking Samuel Hoffenstein above the bedlam and inquired in his velvety brogue, "Is that the voice that launched a thousand quips?"

Others who might be found at worthwhile parties were Carl Van Vechten, Gertrude Atherton, Carl and Irita Van Doren, Henry Seidel Canby, John and Margaret Farrar, W. E. and Helen Woodward, Nancy Hoyt, Konrad Bercovici, Fannie Hurst, Dawn Powell, Amy Loveman, Lewis Gannett, Harrison Smith, May Lamberton Becker, Edna Ferber, Hendrik Willem Van Loon, Frieda Inescourt, Whit Burnett, Thyra Samter Winslow, George Jean Nathan, Anne Parrish, Laurence Stallings, Robert Benchley, Martha Foley, Harry Hansen, Christopher Morley, Anita Loos, Donald Ogden Stewart, Burton Rascoe, and Ben Ray Redman. Ever present was sharp Isabel Paterson, making notes for her weekly "Turns with a Bookworm" column in the *Herald-Tribune.*

To Ben Hecht, a man who attended his quota, the literary cocktail party was "a shower of anecdotes." Others might prefer to say a shower of egos, for under the strident stimulus of bootleg booze, self-love blossomed. One who attended these gatherings with full humility, however, was Ellen Glasgow, author of fifteen novels. Now, at age fifty, she believed her work was becoming stale and she herself losing contact with a lively life. Her antidote was to accept all party invitations in New York, thus mingling as often as possible with younger minds. Her own vigor and charm did much to brighten the affairs she attended, and her next two novels, *The Romantic Comedians* and *She Stoops to Folly,* were sharper than their predecessors. Miss Glasgow credited her gadding about.

Often the author who was the nominal reason for a publisher's bash became the forgotten man as the literati milled about, swapping gossip, anecdotes, and barbs while downing Manhattans, Bronxes, and martinis. Not a few writers of first novels found this well-oiled excitement too much and quickly passed out in convenient chairs.

One budding novelist was the first to turn up at his shindig, and became so nervous that he bolted three quick drinks and passed out on the nearest sofa. Arriving guests found it amusing to drop hats and coats atop the guest of honor, who was all but smothered until a sympathetic young girl noted his limp, dangling hand and uncovered him. He was so grateful that, in time, he married her.

At the opposite extreme stood the kind of party where an overstimulated author chose to neglect the faithful wife who had nursed him through the labor pains of his book. Leaving her in tears, he vanished into the night with one of the female camp followers who at the time pursued writers as vigorously as bobby soxers and groupies later chased movie stars and rock musicians.

Literary cocktail parties appeared especially glamorous to those not invited. Among left outs was a prosperous lawyer named Charles Studin, who had consulted a doctor because his life was losing its zip. "What would you most like to do?" the doctor asked him. Studin made the odd confession that he'd like to attend bookish get-togethers.

The doctor rose to this challenge. "You've got the money," he stated. "If you don't get invited, give 'em." Studin contrived to meet a few writers for whom he threw parties. Then he tossed more for their friends, along with friends of their friends. It was a policy he continued over the next fifteen years.

For all their rich excitements, the literary parties tossed by publishers failed to be rated as the top affairs of the era. This distinction went to the parties tossed by Carl Van Vechten. Indeed, as the Twenties reached mid-point Van Vechten (now that Scott and Zelda had departed) in many ways served as literary symbol of the era. At age forty-five, Carlo more than anyone else appeared to represent the indulgent aspects of his time. "He roared along with the Twenties," writes his biographer Bruce Kellner. Van Vechten himself saluted the decade as "the splendid, drunken Twenties," and went on to boast, "I never went to bed in those days."

Van Vechten was a copious drinker of side cars—equal parts of Cointreau, Cognac, and lemon juice, shake over ice, strain into cocktail glass. One of the fortunate human beings who never suffered a hangover, he drank around the clock and further boasted that he was drunk every day and night during the winter of 1925-6.

The parties tossed by Van Vechten and his wife Fania Marinoff were *crème de la crème* affairs which usually began after the theater and continued into the next day, or days. Top talent was the ideal card of admission, and when in full swing, a Van Vechten party resembled a speakeasy de luxe peopled by literary figures, stage and screen celebrities, prizefighters, dancers, elegant homosexuals, and Lorelei Lee gold diggers.

To Emily Clark of Richmond-in-Virginia, friend Carlo's parties had "an iridescent quality." She recalls one at which George Gershwin sat at the piano tirelessly tinkling and singing his hit songs. In a corner Theodore Dreiser watched broodingly, running a handkerchief through his fingers. Elinor Wylie was present, looking "aloof and lovely." In time, Paul Robeson rose to sing in his pipe-organ voice. James Weldon Johnson followed, reciting his poem "Go Down, Death."

As a host, Carl Van Vechten could be "benevolent and shining." Yet the man who worked so hard to shock his public also enjoyed unsettling guests. There was always a dash of the debauch in Carlo's parties, with some decadent guests eager, with the host's apparent approval, to corrupt anything youthful in skirts or trousers—it hardly mattered which. An adventurous young actress who attended one Van Vechten party said, "I went there in the evening a young girl and came away in the early morning an old woman."

The Champs . . *Ernest Hemingway* .

Lewis . . *Fitzgerald* . . . .

In the early afternoon of February 9, 1926, a vital young man strode along West 48th Street toward the office of Boni and Liveright. Big and broad-shouldered, he had black hair, a small moustache, and (when it appeared) a wide, dimpling grin that sliced across a round, ruddy face to expose shiny white teeth. Even when walking, he radiated an animal vigor, as if so proud of his strong, vibrant body that he could hardly restrain himself from indulging in the jabbing, feinting, and ducking of the shadowboxer.

Ernest Hemingway had arrived that morning from Paris aboard the *Mauretania*. After registering at the Brevoort on lower Fifth Avenue, he was making haste to see Horace Liveright, the publisher who just a few months before had brought out *In Our Time*, Hemingway's book of short stories.

Like every author, Hemingway had expected his first book to make him rich and famous. But it sold only five hundred copies in the first year, and his name was still largely unknown in the United States. Unlike Hemingway, the experienced Liveright had not expected to profit from this volume, but it was considered smart publishing policy to bring out short stories by promising writers in the expectation of cashing in on eventual novels. Though Liveright had printed only thirteen hundred copies of *In Our Time*, he made it an attractive book with a jacket featuring a blurb by Sherwood Anderson and shorter praise from John Dos Passos, Gilbert Seldes, Waldo Frank, and others.

Published late in 1925, *In Our Time* had almost been lost in the inundation of the year's books. Yet it earned a few reviews, one noting the "lean, pleasing, tough resilience of the writing." Another thought Hemingway "drove to the crux of the matter with merciless bareness." Less perceptive minds compared his stories to Sherwood Anderson's, thereby infuriating Hemingway, who still seethed over what he considered the disgraceful deficiencies of *Dark Laughter*.

Liveright had been pleased by the reception given *In Our Time* and congratulated his own astuteness in contracting for the first three books written by this promising resident of the Left Bank; if anything went wrong with one, his firm always had options on another. Liveright's satisfaction increased as he learned by mail that the young author was close to finishing a full-length novel called *The Sun Also Rises*, which was to deal with the life of Hemingway's fellow expatriates in Paris and elsewhere.

So Liveright was astounded to receive, following publication of *In Our Time*, the manuscript of a completely unexpected and undiscussed Hemingway book. Titled *The Torrents of Spring*, it was an obvious parody of Sherwood Anderson, even though occasionally it contained typical, Hemingwayesque lines like "Say, are you a fairy?"

In the smug words of the author, this new effort "made a bum out of Anderson." Usually a slow writer, Hemingway had completed his unlikely effort in a ten-day burst of mixed inspiration and rancor. Some of the friends to whom he read the work—authors liked to read aloud in those days—considered it funny, Dos Passos among them. But all of them, together with his wife, begged Hemingway to drop the project, especially in view of Anderson's feelings. Yet he persisted, and dispatched the manuscript to New York.

Torrents of Spring placed Liveright in an acutely uncomfortable position. Next to Dreiser, Sherwood Anderson was probably the most respected domestic author on his list. More than this, *Dark Laughter* had been a top seller of 1925.

Nor did the Liveright editors consider *Torrents of Spring* a successful parody, or even a very good book. Still, Liveright and his staff were not unduly concerned over the manuscript, remaining serene in the belief that the contract with Hemingway gave them the right to publish his first three novels, no matter what happened. Thus emboldened, Liveright cabled Hemingway, "REJECTING TORRENTS OF SPRING. IMPATIENTLY AWAITING SUN ALSO RISES. WRITING FULLY."

Ernest Hemingway failed to share his publisher's opinion. Instead, he thought—or professed to think—that rejection of any one book by the firm abrogated the whole three-book contract. Some of his Paris intimates believed Hemingway had worked overtime to convince himself of this, and that he wrote *Torrents of Spring* largely as a contract breaker, with the hidden purpose of abrogating the Liveright arrangement. He had become friendly with Scott Fitzgerald, and appeared envious of Scott's warm relationship with avuncular Maxwell Perkins of Scribner's. Louis Bromfield had also praised Alfred Harcourt of Harcourt Brace, and Hemingway may have considered such benevolent publishers capable of a closer rapport with a young writer. Or he may have doubted that Liveright did a good job of selling *In Our Time*.

There is also the consideration that, from this point on, Hemingway made a policy of turning against those who aided him. "He seemed determined to prove to the world that he needed no help," writes Myrick Land in *The Fine Art of Literary Mayhem*. Hemingway had commenced this pattern by turning against Anderson, the man who had encouraged him to write in Chicago, persuaded him to settle in Paris, and written a glowing appreciation of *In Our Time*. Soon Hemingway would turn on Gertrude Stein, with whom he had enjoyed a warm if somewhat peculiar friendship. Miss Stein privately considered young Hemingway a homosexual because he paraded his masculinity so blatantly and talked so much sex. She was also inclined to join Alice B. Toklas and other of her friends in objecting to the way Hemingway encased his outsize feet (they were like snowshoes, someone said) in heavy mountain boots, then rested them on her furniture. But despite these irritations, she admired the aspiring author and was quick to see the intrinsic value of his work. He repaid the compliment by vastly admiring her—for a time.

Hemingway also worked hard to find ways of resenting Ford Madox Ford, the man who employed him in Paris and printed his early short stories in *transatlantic review*. And with *Torrents of Spring*, Hemingway might be said to be turning against Liveright, who had the courage to publish his first book.

In the still uncompleted pages of *The Sun Also Rises*, the vindictive author was also squaring accounts with Harold Loeb, the close friend who had brought him to Liveright and carried the manuscript of *In Our Time* across the Atlantic. *The Sun Also Rises* contained a vicious portrait of Loeb, under the name of Robert Cohn. Loeb's offense had been that he dared bed down with a woman Hemingway (though a faithful husband and father) liked to consider his own platonic property. In real life her name was Lady Duff Twysden; in the novel she is promiscuous Lady Brett Ashley. Incredibly, Hemingway had met Lady Duff through Michael Arlen, who on occasion visited the Left Bank to ascertain how his Bohemian fellow craftsmen fared.

By January 1926, Ernest Hemingway's literary life had grown so tangled that a quick trip to New York seemed to be the only solution. And now, immediately after landing, the burly author was proceeding toward a showdown with Horace Liveright. Yet it was not much of a showdown. Liveright, riding high with *An American Tragedy* and *Gentlemen Prefer Blondes*, was apparently too busy to consider Hemingway a major problem.

Instead, the two men took an immediate liking to one another, and after a short talk adjourned to the nearby speakeasy for drinks. But even in this friendly atmosphere Hemingway was adamant on the contract matter. Liveright, who in his own opinion had ample reason for anger, did not seem disposed to fight for his rights. When the two parted, Hemingway had achieved his desire—to all intents and purposes, he was an author without a publisher.

Next morning he had an appointment with Maxwell Perkins of Scribner's, an editor who proved as compatible as Fitzgerald predicted. Perkins approved *The Torrents of Spring*—Donald Ogden Stewart had brought it to him from the Liveright office—and was prepared to contract for it and *The Sun Also Rises,* paying an advance against royalties of fifteen hundred dollars and offering the unusually generous royalty rate of a straight 15 percent. Hemingway was pleased but still felt obligated to see Alfred Harcourt, the man extolled by Louis Bromfield. Harcourt miffed the rugged writer by praising the talents of Glenway Wescott, an expatriate Hemingway despised as effete (Wescott considered Hemingway "an ugly customer"). He and Harcourt thus failed to strike it off, and by nightfall Ernest Hemingway was safely in the Scribner fold.

Ernest Hemingway had been in New York twice before. The first time came immediately after the war as he hobbled down the gangplank of a troop transport with his bad leg wound. The second had been in December 1921 as he and bride Hadley sailed for Paris. Two brief visits had not made Hemingway overly fond of New York; nor, indeed, was he attached to the United States. He respected the metropolis as a shining symbol of a materialistic era but thought it did terrible things to its inhabitants—"the damndest-looking people," he called them.

In view of such feelings, he did not expect to enjoy his 1926 visit and planned to remain only a week. To his surprise, however, he found the city "joyously hectic," a spot for hearty reunions with friends from Paris, the war, and the Middle West. Everyone he encountered seemed to know a bootlegger or possess a speakeasy card. He met "any hell's amount of people," among them Dorothy Parker, Robert

Benchley, and elegant (but never effete) Ernest Boyd. With the last named, he consumed three full shakers of cocktails before a notable luncheon. He went to prizefights at Madison Square Garden, saw the Broadway production of *The Great Gatsby*, tasted the delights of Greenwich Village, and became infatuated with beauteous Elinor Wylie. When he departed after a sojourn of nineteen days, the poetess accompanied him to the midnight sailing of his liner.

In Paris, Hemingway not only had to finish *The Sun Also Rises* but also cope with a distressing family situation. For he had decided to leave his first wife and their child—was he thereby getting even with helpful Hadley? He planned to take as his second wife a woman who had insinuated herself into the domestic circle as the best friend of all and then, with terrierlike persistence, torn Hemingway loose from Hadley.

By mid-March Hemingway wrote the final lines of *The Sun Also Rises*. To him, the act of writing involved such deep concentration that he was often exhausted after two hours of work. (Reputedly, he envied Scott Fitzgerald his ability to work for long periods, amidst distractions.) For Hemingway, each sentence was an intense search for perfection—to find "the truest sentence you know." He also maintained, "The only writing that was any good was what you made up, what you imagined."

Yet in *The Sun Also Rises* and other novels he rudely shattered this last edict by writing of actual happenings, with recognizable characters. The events of *The Sun Also Rises* were lived—or endured—in July 1925, as Hemingway led a group of Paris cronies to the bullfights at Pamplona, Spain. Several years before, Ernest and Hadley had spent an idyllic vacation there, but this time everything turned sour. The novel begins in Paris, where identities are established, moves to a masculine fishing interlude in the Pyrenees, and winds up in festive Pamplona. Except for certain dramatic moments, the Hemingway characters speak tersely, keep emotions under tight control, and drink heavily. Indeed, there was so much consumption of alcohol in the book that Sinclair Lewis, no mean imbiber himself, accused Hemingway of "extolling drinking as one of man's eternal ways to happiness."

In *This Side of Paradise*, Scott Fitzgerald had shocked the world by picturing indiscriminate kissing. With Hemingway's characters, the pastimes were drinking and fornication. Thus, if Fitzgerald put America's Younger Generation on the map, Hemingway did the same for the Lost Generation. Their credo, according to him, was "a cool manner under stress and drinks." Far more than the native Younger Generation, these Americans-in-Paris considered themselves exceptional, uniquely aware of what has been called "the pathos of post-war experience." Living close to onetime battlefields, among a population whose males had been decimated, they were constantly reminded of the futilities of the so-called Great War.

This only sharpened the disillusionment they brought from the United States. Many of them also nursed feelings of guilt about abandoning their homeland, and as a consequence were fiercely critical of it. Wrote Kay Boyle, "In America, each citizen functions with pride in the American conspiracy against the individual." The noisy hordes of Yankee tourists who had started to invade Gay Paree during summer seasons only increased the expatriates' distaste for their land of birth.

Living in the pleasantest city on earth, with time a-plenty and complete freedom to do anything they desired, Hemingway's expatriates seemed to do little but drink and discourse on the futility of life. This is inherent in the book's title, which derives from Ecclesiastes—"The sun also ariseth, and the sun goeth down, and hasteth to the place where he arose." To live this life successfully required less accomplishment than attitude—coolness under stress and liquor. Nothing was new to the Hemingway expatriate, so why not dwell in the splendid isolation of the lost? The "hero" of *The Sun Also Rises* is Jake Barnes, an unfortunate whose genitals were shot off in the war. As Jake saw life, "I had the feeling as in a nightmare of it all being something repeated, something that I had been through and that I must go through again."

In one of his short stories, Hemingway has a girl say, "I

don't feel . . . I just know things." Hemingway's Lost Generation seemed to "just know"—nothing else was worth learning, achieving, or really liking. The trick was to live on the surface, speaking quick words which never betrayed emotion, trying to get all pleasure possible from life within the tight sphere of the spiritually lost. It was good to be slightly drunk; once in a while it was better to be drunk and briefly in bed with a lost soul of the opposite sex.

In *The Sun Also Rises*, Hemingway drew on the lives, appearance, and philosophies of many early Left Bank figures. In addition to Harold Loeb and Lady Duff Twysden, those easily recognized include Ford Madox Ford, Waldo Peirce, Donald Ogden Stewart, Glenway Wescott, Robert McAlmon, Laurence Vail, Allan Ross MacDougall, and Harry Crosby.

Few were treated kindly; next to Loeb, the cruelest pen portrait is that of Harold Stearns, who appears as Harvey Stone. The onetime editor of *Civilization in the United States* had proved a conspicuous example of the American destroyed by Left Bank life. Stearns eked out an existence by writing a racetrack column for the Paris edition of the Chicago *Tribune*, under the by-line "Peter Pickem." He also borrowed money on a grandiose scale. Nightly he drank himself into a stupor while seated in the Dome or Select, usually passing out with a pile of saucers indicating drinks consumed rising before him like the Eiffel Tower. American tourists who recognized him were able to parade their erudition by saying, "There lies Civilization in the United States."

The manuscript of *The Sun Also Rises*—ninety thousand lean words—reached the Scribner office early in April 1926. After reading it Maxwell Perkins declared, "No one could conceive of a book with more life in it." He passed the typescript along to Charles Scribner, and here, perhaps, is the genesis of a story which delighted the publishing world for years to come. Anxious to be a fearless trailblazer, Hemingway had used a few four-letter words in his book. Scribner was upset and, as he read, jotted down the offending words on a desk calendar. When he went to lunch, his prim, spinsterish secretary began to straighten his desk and her eyes fell on the calendar heading "Things To Do Today" and the list below—"piss, . . . shit . . . fuck."

In the south of France, Hemingway was nervous about his first novel. He showed a carbon to Scott Fitzgerald, who recommended removal of a first section giving the background of Jake and others. Hemingway did so; it was the last time he considered Scott, or any writer, worthy to counsel him. The novel was published in the fall, and Hemingway got upset because initial reviews focused on his casual, hard-boiled characters. His intention, he declared, had been to write "a damn tragedy with the earth abiding forever as the hero."

Few got this particular message, but his fellow writers were vastly impressed by the stunning bareness of his prose, while the reading public was titillated by his characters' easy immorality. Some were offended, with a critic citing "extreme moral sordidness." Author Robert Herrick took it upon himself to declare, "It would not be too strong to call this book mere garbage."

Among culture hounds, however, the book was a sensation. On college campuses, girls began to pattern attire and attitude, if not morals, after dashing, defiant Lady Brett. Boys tried to talk in terse understatement. Yet with all this *The Sun Also Rises* had no great sale. In its first year only twenty-three thousand copies were disposed of, a good but not great sale for a first novel with a sensational theme. Hemingway, of course, had expected the book to make his fortune. When it failed, even at a straight 15 percent royalty, he followed other versatile authors of the day by beginning work on a volume of short stories to be called *Men Without Women*.

Disappointment with sales never caused Ernest Hemingway to depreciate his own gifts. He fully realized that his terse style had charted a new course in fiction writing; as the French say, he had broken the language. Novelists on both sides of the Atlantic were attempting to imitate him, though some were not, and in Manhattan a novel by P. J. Wolfson was promoted by ads which read "WOLFSON IS NOT HEM-INGWAY, WOLFSON IS WOLFSON!" But critics hailed Hemingway's prose style as truly individual, with one stating:

> *That style is stripped bare; it is hard, simple, direct, staccato. Monotonous when thus described, it is in Hemingway's hands surprisingly flexible . . . and he turns it into passages of great power.*

And another:

> *Like a mental surgeon in a sardonic mood, Hemingway cuts away ideals, introspection, analysis, subtlety, national or class roots, and leaves his characters reduced to the simplest terms.*

Hemingway never saw fit to explain the origins of his breakthrough prose. Instead, he left some to believe it might derive from the city room of the Kansas City *Star*, where basic rules were "Use short sentences—Use short paragraphs —Use vigorous English—Be positive, not negative."

Others credited the influence of Gertrude Stein, for in early Paris days Hemingway had persuaded Ford Madox Ford to publish her *Making of Americans* in his *transatlantic review*. This work had been written in 1911, and Hemingway laboriously assisted Miss Stein in making a new handwritten copy legible to the printer. Miss Stein thought this tiresome chore had shaped the Hemingway style—"He learned the value of repetition in writing," she said. Still others traced his inspiration to admiration for the unencumbered language of Spain.

While the world wondered, Hemingway remained secure in the personal knowledge that he was good—no, not good, the *best*! The burly fellow who liked to shadowbox as he walked enjoyed challenging other males (even short ones with glasses) to bouts of fisticuffs. He thought and talked in prizefighter parlance, and knew that the word for him was "champion." In the writing racket, Hemingway considered himself champ.

Yet the world of the 1920's did not regard him as such, and would not until 1929, when A *Farewell to Arms* raised him to the big time. It is odd indeed that Hemingway, who in retrospect seems to dominate the era, was still a hero mainly to other writers and to the restless young. Instead, the recognized champ during nine tenths of the decade was Sinclair Lewis. This fact was never truer than in the years 1926 and 1927, for during this period Red Lewis carried on in a manner thoroughly consonant with the Era of Wonderful Nonsense.

All across the nation Americans were drinking their heads off, impelled by reasons like incredible Wall Street paper profits, the general unpopularity of the Prohibition law, and the demoralizing obbligato of crime that accompanied Prohibition. For these and other reasons, Sinclair Lewis was likewise consuming far more than his personal share of bootleg hooch. One particular reason, naturally, was his personal life. Sinclair and Grace Hegger Lewis still teetered on the brink of divorce, with neither quite daring to jump off the edge of the ledge. For long periods they lived apart, then came together for attempted reconciliations which ended in fiercer conflict.

Observers of these domestic battles accorded them the status of draw. Lewis was rude to his wife in public, and sometimes made amorous passes at other women before her eyes. Grace, on the other hand, possessed a cutting tongue which made a worthy opponent. She had met a man actually named Casanova who seemed anxious to marry her if she ever quit Lewis. In lucid moments, Lewis realized this would be the best solution. At others, he put his head in her lap and sobbed out impossible hopes for the future.

Lewis lived in terror of solitude and when not residing with Grace, preferred to live in hotels—he could meet drinking companions of both sexes in the lobby, while it was easy for a steady procession of friends and admirers to find his suite. At these gatherings Lewis was ever the dominant figure, in perpetual motion as he leaped from his favorite perch on the corner of the bed to test a chair for a moment, then pace up and down while giving his latest imitation of Calvin Coolidge. When, inevitably, he passed out, friends either tucked him in bed or continued the festivities over his prone body. Stories of this dedicated drinking spread, and quite a few Americans were aware that the foremost novelist of the era was, in Mark Schorer's careful words, "a considerable drunkard."

Lewis further reflected the Turbulent Twenties by manifesting an urge to make fast money. All at once the writer whose literary integrity had been exceptional since 1920 made up his mind to write a piece of inferior fiction, certain to sell because of his name. Yet money alone may not have been the basis for this decision. Lewis perhaps envied the way authors like Scott Fitzgerald and Hemingway put their own experiences into books.

In 1925 he and his doctor brother had been allowed to accompany a Canadian government agent on his annual swing through the Indian reservations and settlements of Saskatchewan and Manitoba. This was known as one of the loneliest and most rugged expeditions on earth, and Lewis hoped for "a long and husky rest." He was the first world-famous author ever to pass through the Canadian Northland, and in towns en route booster clubs lionized him, the members pouring potent beverages in his honor. Then, deep in the wilderness, the absence of booze and conviviality upset the would-be explorer, and he abruptly quit the party.

Nevertheless, he had penetrated partway into a territory familiar only to the most robust adventurers, and the temptation to utilize the background in a hastily written book proved tempting. *Pictorial Review* had offered him fifty thousand dollars for the serial rights to his next novel, and he determined to write a quickie with a Saskatchewan background—"a swell piece of cheese to grab off some easy gravy."

The result was *Mantrap*, which *Pictorial Review* read in manuscript and flatly rejected. However, *Collier's* bought it for $42,500, and Hollywood grabbed the book for a film starring pert Clara Bow and gawky Ernest Torrance. Today

Mantrap is all but forgotten; if not the worst book Sinclair Lewis ever wrote, it was his worst in the Golden Twenties.

With *Mantrap* behind—for better or worse—the tempestuous author began to research *Elmer Gantry*, his fourth major work of the decade and a real challenge to his skill. After finishing three books in luxury hotels, thatched English cottages, Swiss chalets, and Italian lakeside villas, Lewis was once again writing in his native land, and it proved a task unlikely to sooth the spirits of a man prone to personal frenzies.

Like H. L. Mencken—to whom *Elmer Gantry* was eventually dedicated—Lewis had only contempt for religion and its American practitioners. The two men doggedly believed that few, if any, men of the cloth truly believed in God, but were only bamboozling the public and obtaining soft livings by spreading the Holy Scripture.

They detested particularly those evangelists who used extrovert personalities and glib tongues to sell religion to their flocks and often raised them to heights of ecstacy. Such types were to be found in all denominations, with the possible exception of the Roman Catholic and High Episcopal. Most of all, Lewis and Mencken hated the religious revivalists who pitched tents on baseball diamonds or vacant lots, then exhorted the faithful to be washed in the blood of the Lamb. The character of preacher Elmer Gantry, a rich compound of all these, was not likely to be a pleasant mix.

In piecing together *Elmer Gantry*, Lewis decided not to do his research among topflight evangelists like Billy Sunday, Aimee Semple McPherson, or even Uldine Utley, a girl revivalist. Rather, he sought out those of lesser fame, picking Kansas City as his hub of operations. So great was Lewis' reputation, as well as the nation's worship of celebrities, that local clergymen gave the warmest of welcomes to the irreverent satirist. He stayed at the homes of several for long periods, took long auto trips with others.

Finally, he set up headquarters in the Ambassador Hotel, where more clergymen swarmed to see him. He immediately plied them with drinks and extracted priceless bits of data while they were in varying stages of inebriation. Actress Ethel Barrymore, temporary resident of the Ambassador, has recalled:

> ↭ *On the way to my suite, I would have to pass the open door of his. It was always full of ministers of every denomination whom he was bullying, in the hope, I suppose, of extracting something for his book. He would stride around the room, pointing a finger at one of them after another, and saying, "You know you don't believe in God."*

For a man who loved drinking himself, as well as mimicking his fellowman, this added up to enjoyable research. Soon Lewis had built up a store of mock sermons, a few of which appeared on the pages of the novel. Meanwhile, newspaper reporters kept tireless track of him. One Sunday a friendly preacher gave him an opportunity to speak from the pulpit at an informal evening forum. Lewis was delighted by an offer which, he said, "gave him a chance to speak to papa God." Mounting the pulpit, he ostentatiously took out his watch and gave God Almighty fifteen minutes to prove His existence by striking him dead. Newspapers erroneously reported this provocative episode taking place at a Sunday morning service, and cries of outrage resounded to the East Coast, where *The New York Times* editorialized on blasphemy.

A larger tidal wave of Sinclair Lewis publicity swept the land as he refused the Pulitzer Prize for *Arrowsmith*. Here was a moment he had anticipated for five years, since the Prize had been snatched from *Main Street* in what Lewis called "a burglary." His anger had mounted in 1923, when *Babbitt* was passed over. Lewis now heard through the literary grapevine that *Arrowsmith* would win the prize in 1926 and chortled, "I am ready for them."

When the award duly arrived, he rejected it in a letter which claimed that literary prizes ruined the integrity of writers. Citing the baleful influence of the French Academy, he went on, "Only by regularly refusing the Pulitzer Prize can novelists keep such a power from being permanently set up over them." Never before had anyone refused a Pulitzer

Prize, with its thousand dollars of convenient cash, and the United States was agog.

Lewis wrote *Elmer Gantry* in Pequot, Minnesota (where folk from all over his native state came to look at him), and in New York hotel suites usually full of bibulous companions. Completing the book just before Christmas 1926, he joined his wife in Washington for the holidays. Now came their final breakup, and shortly after, Lewis set off alone for England.

While overseas he learned that the American clergy, which had always helped Mencken by overreacting shrilly to his blasts, was according him the same favor. Advance proofs of *Elmer Gantry* had been sent to one Kansas City preacher who had opened his home to Lewis. He responded by calling in reporters and, after claiming that the novel was full of unspecified errors, stated that Lewis had been drunk through his entire Kansas City sojourn; that Sunday he rose to deliver a sermon on the text "Ben-hadad was . . . drunk." National headlines were increased as Billy Sunday got hold of a set of galleys and branded Lewis "Satan's cohort." Hugely encouraged by this, Harcourt, Brace went ahead to order a first printing of 140,000 hard-cover copies, the largest edition ever.

Lewis returned from abroad a few days after publication to feast his eyes on a sight permitted few authors. His publisher had taken five billboards in mid-Manhattan to promote the book. *Elmer Gantry* had also been selected by the Book of the Month Club. First-day reviewers found Elmer a slanted, one-dimensional figure, and saw little worth in him, but they admitted that, in the lesser characters and in his teeming background, Sinclair Lewis was his old, stimulating self.

Then criticism was swept aside by a torrent of news stories and editorials which made the book a number-one topic of conversation across the country. *Gantry* was quickly banned in Boston, while Sauk Center's most respected preacher attacked it, thus returning Harry Sinclair Lewis to the local doghouse. Lewis personally received bales of hate mail of the type usually addressed to Mencken.

It was hectic, it was glorious fun!—and for several months Sinclair Lewis reveled in it. Then he again sought refuge in Europe. He had left Grace for good—or she had left him— but neither seemed in a rush for a divorce. This remained the situation until Lewis set eyes on the classic beauty of foreign correspondent Dorothy Thompson in Berlin. Suddenly he could not get his divorce fast enough.

Scott and Zelda Fitzgerald returned to the United States with little Scottie in December 1926. This was a visit more remarkable for its episodes than its accomplishments.

In Paris, Scott had assuaged disappointment over sales of *The Great Gatsby* by increased drinking—though some might have believed this impossible. After week-long benders he sometimes woke up in places like Brussels, with no recollection of arriving. He sometimes drank until his face turned dead white, his eyes rolled up into his head, his skin pulled tight, and his pores oozed perspiration. Hemingway witnessed one of these seizures and was appalled. A closer friend of Scott's assured Hemingway they were routine and hauled the inebriate home to bed.

At long last, Scott could be labeled an alcoholic, the kind of person unable to control his need for drink. It has been said that the five stages of drunkenness are jocose, bellicose, morose, lachrymose, and comatose. Scott covered all these. He knew it and often acknowledged introductions by saying, "I'm very glad to meet you—you know, I'm an alcoholic." He was especially defensive about the changes time and alcohol had wrought in his once shining image as laureate of the Jazz Age. If anyone brought up *This Side of Paradise,* he might snarl, "If you mention that book again, I'll knock your block off!"

Meanwhile, Zelda was pointed toward actual madness. Shortly after meeting Hemingway, Scott had proudly taken

Ernest home to meet her. It was not a happy inspiration, for as Hemingway left, he took his host aside to say, "But, Scott, you realize, don't you, that she's crazy."

Among other things, Zelda was intrigued by the idea of *chaos*. She liked to explain that she drank so much because "the world is chaos and when I drink I'm chaotic." After drinking to a point where friends feared she had dt's, she shrieked, "I want chaos, I want chaos!"

Yet it was hard at this point to tell which of the Fitzgeralds was the drunkard and which mad. Mary and Padraic Colum, then in Paris, couldn't. "Each seemed as deranged as the other," Colum has said.

One night on the Riviera, Zelda decided Isadora Duncan was making passes at Scott and suddenly flung herself over a parapet and down a flight of stone steps. With the luck of the inebriated (or the insane), she suffered no more than scraped knees. Scott matched this unbridled behavior during a taxi ride in Paris when he began stuffing his mouth with hundred franc notes (then worth about twenty dollars) and spitting them out the window. The cab driver stood it as long as he could then braked the taxi to a halt and rushed back to retrieve the money. With this, Scott commandeered the cab and drove wildly toward the Seine. A companion on the rear seat finally wrestled the wheel away from him.

Scott was working erratically on a novel dealing with the curious subject of matricide; some thought he had been pointed in this grim direction by reading *An American Tragedy*. He and Zelda were anxious to return home, if only for a visit, but as usual lacked the wherewithal, "We want to come back, but we want to come back with money saved, and so far we haven't any," Scott wrote John Peale Bishop.

Then from Hollywood came an offer for Scott to write the scenario of a film starring comedienne Constance Talmadge. Arriving in New York, the pair hastened through the temptations of the metropolis, and on the West Coast made the exhilarating discovery that the film capital rated them as visiting royalty.

With this, the two began enacting the roles they had played

in New York during the early part of the decade. Self-enchanted, usually drunk, they amused themselves by outrageously teasing and insulting people. Once they told the egotistical artist James Montgomery Flagg, "God, but you look old!" Even in Hollywood such antics seemed out of date—this might be the Era of Wonderful Nonsense, but the nonsense had a more sophisticated flavor than before. All at once Scott and Zelda Fitzgerald seemed a trifle passé.

Again, it was impossible to tell which was drunk or sane. One day Zelda piled her clothes in the bathtub and set them afire. At a party Scott, lurchingly drunk, collected the ladies' pocketbooks and compacts from the bedroom and took them to the kitchen. There he placed them in a pot, emptied a can of tomato paste on top, and set the pot on a lighted burner. He was gleefully stirring this mess when the stench summoned the other guests.

In France, while Scott was working hardest on *The Great Gatsby*, Zelda had become interested in a dashing French aviator. To break up this illicit romance, Scott had locked his wife in a room. Scott's turn came in Hollywood, where he became infatuated with the eighteen-year-old movie actress Lois Moran. His own word for their relationship was "affair," which might mean anything. But it was upsetting to Zelda, if only because Lois Moran was ten years younger and a beauty.

But Scott's real mistake in Hollywood was to treat his film assignment lightly—he later admitted being "confident to the point of conceit." His final scenario for Constance Talmadge was curtly rejected by the studio. This was a multiple tragedy, for Scott had always been interested in screen writing; had he succeeded in this one project, the high-paying career of script writer would have opened up for him just as talking pictures came in. Instead he goofed, and his failure was known all over Hollywood.

The Fitzgeralds quit California ingloriously, actually crawling on hands and knees to their train compartment in an effort to slip away undetected. Yet one member of the film colony was sorry to see them go. Delicious Lois Moran telegraphed to the Santa Fé Chief: "BOOTLEGGERS GONE OUT OF BUSINESS. COTTON CLUB CLOSED. ALL FLAGS AT HALF MAST . . . BOTTLES OF LOVE TO YOU BOTH."

In the East, they leased a Southern mansion called Ellerslie, outside Wilmington, Delaware—a region appealing to Fitzgerald because of his kinship with Francis Scott Key. Scott was past thirty, "and sore as hell about it." He talked a lot about the matricide novel, but did little work on it. It was still possible for him to make thirty thousand dollars a year from his short stories, most of them for *The Saturday Evening Post* at twenty-five hundred dollars apiece. Yet as usual the work depressed him. His drunkenness at this point was described as "sardonic and sadistic." Twice he was jailed for public intoxication, and fights with Zelda increased in bitterness and frequency.

In the midst of this, Zelda began acting in a way that could really be called demented—no doubt the Lois Moran episode had provided the flame to ignite the tinder of her madness. Scott's infatuation had been bad enough, but now during domestic brawls he kept rubbing into Zelda that young Lois was making something of *her* life. Zelda had written a few clever short stories and sketches; some friends thought she wrote as well as Scott. She had also tried painting. But for the most part, she appeared content to let Scott stand forth as the family genius.

Now, however, she began to envision a career of her own, with triumphs transcending his. She had always loved dancing, excelling in the strenuous Charleston and Black Bottom. Ordinarily, this might have led her toward stage dancing, but her seething dreams fed on a grander fare. Ballet must be her career.

Visualizing herself turning into a world-famous ballerina, the twenty-eight-year-old woman began studying with Catherine Littlefield in Philadelphia. On the Fitzgeralds' return to Paris in the summer of 1928 she devoted herself to ballet lessons with demonic intensity, totally neglecting husband and child. In time she described this phase of her life in her novel, *Save Me the Waltz*. It is hard to read it without joining

Ernest Hemingway in the belief that envy of Scott's creativity had festered inside Zelda for years.

Two poignant episodes emerged from this American foray. The first occurred when Scott met the aristocratic Mrs. Winthrop Chanler, also a writer. The two quickly charmed each other, and Mrs. Chanler inquired what Scott desired most in life. "To stay married to Zelda and to write the greatest novel in the world," he answered. "Then," she told him, "you'll have to do something about your drinking." Scott said not a word.

The second came when Scott visited New York alone. Mencken and Charles Angoff visited his hotel room, finding him so drunk he could barely stand. He tried to embrace Mencken, who was annoyed at the attempted intimacy. With Scott so befuddled, there seemed little point in remaining. Yet as the two started to leave, Scott pulled himself together and began to outline an idea for a novel. It was, he said, "about a woman who wants to destroy a man, because she loves him too much and is afraid she'll lose him. Then she gets jealous of him, because of his achievements in some line she thinks she's also good in. . ."

Mencken broke in, "Why, it's your wife Zelda all over again."

Scott reacted violently. "I spill my guts out to you," he shouted, "and you answer with Zelda. Of all the times to mention Zelda to me! Of all the goddam times . . ."

Hurling himself on the bed, he burst into tears.

Nonfiction Has Its Day ...
Richard Halliburton . . William Seabrook . . . . .
Trader Horn . . . .

In May 20, 1927, Charles A. Lindbergh, Jr., began his one-man flight from New York to Paris. It was a heroic feat, accomplished with unerring skill by a clean-cut, unassuming young American. And in addition to its trailblazing aspects the solo flight had unusual repercussions on the nation's culture.

At the moment of the Lindbergh flight, America had reached an all-time low in taste, with the Era of Wonderful Nonsense serving up idiotic sensations like the marriage of fifty-five-year-old Daddy Browning and his plump, fifteen-year-old Peaches. When this thrill ended in a court trial for separation, headlines were immediately grabbed by the sordid Snyder-Gray husband killing. America's culture had reached its nadir—the low point of Scott Fitzgerald's "grandest, gaudiest spree in history."

But as the Lone Eagle flew through day and night, Americans felt spirits ennobled, as if some forgotten decency in them had revived. Yet for all its uplifting qualities, the Lindbergh flight did not—could not—cleanse the atmosphere overnight. Not until the Depression of the next decade did the nation really sober up.

One effect of the Lindbergh flight was particularly interesting to the book world. The flier returned in June to receive

the most tumultuous reception ever accorded a single human
being, then was whisked to the Harry Guggenheim estate on
Long Island, where he placed himself in the hands of ghost-
writer Charles J. V. Murphy. In record time *We*, a book on
his flight, was completed and rushed through production with
such rapidity as to be ready for the public in September.
Needless to say, *We* became a best seller of the 1927–28
season.

The Lindbergh flight also highlighted a change which had
taken place in the reading habits of Americans. During the
first half of the decade, people had been busy casting off
inhibitions and adjusting to the three P's—Prosperity, Prohibition, and Promiscuity. Americans then had been interested
in the emotions and ideas that are customarily found in fiction. But with adjustment to the three P's more or less accomplished, the reading public became less reflective and
started demanding facts, thrills, and deeds. The wild excitement of the Lindbergh flight, a *deed*, only reflected this.
However, it cannot be said that excellent fiction was not published between 1925 and 1930—only that this turned into an
era of nonfiction.

This change in taste was duly noted during 1927 in a
speech by the president of the National Association of Book
Publishers. First the speaker assured his listeners that America led the world in the printing and purchase of books and
that an even greater upswing was to be anticipated. Then he
reported that "Americans have suddenly become conscious of
the value of history, biography, psychology, science, and
other types of nonfiction."

Concrete proof was visible in the type of books published
in the latter half of the decade. Never before, for example,
had expensive, two-volume works been so cheerfully purchased, to be appreciated and discussed in thoroughly normal
fashion. Possibly the outstanding nonfiction book of the time
was Charles A. and Mary Beard's *Rise of American Civilization*. A two-volume work, priced at $12.50, it ran to sixteen
hundred cogent pages. The Beards carried American history
from colonial times to Harding normalcy, with critics assur-

ing the public that in their hands interpretation became drama—"It satisfies until it excites," wrote Carl Van Doren. The public retaliated by buying the set, overlooking bulk and price to concentrate on ideas and readability.

Another respected two-volume work was Vernon L. Parrington's *Main Currents in American Thought*. Somewhat smaller than the Beard epic—880 pages altogether, at eight dollars for both—this was really cultural and social history, told in literary terms, evaluating American authors of the past with freshness and brilliance, while uncovering forgotten talents. These first two volumes—*The Colonial Mind* and *The Romantic Revolution in America*—were only part of a projected three-volume work, but the author died before finishing volume three, which, though incomplete, was brought out posthumously.

History of a lighter, brighter sort arrived with Mark Sullivan's *Turn of the Century*, the first volume of his *Our Times*, a project expected to continue until the author caught up to himself. Covering the spectrum of each period since 1900, the esteemed Washington columnist and correspondent planned to depend heavily on his own knowledge and experience in the books, while leavening the prose with lively items from newspapers, popular songs, and personalities of the recent past. Those who preferred a more conventional approach to popular history found it in the works of James Truslow Adams, currently occupied with New England and the colonial period.

From overseas came books which proved the American public ready to grapple with intellectual pretension. Oswald Spengler's *Decline of the West* had been published in Germany eight years before. Intellectuals able to read German had been quoting Spengler ever since, with one of them writing, "It has always been my impression that it is very wrong to read Spengler from a moralistic standpoint, if we are to read him profitably."

Now this formidable single-volume work was available to the American public, with Ernest Boyd hailing it as the greatest book of philosophy out of Germany since Nietzsche. Another critic called it "stupendous, formidable, lugubrious, passionate." Readers found that Spengler had "periodized" world history in a way childishly easy to comprehend, though the text itself was rough going. He had divided the history of our civilization into the same ages that ruled human life— Youth, Maturity, Old Age, Death. It was his belief that by the 1920's civilization had reached its next-to-last phase. After that, Death!

André Siegfried's *America Comes of Age* took a brighter look. A highly respected French historian, this author had made several tours of the United States and in his resulting book covered industrialization, race relations (even then!), Prohibition, foreign policy, culture, religion, and kindred subjects. Reviewers found it the best evaluation of American life since Alexis de Tocqueville's *Democracy in America*. Politically minded Mencken rated it higher. "This book," he burbled, "is so good it almost seems incredible!"

The Nonfiction Era naturally saw the publication of notable biographies. Outstanding was Carl Sandburg's *Abraham Lincoln: The Prairie Years*—two volumes at ten bucks— which covered the first fifty-one years of Lincoln's life, bringing him up to the Presidency. Here was a true milestone in American biography, a work by a man who not only loved his subject but the land from which he sprang. One critic wrote, "A glowingly beautiful piece of work, it shifts from paragraphs drenched in soft beauty to stirring recountings of political and legal forays."

Lincoln was viewed from a different angle in an important work by Albert Beveridge, the esteemed biographer of John Marshall. Beveridge chose to offer, with lawyerlike precision, every available scrap of information about Lincoln. If Sandburg's biography had heart, this was all brain, with one critic finding it "mercilessly dispassionate." The Beveridge work brought Lincoln up to 1858, with a second volume projected. But once again an author died before completing a *magnum opus*.

Other figures of the American past were treated to in-depth treatment. Hervey Allen wrote *Israfel*, a colorful account of the life of Edgar Allan Poe; M. R. Werner, biographer of Barnum and Brigham Young, tackled William Jennings Bryan; J. Brooks Atkinson dealt with Thoreau; Heywood Broun and Margaret Leech picked Anthony Comstock, pioneer vice crusader, a job co-author Broun called "a labor of hate"; Van Wyck Brooks charted *The Pilgrimage of Henry James*; E. F. Dakin produced a none-too-flattering *Mary Baker Eddy: A Study of a Virginal Mind*; W. E. Woodward wrote *George Washington: The Image and the Man*; Rupert Hughes also covered Washington, using a hatchet on the chopper of the cherry tree; Edgar Lee Masters tried to expose flaws in Lincoln; Joseph Wood Krutch also examined the chaotic life of Poe, subtitling his book "A Study in Genius."

Allan Nevins, already recognized as a historian, turned biographer with *Frémont: The West's Greatest Adventurer*. Lewis Mumford, born in 1895, had begun writing for technical magazines at the early age of fourteen. So far in the Twenties, he contributed to *Civilization in the United States*, written book reviews for the *Freeman*, and produced two books—*Sticks and Stones* and *The Golden Day*. The former reflected the interest in architecture and urban development which would be a keystone of Mumford's distinguished career in years to come; the book analyzed American architecture and the growth of cities as an aspect of our civilization. *The Golden Day*, published in 1926, was a study of the American experience and culture which decided that the era of Hawthorne, Emerson, Thoreau and Melville had been our Golden Day. Now Mumford was working on a biography of Herman Melville. Of it a critic would say, "He uses history, literature, philosophy, psychology, and criticism for a single end: the rounded interpretation of a man's life, his work, and the society in which he lived."

Not all biographies by America-based authors were on domestic figures. Young John W. Vandercook wrote a haunting life of Christophe, King of Haiti; Francis Hackett, Irish-born but well entrenched in America's literary life, produced an exceptional Henry the Eighth; and Ernest Boyd evoked Guy de Maupassant.

From abroad came distinguished biographies which found great favor in America. Emil Ludwig led the procession with *Napoleon,* a Boni and Liveright success which was followed by *Goethe.* André Maurois had laid the cornerstone of a distinguished career with *Ariel* a romanticized life of Shelley, in 1924; now he was represented by a more factual *Disraeli* and in the near future hovered his *Byron.* Lytton Strachey, daddy of them all, contributed *Elizabeth and Essex.* Harold Nicolson covered Swinburne and Verlaine. The highly romantic E. Barrington contributed *The Glorious Apollo,* who was Lord Byron, and *The Divine Lady,* about Emma Hamilton and Lord Nelson.

Most of these biographies, whether native or foreign, contained an element of realism, which *The New York Times* described as "slashing away the underbrush surrounding great historical figures to present biographies of human beings, not copybook heroes." William E. Woodward expressed the feelings of himself and other contemporary biographers when he told an interviewer, "I have a consuming curiosity about the doings of people. I think that most historical writing [of the past] was dull and insipid, and far too scholarly in style, and my impulse is to present history and biography in such fashion that the subjects are readable and entertaining."

Reminded that he had coined the word "debunking," so applicable in this connection, Woodward heaved a gloomy sigh. "In my first book I invented the word 'Debunk' to my regret," he said. "It has now become thoroughly established in the language, but I do not like the word and have never used it since."

Other works of nonfiction boxed the culture compass. After scoring with *The Man Nobody Knows,* Bruce Barton followed with *The Book Nobody Knows,* his jazzed-up look at the Bible. Hendrik Willem Van Loon also offered a bright and vivid *Story of the Bible.* William Bolitho, in *Twelve Against the Gods,* examined unusual personalities of the past. James Jeans unveiled the mysteries of outer space in *The Universe Around Us.* The astoundingly prolific William

Beebe seemed to bring out an account of his own scientific adventures each year. After writing of dry land exploration in *Edge of the Jungle, Galapagos, Jungle Days,* and *Pheasant Jungles,* he had proceeded to open up new vistas in *The Arcturus Adventure,* which described his participation in the New York Zoological Society's first deep-sea expedition. His next effort would be *Beneath Tropic Seas,* about deep-sea diving off Haiti.

Dr. Paul de Kruif, on his own again after aiding Sinclair Lewis with *Arrowsmith,* had written *Microbe Hunters.* Katherine Mayo in *Mother India* closely scrutinized that crowded country; some declared she looked too hard, accenting the negative and lurid in order to woo readers. In *Coming of Age in Samoa,* young Margaret Mead offered up a popular mixture of anthropology and sex, to make one of the few nonfiction books of the Twenties which has never gone out of print. Another is H. W. Fowler's *Modern English Usage.*

Yet the most appreciated nonfiction book of the era was probably Dr. Will Durant's *The Story of Philosophy,* a top seller which set the fledgling firm of Simon and Schuster firmly on its feet. In 577 pages, the author covered seventeen of the world's great philosophers from Plato to John Dewey. Critic Stuart P. Sherman capsuled its contents better than the publishers' blurb by writing, "Straight at the average man he addresses this lucid and entertaining account of seventeen famous attempts to see life steadily and see it whole."

The public cheerfully bought this book at five dollars, though unfavorable publicity was given the fact that much of it had already appeared (written by the same author) at five cents a copy in the Haldeman-Julius Little Blue Books. Emanuel Haldeman-Julius was known as the Henry Ford of publishing, but Simon and Schuster scored by giving Dr. Durant the Rolls Royce treatment.

Readers were free to do their own philosophizing after perusing Abbé Ernest Dimnet's *The Art of Thinking.* Dr. Axel Munthe also helped with his reflective *The Story of San Michele.* Readers kept track of themselves in G. A. Dorsey's *Why We Behave Like Human Beings,* A. E. Wiggams' *Ex-*

ploring Your Mind, and Harry A. Overstreet's *Influencing Human Behavior.*

Highly popular with average readers were the works of Dr. Joseph Collins, a practicing physician who liked to read books and ponder the contents. Having done so, he wrote his own books under the title *A Doctor Looks at* ———. The good doctor specialized in no-nonsense opinions, which caused Burton Rascoe and other critics to brand him a "moralist." At the same time he was skilled at working sex into his discussions of "psychology." In his latest best-seller, *The Doctor Looks at Love and Life,* he made the flat statement that Prohibition had turned his countrymen into "a nation of lawbreakers who are fast becoming drunkards." Critics who liked to judge books with highball in hand were infuriated, but the public approved the doctor's dogmatism.

Those pointing with pride to excellent nonfiction were forced to admit that with the superior books came many inferior—Americans, of course, are notorious for taking the bad with the good. In an editorial extolling the quality of contemporary nonfiction, *The New York Times* saw fit to conclude:

> ►§ *If all the non-fiction referred to were as good as the best of it, or even half of it were as accurate and well written, the situation would be more encouraging. The success of the first philosophical and biographical works, well deserving of substantial rewards, has led to the publication of clap-trap imitations. They are written in the manner of bright, careless gossip, whose chatter is probably entertaining for a time but is certainly worthless.*

More than in the philosophical-biographical field, though, the wide variation in quality was apparent in the books of adventure-travel, or travel-adventure, which constituted not only the latest nonfiction category to open up before a delighted public, but the most popular area of contemporary escape reading.

Until 1920 only wealthy Americans had traveled for pleasure, but World War I made Europe appear closer, and Coolidge-Hoover prosperity now made it possible for Americans to get there. In the summer of 1927, twenty thousand members of the American Legion, most with wives and some with children, flocked to Paris to celebrate the tenth anniversary of the landing of the wartime American Expeditionary Force. *Tout Paris* turned out for the big Legion parade which, among much else, gave Europe its first glimpse of American drum majorettes.

As promised in glowing steamship ads in magazines, Europe had become America's playground. And as Europe became familiar, the idea began to spread that Americans might go anywhere. In old days, explorers had seemed eccentric oddballs, but suddenly everyday men began writing travel books which made favored armchair reading in winter and hammock reading in the heat.

In the classic tradition of adventure-travel were the books of the foreigners Sir Francis Younghusband, Vilhjalmur Stefansson, and Dr. Sven Hedin. Admiral Richard E. Byrd's *Skyward* (along with Lindbergh's *We*) introduced the flying explorer of a new age who usually was an American. The tradition of the roving Yankee newspaper correspondent, once the private preserve of Richard Harding Davis, was perpetuated by youthful Vincent Sheean, in his *An American Among the Riffi.*

A blockbuster of 1927 was T. E. Lawrence's *Revolt in the Desert.* Shortly a limited edition of Lawrence's *Seven Pillars of Wisdom* appeared—a *very* limited edition because of its shocking homosexual scene. Yet it is ironic to note that the great vogue of the mysterious Colonel Lawrence was abetted in the United States by the popularity of Lowell Thomas' *With Lawrence in Arabia.* In *Count Luckner, Sea Devil,* Lowell Thomas—whose career as author-traveler-broadcaster has spanned nearly fifty years—performed the considerable feat of making large numbers of Americans read about a German war hero.

But in handsome, boyish Richard Halliburton, America

found its outstanding new-image travel writer. Fresh faced, with an engaging grin and the lithe body of an expert swimmer Dick Halliburton had, in the neat phrase of the era, personality plus. The young man seemed to be cast in the mold of both Slim Lindbergh and (yes!) Scott Fitzgerald. Born in 1900 and raised in magnolia-scented Memphis, Halliburton had been a Princeton freshman in the fall of 1917 while Scott, a junior, was making up his mind to join the Army.

If Scott nursed hopes of becoming the greatest novelist of his time, Dick had even more effulgent dreams. As he wrote later:

> ✑ *Let those who wish have their respectability—I wanted freedom, freedom to indulge whatever caprice struck my fancy, freedom to search in the farthermost corners of the earth for the beautiful, the joyous, and the romantic. . . . The* romantic . . . *that was what I wanted!*

He got it. Because of wartime Navy service, Dick did not graduate until 1921, the exuberant possessor of everything necessary for travel except money. Yet a few footloose vacations had taught him how easily he could charm people into assisting him and that he could grin his way out of most predicaments. He had likewise discovered a fellow classmate who shared his Rover-boy dreams of scaling the Matterhorn, though neither had yet climbed anything higher than a flight of stairs.

The two signed on a European-bound freighter as able seamen and on landing used their wages to buy bicycles. Arriving broke at the foot of the Matterhorn, they charmed the guides into assisting them and lending the necessary climbing gear. Slowly, they ascended the 14,780 feet of what Dick thought of as "the incorrigible mountain." At the top he felt a "fierce joy," but his companion experienced less exalted reactions. "Oh, Dick," he shouted, "at last, after talking about it and dreaming about it all these years, at last I can *actually* SPIT A MILE."

After the Matterhorn his Princeton friend left him, and

Dick pressed on solo, sometimes joining up for short periods with adventurous youths infected with his own wanderlust. He had arranged with a few small-town newspapers to file occasional stories on his travels, and the sums received from this were barely enough to keep him going. In Paris, he stayed at a pension whose guests included a young man of his own age and an exceptionally pretty girl. She seemed so shy and demure that the boys dared not approach her; instead they christened her Miss Piety.

One night the two got enough francs to attend the Folies Bergère, and suddenly Miss Piety appeared before their astounded eyes as a nude dancer in a harem scene. Now they felt free to speak to her, and she answered prettily, "When I am demure at our table, you scorn me; when I am an oriental, you rush to meet me. Wretches!"

What use did the two wretches make of bold Miss Piety? Nothing sexual, you may be sure. Instead, they persuaded her to use her sweet wiles on the crusty gatekeeper of the Trocadero Tower, who let them slip inside for an illicit midnight view of Paris the Beautiful. It was another first for Dick Halliburton.

An author who wrote with a somewhat limp wrist, Halliburton often contrived to weave pretty girls into his narratives, thus adding a soupçon of sex to his rhapsodic prose. But if he dramatized high spots of his adventuring, no one ever accused him of outright falsification. Now, from Paris, he proceeded to the south of France, where he lost his few remaining francs at the Monte Carlo casino and (inevitably) encountered an attractive *femme fatale* who had dropped thousands.

Advancing to Luxor, he swam the Nile, then headed in the direction of darkest Africa, greeting those he met with a flashing smile, outthrust hand, and the disarming words, "I am Richard Halliburton, Princeton graduate last June—out in quest of the pot of gold at the end of the rainbow." In Asia, he crossed the Himalayas and fulfilled another boyhood dream by spending a night in the Taj Mahal. This was strictly forbidden, but Dick hid until the gates were shut, then emerged to have a ball until the first cat's-paw of dawn. Suddenly a creepy spell seized him:

> ⋞ *Alone, in all this supernatural beauty, resting by the pool before the phantom Taj, I felt myself transported to some previous existence that knew neither time nor space nor substance. I and all that I beheld was myth. The subconscious mind was master, linking me with previous incarnations in the dim past. A strange ecstacy came to me. I heard myself laugh deliriously.*

The spell passed, leaving him in a state of shivering terror. Running to the gates, he shouted for the guards, who hauled him before the officer in charge. By now Dick was himself again, and he talked his way to freedom.

Next stop Bali, to live the lightsome beachcomber life and make joyous note that local girls went bare-breasted. In Japan he was warned of the impossibility of climbing Fujiyama in midwinter; no one had ever done it. His twenty-third birthday found him at the summit, shouting into frigid winds, "Here I am on Fujiyama."

Back home he set his experiences into bouncy words, only to have the manuscript rejected by nine publishers. One day he was in New York's Princeton Club regaling members with stories of his travels. A representative of the Bobbs-Merrill publishing company heard him and said, "You should write a book." As always Dick had a ready answer. "I have," he said. Bearing the Bobbs-Merrill imprint, *The Royal Road to Romance* went into twenty printings and several languages.

For a time Dick tried to live the life of effete city dweller, but found it intolerable. "This slippered ease before the hearth," he told himself, "how barren and profitless, it seems. . . . I envy every sailor that will wave his farewell to the skyline of New York and turn his salt-stung face to some strange enchanted land beyond the far horizon."

He had long dreamed of traversing the path of Ulysses in the *Odyssey* and now did so for a second book called *The Glorious Adventure*. He swam the five-mile Hellespont, nearly drowning in its wicked currents. Setting out to dupli-

cate Pheidippides' classic dash from Marathon to Athens—
"one of the most romantic events in the record of athletic
achievement"—he found progress difficult because of pedes-
trians, carts, and autos on the road.

After jogging twelve miles, he developed a sharp thirst and
paused at a tiny hamlet for water. There was no water, only
wine, which he quaffed copiously. Suddenly he was a stumbling, foolish drunk. "Running is too ridic'lous," he muttered,
and jumped into a passing taxi, completing the journey while
singing lustily on the back seat. His legion of readers doted
on this naughty escapade.

Still on Ulysses' trail, he tried swimming from Charybdis to
the rock of Scylla. Here his dependable charm turned rancid.
Natives did not like him, calling him "the crazy foreigner."
Currents proved too strong, and on his dejected return to the
starting point, he found the local police—unfriendly boatmen
had reported that he cheated them. Dick passed the night in a
crummy jail and in the morning gave up all his money as a
fine. Alone, he set out to walk five miles to a ferry, confident
that his charm would be working again when he got there.
And it was!

Next he met an English girl named Jimmy—"a merry
Amazon, a jollier companion never lived. . . ." The two carefully stayed at different hotels, but climbed Mount Vesuvius
together. No one quite knew where Ulysses' sirens had sung,
but Dick and Jimmy felt sure they found the place in the Blue
Grotto on Capri:

> *As we looked with dreamy eyes out over the ocean,*
> *from within the cavern faint music came to us softly*
> *through the darkness. . . . We knew it was the soft voices*
> *of Ulysses' sirens—singing.*

Fittingly enough, Dick completed his travels at Ulysses' castle, for the last time tucking his worn copy of the *Odyssey* in a
pocket:

> *And now, once more, the darkness creeps on Ithaca—*
> *and me. The scarlet fades. The evening stars come out.*

I pocket my faithful little book and leave the twilit stage.
My Odyssey—is ended.

After *The Glorious Adventure,* the effervescent adventurer made plans to swim the Panama Canal and spend a summer on Devil's Island—both of which were part of a later volume.

Halliburton's books brought lighthearted adventure to young and old, but perhaps their finest tribute came when a Clean Books League in Seattle tried to ban them as "unfit for children." On what conceivable grounds? Because they "excited to wanderlust."

Richard Halliburton never claimed to write literature. Instead he was content to provide the most obvious sort of escape. But an adventure book hailed as true literature was *Trader Horn,* written by Alfred Aloysius Horn, with the expert assistance of the South African novelist Ethelreda Lewis. It first appeared in England with a warm introduction by austere John Galsworthy, who wrote, "This is a gorgeous book, more full of sheer stingo than you are likely to come across in a day's march among the bookshops of wherever you may be."

Trader Horn recounted the life story of an Englishman who went out to South Africa "with the milk of his English grammar school education still on his lips." Over fifty lusty years he had been ivory trader, gorilla- elephant- and diamond-hunter, as well as jungle explorer and pal of pygmies and cannibals. He claimed to have saved the life of Cecil Rhodes in a crocodile swamp, and rescued the fair-haired octoroon Neva from a joss house where she was imprisoned and worshiped as a love goddess. Reduced in old age to selling pots and pans from door to door, he reached the home of Mrs. Lewis, who offered him a soothing glass of water. He began to talk and so intrigued her with his stories that she persuaded him to write down an episode a week. After he brought her the rough material, she reworked it into a book.

Word of *Trader Horn* reached the ears of Simon and Schuster, and the book became one of that firm's amazing succession of best sellers which dazzled both book trade and public in the latter Twenties. Simon and Schuster merchandised books with what was described as "wild and honest enthusiasm." In some mystic way they were able to make people consider their lives empty unless they had read the latest Simon and Schuster publication. In this case, Max Schuster, promotion genius of the firm, announced *Trader Horn's* acquisition with a signed full-page ad which began:

> ✎§ *I am going to buy* Trader Horn *today! I shall sail far beyond the sun . . . wildest Africa will be my home, swift rivers my daily course, apes and peacocks my stock in trade. . . . Romance will run amuck. . . .*

On publication, *Trader Horn* was hailed in terms as glowing as the advertisement. *The Saturday Review of Literature* paid tribute to its "unusual charm" and called the white-bearded trader "an individual of astounding saltiness." Another called it "a wise and witty work of art, surprising in its freshness." Elsewhere *Trader Horn* was labeled a combination of "The Ancient Mariner" and the Leatherstocking Tales. William Lyon Phelps in *Scribner's* found it almost too good to be true, declaring, "This is a diamond mine of such astonishing richness and brilliancy that I would not believe the gems were genuine, if it were not for the guarantee of John Galsworthy."

Following this, Simon and Schuster decided to bring Trader Horn himself to these shores, and cabled the fare from Johannesburg. It may have been a mistake, for in the flesh the old codger failed to jibe with the stimulating character in the book. Some were uncharitable enough to say he was more like a Bowery bum. The whiskered gaffer shone at cocktail parties, where he consumed every libation in sight. In his cups, he liked to confide to the ladies that he slept with beard tucked inside his nightshirt.

With this, the literary world developed a certain distrust of *Trader Horn*. *Forum Magazine* ran an article which attacked his book as "senile drivel touched up, with much skill, by a third-rate novelist." A publication called *The Independent* declared, "This volume represents an artistic, clever, convincing swindle. . . . As an authentic document it assays about nineteen percent gold."

But by now *Trader Horn* had sold 170,000 copies, and there was nothing, really, to be done. Even if a fraud had been perpetrated, Simon and Schuster had been taken in with everyone else. Also, for all his crudities, the old Trader had been an agreeable tosspot, and his book, whatever its veracity, undeniably entertaining. So *Trader Horn* was allowed to fade away unchallenged.

Two years later, when Simon and Schuster brought out Joan Lowell's *Cradle of the Deep*, critics were rougher. Perhaps it was simmering resentment over *Trader Horn* that increased the fury of their attack. As for Alfred Aloysius Horn, whose right name turned out to be Smith, he made $100,000 from *Trader Horn*, its sale to the movies, and other volumes which followed it. Four years later he died, leaving an estate of only eight thousand dollars. Americans who recalled him wondered if he had drunk up the difference.

Those partial to gut-level adventure discovered rich rewards in the books of William Seabrook, author of *Adventures in Arabia*, *Jungle Ways*, and *The Magic Island*. Son of an Atlanta minister and a lifelong mother hater, manly William Seabrook was encouraged to write and travel by Mencken. Seabrook's prose was far more rugged than Richard Halliburton's, but at times he could be florid and over-dramatic. Theodore Dreiser, whom Seabrook greatly admired, once rudely called him "a yellow journalist" and turned his back.

Seabrook's writing also exposed the thin line between fact and fancy in adventure tales. Novelist Marjory Worthington, his devoted wife, once admitted that on occasion her husband "decorated the truth." But she claims he always saw things through different eyes—"*his* truth," she calls it.

In *Jungle Ways*, which dealt with the fiercest tribes of Africa, Seabrook told of joining cannibal rites where he ate human flesh, which was known to the natives as "the long pig." The success of *Jungle Ways*, and possibly Seabrook's entire career, stemmed from this stomach-turning episode. Yet Mrs. Seabrook reveals that her husband did not actually devour flesh in Africa. Rather, he dreamed up the episode in Paris, then set out to make it true. Through a friendly hospital intern he was able to secure a hunk of flesh from the body of a young man just killed in an accident. This Seabrook ceremoniously cooked and ate. So his account was part truth.

In *Adventures in Arabia*, Seabrook consorted happily with Bedouins, Druses, whirling dervishes, and Yezidi devil worshipers. In *The Magic Island*, he joined Haitians in voodoo rites and introduced the word "zombi" to the American tongue. But when examined from the vantage point of the 1970's, Seabrook seems less arresting as a writer than as an individual; indeed, he might have stepped from the pages of an erotic novel or film of the sex-ridden Seventies. A heavy drinker to begin with, William Seabrook was also a disciple of the Marquis de Sade, who enjoyed hurting and humiliating women. Dr. A. A. Brill believed hatred of his mother made him want to punish all females.

His long-suffering wife remained at his side, viewing his abnormalities as sick rather than sinister. "We were physically drawn to one another," she has written, "and yet I was totally unsympathetic to the business of chains and leather masks that were so important to him." Again she says, "I had cultivated an ability to be present with the body and absent with the spirit."

In his travels, Seabrook had many opportunities to indulge his kinky passions. Yet Paris, with its large prostitute population, was his favorite stamping ground. There he gave a famous party at which a beautiful girl, naked to the waist, hung suspended from a balcony by chains, her toes just touching the floor. Embarrassed guests pretended not to notice.

Returning to New York City in the late Twenties, Seabrook could be seen in Greenwhich Village leading on a leash girls whose faces were covered by leather masks, or whose hands were locked behind with pearl-studded handcuffs. But he did not always pay money for his rare pleasures. Once he boasted that two out of five women he met socially were responsive to the cruelty inherent in his overtures.

Seabrook's mind teemed with other sadoerotic fantasies, such as shutting naked young women in outdoor cages, which he did. But at the same time his character displayed the curious ambivalence often found in sadists, masochists, and athletes of the abnormal. At one point, the considerable sums of money earned from his books allowed him to rent a villa on the fashionable Riviera, where he mixed with posh people and proudly flaunted his aberrations. Soon a group of wastrels decided to play a joke on the self-professed sadist. Grabbing an unpopular member of their set, they plied her with drinks, stripped her, and in the middle of the night chained her to a tree before Seabrook's villa. When Seabrook woke in the morning, he was all minister's son, outraged at being the butt of a crude joke, full of pity for the wretched, chained girl. When *he* did such things, it was fun. When done by others, it was wrong—and cruel!

In August 1927, the literary world suddenly began to write its own non-fiction book, as in Boston the execution of the alleged anarchists Nicola Sacco and Bartolomeo Vanzetti drew irrevocably closer.

Writes John Dos Passos, "It is hard to explain to people who never lived through the early Twenties the violence of the revulsion against foreigners that went through the United States after the first World War."

Because of his unusual name, Dos Passos had been involved in several unpleasant episodes of his own. Thus he felt a special sympathy for fish-peddler Vanzetti and factory-worker Sacco, who had been caught up in the seething Red Scare of 1920 and charged with murder in a case intellectuals in nearly every field considered a frame-up. Presiding at their two trials was Judge Webster Thayer, who openly displayed contempt for the foreign-born, especially the Italians he called "Wops" and "Dago sons of bitches."

The plight of Sacco and Vanzetti became a *cause célèbre* among the literary after Robert Benchley, then drama critic of *Life* and seemingly the least political of men, heard of Judge Thayer gloating to friends, "Did you see what I did to those anarchist bastards?" Digging deeper, Benchley grew so outraged over the Judge's utterances about Sacco and Vanzetti that he filed a writ of protest with the court. Through him, Dorothy Parker became interested in the unfortunate pair. Heywood Broun, whose column in the New York *World* had become increasingly liberal (to some, radical), had long been disturbed by this example of Massachusetts justice. Edna St. Vincent Millay, John Dos Passos, Babette Deutsch, Upton Sinclair, and Mary Heaton Vorse were among those who arrayed themselves on the side of Bart and Nick, as American partisans quickly dubbed them. No one who talked to the two doomed men could conceive of them as murderers. To John Dos Passos, Sacco was a simple, outgoing man, Vanzetti "gentle and cogitative."

Neither the protests of intellectuals, nor the legal help of lawyers like Professor Felix Frankfurter of Harvard, stayed the relentless progress of the law. Sacco and Vanzetti were sentenced to die on the night of August 23, and on that day Boston resembled an armed camp.

Boston Common, for the first time in history, was closed to orators. The local police force, on twenty-four-hour duty, roamed midcity, arrested picketers and protesters. Riot squads equipped with automatic rifles, hand grenades, and tear-gas bombs busily broke up street-corner meetings. Among those arrested were Dorothy Parker and Edna St. Vincent Millay, both charged with disturbing the peace. John Dos Passos was accused of "sauntering and loitering."

Sacco and Vanzetti were electrocuted on schedule— "ROASTED ALIVE," read the headline on New York's infamous tabloid *Graphic*. Among the many side effects of a supremely controversial case was a change in America's conception of its writers. The literary lights who walked Boston picket lines had been the topmost celebrities involved in the protest, and newspapers played them up in text and picture. So, among everything else, the Sacco-Vanzetti case acted as a harbinger of the Thirties, when authors associated themselves freely with political causes.

But even at the moment, the American writer no longer seemed just the hard-drinking, hard-playing possessor of talent. A shadow had fallen across this carefree image, and it indicated a reviving concern among the literary for simple justice and the underdog.

"This Manuscript MUST Be Published!". . . . *Thornton Wilder* . . *William Lyon Phelps* . . *Maxwell Perkins* . . . . *Thomas Wolfe* . . *William Faulkner* . . . . . .

◈▭◈▭◈▭◈▭◈▭◈▭◈▭◈▭◈▭◈

Included in the promise sweetening the atmosphere of the early part of the Literary Decade had been the expectation that novelists of the time would write their best books during the ten-year span to come.

This was still true as the decade began to wane. For these were the days when Willa Cather wrote *Death Comes for the Archbishop*, certainly her best-known, if not necessarily her best, work; Ellen Glasgow, her mind sharpened by contact with cocktail-party literati, did *The Romantic Comedians*; Louis Bromfield, still a delighted expatriate ("Strange to say, I feel more American than before") provided *The Strange Case of Miss Annie Spragg*; and Elinor Wylie, who died in 1928, was represented by *The Orphan Angel*, a fictionalized story of her beloved Shelley, and then by *Mr. Hodge & Mr. Hazard*, a novel of England following its rejection of Shelley.

It was also the time of Elizabeth Madox Roberts' *The Time of Man*, Mazo de la Roche's first work on Jalna, Oliver La Farge's *Laughing Boy*, Edith Wharton's *Twilight Sleep*, Julia Peterkin's *Scarlet Sister Mary*, DuBose Heyward's *Porgy*, T. S. Stribling's *Teeftallow*, Glenway Wescott's *The Grandmothers*, Carl Van Vechten's *Nigger Heaven*—and

Booth Tarkington's *The Plutocrat*, not to mention Edna
Ferber's *Show Boat*.

From abroad arrived Warwick Deeping's *Sorrell and Son*,
D. H. Lawrence's *The Plumed Serpent* and his under-the-
counter *Lady Chatterley's Lover*, Thomas Mann's *The Magic
Mountain*, Virginia Woolf's *To the Lighthouse*, Aldous Hux-
ley's *Point Counter Point*, and Evelyn Waugh's *Decline and
Fall*.

In the field of poetry *John Brown's Body*, by Stephen Vincent Benét, was an immediate success, aided by the Book of
the Month Club. Weaving a web of the Civil War past over
readers, Benét's hundred-thousand-word poem found favor
with critics except for a few like Max Eastman, who thought
it "lacking in rapture and perfection." Such carping, however, failed to deter eager readers, many of whom had never
before read a narrative poem from beginning to end. To them
and others *John Brown's Body* proved as engrossing as any
historical novel, and far more inspiring.

Ezra Pound's collected poems came out under the title
Personae, with Ford Madox Ford hailing the expatriate
American as "the greatest living poet." Another reviewer
saluted him as indeed ". . . a poet that doth drink life/As
lesser men drink wine." Edwin Arlington Robinson, so long a
single-minded fighter for poetic integrity, won a gratifying
(one assumes) Literary Guild selection with his romantic
Tristram, a four-thousand-line poem on Isolt of Brittany.

With all these books, though, the one that most satisfied
the contemporary reading public was *The Bridge of San Luis
Rey*, by Thornton Wilder. If nothing else, this successful
novel once more highlighted the change in the reading habits
of Americans, who in the first part of the decade had favored
Main Street, *This Side of Paradise*, *Bunk*, and other books
reflecting the mores of the time. Seemingly the same readers
now preferred escape fiction, provided it had implications.
This magic formula was brewed to full potency in *The Bridge*

of San Luis Rey, with its author hailed by Sinclair Lewis as one who "in an age of realism dreams the old and lovely dreams of the eternal romantics."

Thornton Wilder was thirty years old at his moment of initial success. Born in Madison, Wisconsin, he had spent eight formative years in Shanghai and Hong Kong, where his father served as consul general. In the United States he attended Oberlin College, served in the wartime Army, and returned to finish his studies at Yale. After graduation, he passed a year at the American Academy in Rome, coming back to teach at Lawrenceville prep, where his subject was French in order to keep a clear mind for writing English.

His first novel had been *The Cabala,* about a group of sophisticates observed in Rome; published in 1925, it made only a mild impression. *San Luis Rey,* two years later, propelled Thronton Wilder to world fame. He begins his novel with a real grabber—"On Friday noon, July the 20th, 1714, the finest bridge in all Peru broke and precipitated five travellers into the gulf below." Every person in the area, perhaps every Peruvian, had at one time or another traversed this picturesque swinging bridge made of osier, or wickerwork willow.

Granted the bridge is old and worn, why does it break at the moment these five diverse people are on it? Brother Juniper, humble friar, witnesses the tragedy and attempts to find an answer to this cosmic question mark by delving into the lives of the quintet. He finds that the life orbit of each has impinged at one time or other on the others. More important, each life seems to have achieved a kind of completion before the fatal accident. His conclusion: "There is a land of the living and a land of the dead and the bridge is love, the only survival, the only meaning."

The lack of pretentiousness in *San Luis Rey* especially delighted reviewers. Like E. M. Forster in *A Passage to India,* Wilder had been content to restrict his canvas and, within its limitations, attempt to write the perfect book. Isabel Paterson thought he had succeeded; she called it "a minor masterpiece." Malcolm Cowley expressed the identical opinion more elaborately: "Nothing falls short of its mark; nothing exceeds it; and the book as a whole is like some faultless temple erected to a minor diety." Clifton Fadiman, in *The Nation*, found "extrinsic as well as intrinsic value." The public responded by buying 240,000 copies over following months. The Pulitzer Prize Committee was so impressed that it shattered precedent by bestowing its fiction award on a book whose locale was outside the United States.

Exceptional authors may be able to sense the demands of the reading public. For even as Thornton Wilder worked on *San Luis Rey*, two other novelists of stature had embarked on books with a similar religio-mystic theme. Willa Cather's *Death Comes for the Archbishop*, published in the same year, uses religion as a means of evoking the past the author adored. Miss Cather tells the story of a Catholic priest who comes to New Mexico as a vicar in the mid-1800's and slowly becomes the archbishop who, with his friend Father Joseph, wins the Southwest for Catholicism. After forty years, the archbishop dies "of having lived."

A Catholic convert, Miss Cather applied her best skills to her cadenced words, and the struggle of the two priests against the forces of heathenism becomes a gripping epic. Her prose, said Rebecca West in the New York *Herald-Tribune*, was "clear as a dewdrop." Yet Miss Cather may have over-idealized the past. *Time* called attention to this by noting the book was "filled with colorful people, rainbow scenery, amazing weather."

Louis Bromfield, having ended his four "panel" novels of Midwest life—*The Green Bay Tree, Possession, Early Autumn, A Good Woman*—also stepped forward with a religious mystery story, amazingly close in concept to *The Bridge of San Luis Rey*. Titled *The Strange Case of Miss Annie Spragg*, the Bromfield opus told of an eccentric American spinster whose death in a shabby Italian *pensione* exposes the miracle of the stigmata on her body. So begins an eerie flashback narrative of religious fanaticism with roots deep in the American Middle West. Critics called it "exhila-rating," "intelligent," and "often brilliant."

As this spate of books poured off presses, Professor William Lyon Phelps of Yale rendered the opinion "There will be more books published in 1928 than in 1927 and there will be more in 1929 than in 1928—for of the making of books there is no end!"

Pontifications such as this were what the world expected from "Billy" Phelps, not only distinguished Lampson Profes-sor of English Literature, but also contributor of the jaunty monthly "As I Like It" column to *Scribner's*, and literary lecturer of such renown that his once-a-month discourses at New York's Town Hall were treated by the *Times* as news stories.

In other parts of the land, Professor Phelps lectured with such frequency and variety, usually before women, that he was called "The Solon of the Ladies' Clubs." In addition, he had authored an almost uncountable number of books, most of them based on his popular lectures. Among them were *The Advance of the English Novel, Happiness, Thoreau, Essays on Russian Novelists, Human Nature in the Gospel, The Mother's Anthology, Marriage, The Courage of Ignorance,* and *The Excitement of Teaching*.

Professor Phelps, sixty-three in 1927, may possibly go down in history as the victim of a buoyant personality. For here was a man whose unbridled enthusiasm for life, along with zest for the seven arts, rendered him a totally indiscrimi-nate individual. By virtue of education, accomplishment, and numerous honors, Billy Phelps displayed ample credentials as a highbrow. Yet this posture was vitiated by an overwhelming acceptance of whatever came his way. As a result, to both peers and public he seemed an unabashed middlebrow.

Certainly he remains the only serious lecturer and book reviewer ("literary critic" is too flattering a term) whose ad-mirers fondly thought of him as "Billy." Yet adulation from the vast American public had made him a personality as newsworthy as Sinclair Lewis, whom he had taught at Yale. Naturally Professor Billy was enormously pleased by the success of Thornton Wilder, another onetime pupil. He responded by saluting *The Bridge of San Luis Rey* with a characteristic string of clichés:

> *This is a work that no other man could have written. One hesitates to use the word genius, but there is something akin to that mysterious essance in the pages of this novel. The author is a star of the first magnitude; he will take his place among the leading novelists of our time.*

Professor Billy was well aware that his wide-eyed approach to books had earned him the dislike, if not contempt, of his fellows in the field. Of him a colleague wrote, "He is one of those for whom the profession of criticism has only one attraction—the pleasure of praising." To the fury of rival critics, Billy loudly sang the praises of Kathleen Norris, Booth Tarkington, Anne Douglas Sedgwick, and A. S. M. Hutchinson. He was capable of devoting one paragraph to praise of Willa Cather's *My Antonia* and the next to extolling the far lesser skills of Ben Ames Williams: "I never neglect a book by Mr. Williams, a born narrator; his latest is full of stirring fights and perilous adventures." He also delighted in singling out obscure writers, once rating an unknown Edith Miniter above Edith Wharton.

Professor Billy was never one to pick a fight—"I dislike controversy because it usually leads nowhither," he wrote. Yet occasionally he struck back at his detractors. Once he said, "Because I am enthusiastic about good things, and make no attempt to conceal it, I am frequently accused, much to my amusement, of saluting every new book with indiscriminate praise—there could hardly be a more inaccurate statement." But on another occasion he sounded wistful, rather than defiant: "It is curious that so many should believe cheerfulness is incompatible with brains."

Professor Billy was also defensive because he had passed his life in a single grove of academe. Born in New Haven, son of a minister, he attended Yale and, after travel and graduate studies, returned there in 1892 to teach. A decade later he became the prestigious Lampson Professor. Phelps was, it must be noted, an excellent teacher, whose enthusiasms fired the imaginations of students, one of whom said, "You soon learned that he was not the Lampson Professor but dear Billy Phelps." Even those who deplored his bounce had to rate him with Chauncey B. Tinker of Yale and John Erskine, Irwin Edman, and Raymond Weaver of Columbia, as the virtuoso professors of the day.

Billy's euphoria went beyond literature to embrace the theater and music, and he could often be seen on the afternoon train to New York, where he fed his insatiable appetite at plays and concerts, at the same time gathering material for his well-paying lecture dates. About Manhattan he raved in true Phelpsian fashion:

> ⋫ *New York may or may not be the largest city in the world. It is certainly the earth's musical and artistic metropolis. Simply stay on Manhattan Island, and you will see every person in the world most worth seeing. Authors, actors, composers, musicians, scientists, statesmen, physicians, prophets, and prizefighters—they all come to New York. And the quality of hospitality is not strained. . . .*

Billy Phelps had been class orator in high school and public orator at Yale. Love of talk was ever visible in his prose, which had the loose, unedited quality of impromptu speechmaking. This increased the vexation of contemporary highbrows. According to one, "His mind hops around like a grasshopper; you never know where it is going to land next. . . . Something seems to start him on one line of thought, but before he has developed it, he thinks of something else. To follow his mental processes becomes a strange, fascinating sort of game."

None of this upset the clubwomen who jammed halls to the rafters to hear his cocksure lectures. Billy was especially fond of saluting seasons of the year, and his audiences reacted with rapture as he declaimed, "June is filled with the reverberations of commencement oratory and the sound of wedding bells." Or, "September is the month of mental awakening: the schools and universities reopen; the symphony orchestras are in active rehearsal; the serious theaters are busy; the churches begin to fill." His little jokes were equally appreciated. Typical of them was the postcard of congratulation sent to Sinclair Lewis after *Main Street:* "Dear Sin: I call you Sin because you are as original as sin."

Billy's chief belittler was Burton Rascoe, who endeavored to ridicule him as a master of the irrelevant, the anticlimax, and the nonsequitur. Rascoe also saw in Professor Billy's mental processes a resemblance to the stream-of-consciousness ruminations of Leopold Bloom as he roamed Dublin. Yet it was always hard to dislike Billy, and Rascoe could not sustain it. In the end, he was forced to admit, "I adore Billy Phelps! He is not urbane but there is no malice to him. . . . He has not soured on his job."

One of Professor Billy's great moments—and a peak incident of the Era of Wonderful Nonsense as well—took place on April 23, 1928, anniversary of Shakespeare's birth.

During the past winter Phelps met Gene Tunney, who had just clinched the title of heavyweight champion of the world by defeating Jack Dempsey in the famous "long count" fight in Chicago. Billy and Gene—as they immediately called one another—were wintering in Florida, and the professor was amazed and delighted to find the prizefighter a Shakespeare buff.

As a schoolboy in a tough section of Greenwich Village, Gene had heard of Shakespeare, but he did nothing about reading him. As a marine in World War I, he got hold of *A Winter's Tale,* generally considered among the Bard's most difficult works. Nonetheless, the Fighting Marine read it ten times before progressing to the less arduous plays. By the time Tunney had become a heavyweight contender, he was hooked on Shakespeare. All this was a revelation to Professor

Billy, who listened with mounting pleasure, then invited the world's champion to speak at Yale on Shakespeare's next birthday.

Tunney looked a trifle sheepish outside Harkness Hall on the morning of the lecture. "An embarrassed grin spread its way across a face burned to mahogany tint by the Florida sun," said one account. He admitted to qualms. "Lecturing is not my métier," he said, in precise diction. "I feel something like Professor Billy would feel climbing into a prize ring. That's not *his* métier."

Still, he did well. Speaking without notes for three quarters of an hour, Tunney told the crowded hall that *Troilus and Cressida* (another hard one!) was his favorite Shakespeare work. He liked this because it could easily be tied into the prizefight racket. He considered that its message was "You have to get up and fight."

In his own parlance, he pictured Achilles sulking in his tent while Ulysses sought to rouse him by threatening to have Ajax fight the Trojan champ Hector. As paraphrased by Tunney, Ulysses taunted Achilles by saying, "You're all through, you are a has-been—you must get up and do something to defend your title." Ajax particularly earned Tunney's scorn. "He was just a great big ambitious fellow who didn't have the stuff—just like Jack Sharkey," the champ said.

The lecture was a huge success, with so many well-wishers crowding around the highbrow pugilist at the end that Professor Billy called out, "I say, Gene, they're not hurting your hand, are they?" That night reporters phoned Jack Sharkey to tell him about Tunney's comparison to Ajax. "You can tell Tunney that there is nothing the matter with me at all," Jack answered.

Tunney's lecture made page one of *The New York Times* and other journals across the country. Stimulated by its success, the champion went abroad, to hobnob happily with George Bernard Shaw and Max Beerbohm, no doubt as a result of letters of introduction from Professor Billy.

While visiting Beerbohm, the champ undertook to describe the sunset to his host, doing it in elaborate and pretentious terms. Later the Incomparable Max recalled, "I had to steel every nerve in my body to meet such sensitivity."

If William Lyon Phelps was familiar to most literate Americans, the name of Maxwell Perkins was unknown beyond the boundaries of publishing. Perkins was, of course, the editor of Charles Scribner's Sons who in 1919 insisted that his sedate firm publish *This Side of Paradise* and then, with the help of Fitzgerald, became Ernest Hemingway's understanding editor. In the publishing world, Perkins' name was revered, and his close relationship with favored authors set the pattern for writer-editor cooperation over the next thirty years.

Maxwell Perkins, forty-four in 1928, had been at Scribner's since 1910. Born in New York City at the corner of Second Avenue and 14th Street, he had the look of a lean, frosty, reserved New Englander. This is hardly surprising, since the Perkins clan belonged to a select group known as the Manhattan Yankees—that is, well-born New Englanders transplanted to Manhattan. Next, the family moved to Plainfield, New Jersey, where Max romped with Van Wyck Brooks. Still, ties to New England remained close. Summers were passed in Vermont, and Max was sent to St. Paul's School in New Hampshire and later Harvard.

After graduation he returned to New York, working for a time as a reporter on the *Times*. Then he drifted—as young men of the day seemed to do—into publishing. First he served as advertising manager of Scribner's, and in 1914 took over an editor's chair. "How long have you been at Scribner's?" he was asked once. "Oh, I've always been at Scribner's," he replied.

During his first five years as an editor, Perkins seemed content to perform with quiet competence in a firm whose major profits derived from English authors like George Meredith, Robert Louis Stevenson, James M. Barrie, and John Galsworthy. Scribner's top American writers were Henry James, Edith Wharton, and Teddy Roosevelt, the last of whom was to some members of the firm a dangerous radical. Perkins' services to the company became of such value that he was made secretary and director. To all intents and purposes he was, from that point on, editor-in-chief.

As the postwar era dawned, Perkins alone seemed to realize the changes taking place outside the firm's Victorian chambers on Fifth Avenue. As a one-man revolution within the company, he fought with determination for Fitzgerald and other new-day writers. Publisher Charles Scribner considered *This Side of Paradise* "frivolous," while others on the staff refused to carry the book home for fear of corrupting wives and children. Nor did Perkins' troubles end after Fitzgerald was a success. A few at Scribner's wanted to reject *The Great Gatsby* because it contained the words "son of a bitch."

It's hard to believe now, but by fighting for Fitzgerald's first novel Perkins changed the image of American publishing. If the third oldest firm in the country (Harper's and Lippincott are older) could place its dignified imprimatur on a jazzy, pace-setting novel like this one, other old-line firms felt impelled to follow. "The monarchy of Scribner's had joined the revolution," one pundit said.

Having scored with Fitzgerald, Perkins went on to sign vigorous writers like cowboy Will James, and the ex-marines James Boyd (*Drums*) and John W. Thomason, Jr. Instead of continuing to avoid such up-to-the-moment authors, entrenched firms began scrambling to find them.

For these and other deeds of intellectual derring-do, Perkins was often cited for farsightedness. Yet as a person he held tight to the old-fashioned virtues of honor, loyalty, and friendship. Perkins turned his pet authors into close workaday friends, and in two instances—Fitzgerald and Thomas Wolfe—temporarily made them sons. The presence of five Perkins daughters at home may have made this process easier.

In a world rapidly becoming high-pressure, Perkins sought to avoid editorial meetings, publishers' conferences, booksellers' conventions, and literary cocktail parties. He preferred to keep his time free for manuscript reading and conferences with potential authors or those already under contract to the firm. As an editorial adviser, Perkins was given to long, pregnant silences which he did not find embarrassing. Nor, it seems, did those with him at the time. "You got confidence just being near him," one said.

In his approach to authors, Perkins believed he operated differently from others in his field. "The trouble with most editors," he commented, "is that they are disappointed writers." Perkins viewed his own function as that of the obstetrician, or midwife, who assisted valiantly during pregnancy and delivery, but had no final responsibility for the job. "The source of a book is the author," he liked to say. "You can only help him produce what he has in his compass."

This does not mean Perkins failed to work hard with writers. He was particularly helpful to authors lost in the jungles of inspiration, and sometimes wrote thirty page memos to assist them. Yet he preferred to improve a manuscript by discreet suggestion, rather than issuing orders, as a disappointed writer might do. Basically, Perkins sought to stimulate an author's imagination, leaving him to evolve his own way out of an impasse. To Roger Burlingame, Scribner editor turned author, the process ran like this: "He suggests to you, in an extraordinary inarticulate fashion, just what you want to say."

Once a manuscript was done to his satisfaction, Perkins handled it with a respect amounting to reverence. For a while he went so far as to advocate that books be printed with the author's own spelling, grammar, and punctuation intact.

This superbenevolent attitude came a cropper with *This Side of Paradise*. For Scott Fitzgerald was not only unable to spell, but his grammar was often atrocious and his punctuation grotesque. For example, when offered a chance to act in the film version of *This Side of Paradise*, he wrote of the project as "a movie with Zelda and I in the leading rolls." He also spelled Nietzsche Nietche. The first edition of *This Side of Paradise* contained nearly one hundred errors of ignorance, which upset the purist Franklin P. Adams. In "The

Conning Tower," F.P.A. branded Scott "sloppy and arrogant," and had little use for his work thereafter.

Fitzgerald's novel had to be copiously corrected in its second edition, and this expensive process wrung from Perkins grudging admission of the worth of copy editors. Yet he went on viewing works in progress more from the author's angle than the firm's. As one writer put it, "He steps into the author's shoes and sees the book as he does." Not unexpectedly writers like Fitzgerald, Van Wyck Brooks, and Arthur Train dedicated books to him.

In the best New England tradition, Maxwell Perkins was a bit of an eccentric. At his best, he looked distinguished, but seemed to take a sly pleasure in appearing his worst in suits shabby and unpressed. The possessor of an unusually narrow skull, Perkins had trouble finding hats that fit, and as if to show his indifference, he bought shapeless gray fedoras that fell down on his ears. Incredibly, he liked to wear them in the office.

He was also growing deaf in one ear and to cover up the hearing difficulty, conversed with visitors to his office by tilting two chairs back against the wall, allowing the other person to talk into his good ear. While thus engaged, the two resembled a pair of rubes teetered back on the porch of a rural general store.

Perkins could also be absentminded on a heroic scale, and one afternoon his eccentricities merged when a young writer kept an appointment with him. Perkins sat at his desk, hat enveloping head, while the young man was ushered in. Then he rose, set the two chairs against the wall, and indicated the method of conversation.

The crowning moment arrived as an imposing gray-haired man entered the office and began ruffling through papers on the desk. Perkins felt introductions were in order and without difficulty remembered the young man's name. But he could not summon that of the older man, snapping fingers in exasperation as his mind probed. Finally, the older man supplied his own name. "Charles Scribner," he barked.

Perkins lunched at the same restaurant every day, invariably in the company of an author. Once he had decided on his favorite dish in the place, he ordered it forever more. After work it was his custom to stop, again with an author, at the Chatham or Ritz Bar, where he quaffed a considerable number of martinis before boarding the train to New Canaan, Connecticut.

Yet with all his rigidities of character, Perkins retained an uncommonly flexible mind. He had proved this in the early Twenties; now he did it again during the second part of the decade.

One triumph concerned Willard Huntington Wright, who had been editor of *Smart Set* before Mencken and Nathan. Handsome, arrogant, and irascible, Wright was characterized by Ernest Boyd as "the most interesting and attractive *unlikable* man I have ever known." Wright's tussles with his fellowman were legendary, but the erudition and good taste of his published books on music, literature, and (especially) art won him simultaneous respect. "As a critic," says Carl R. Dolmetsch in his *Smart Set Anthology*, "he was more learned than Mencken and Nathan, if less adroit at phrase making."

During World War I, the perverse fellow made the most of a facial resemblance to the German Kaiser, and even boasted of being related to the Hohenzollerns "in a morganatic way." This loose talk reached the ears of the Secret Service, and his secretary was instructed to spy on him. In an effort to trap the girl Wright fiendishly dictated a letter full of references to "our glorious Kaiser." Then he followed her to a telephone booth as she attempted to report this instance of treason. A wild rumpus ensued, police arrived, and a newspaper reported the fracas under the headline "EXCITING TIME IN A TELEPHONE BOOTH AT CORNER DRUG STORE."

This and other ill-considered acts won Willard Huntington Wright a blacklisting in Gotham's literary world. Reduced to cheap ghostwriting and free-lance newspaper work, he became a drug addict. Somehow he got to a Paris sanitarium known for miracle cures, placing himself in the hands of a therapist who locked him in near solitary confinement and allowed him to read only mystery stories. This simple literary fare was supposed to relax the patient's churning mind and restore his withered ego.

Amazingly, it worked. The Willard Huntington Wright who departed the sanitarium bore the outlines of a new man. Along with a revitalized personality, he carried the conviction that most of the hundreds of whodunits left behind him were trash and that he could do a damn sight better. From Sherlock Holmes he knew the importance of a strong, opinionated leading character. Borrowing from Sherlock and his own potent personality, he created Philo Vance, an elegant, super-cilious, gentleman-detective who languidly dropped his g's, smoked gold-tip Regie cigarettes, and "in a cold, sculptural fashion was impressively handsome." Next he devised three intricate plots for Philo to solve, one involving Mother Goose rhymes. Wright was well aware that mystery stories were looked down upon as fodder for lowbrows and insomniacs. Afraid of tarnishing his splendid reputation as an art critic, he decided to sign his mysteries S. S. Van Dine.

Thus equipped, he visited Horace Liveright, who had published his previous books. Liveright did not relish mysteries or pseudonyms, and probably did not like Willard Huntington Wright, even the new one. For once the publisher-plunger refused to take a risk, and ushered the would-be Van Dine out of his office. Wright took a plunge himself, and went to see Max Perkins, who was receptive. The first three Philo Vance mysteries were *The Benson Murder Case*, *The "Canary" Murder Case*, and *The Greene Murder Case*—the main word in each title containing six letters, like Wright. With these three intellectual mystery novels, the genre at last achieved status. The books also sold well—at least sixty thousand hard-cover copies each—for the house of Scribner.

Yet for Perkins the satisfactions of ineffable Philo were minor compared to another discovery. Even as S. S. Van Dine made the crime story respectable, the Scribner editor-in-chief was immersed in a manuscript which had arrived at his office in two huge bundles. Titled *O Lost*, it was the work of an unknown from the South named Thomas Wolfe. Several other publishers had read and rejected *O Lost*, one of them Covici-Friede, a new company established by the former Chicago bookseller-publisher Pascal Covici and Donald Friede, who had left Boni and Liveright. Appalled at the size of the manuscript, Friede had turned it over to an editorial department reader whose reasons for rejection were similar to those of others:

> A semi-autobiographical novel of well over 300,000 words, relating the history of a family over a period of 50 years. It is fearfully diffuse, and it would be a tremendous piece of work to boil it down. In parts it holds one's interest by its vitality, but it is marred by stylistic clichés, outlandish adjectives and similes, etc. Probably the author could write if he dumped this overboard and began again. I do not believe it would be possible or worthwhile to doctor this up. It has all the faults of youth and inexperience.

Perkins' interest was kindled when agent Madeleine Boyd, who handled the manuscript, told him of reading it in twelve hours of fascinated concentration, then dashing out into the hall of her apartment crying, "I have discovered a genius! I have discovered a genius!" Perkins reacted in much the same way on finishing the mountain of manuscript before him; he thought it "a nakedly truthful autobiographical novel." Fully aware of its diffuseness, he still thought every word had heartbeat vigor. Perkins' time-honored phrase of approval was "This manuscript *must* be published!" Presumably he uttered it now.

Thomas Wolfe, who had begun to think the cause of his book hopeless, had twenty-seven cents in his pocket when Perkins summoned him to the Scribner office. He was so unfamiliar with the publishing business that he addressed the editor as "Mr. Peters." Yet after listening to Perkins for only a few minutes, he thought, "For the first time in my life, I am getting advice I can really use."

In order to reduce the book to one-volume size, it was necessary to cut out at least 100,000 words. Wolfe tried but was unable to do so. "I'd stare at the manuscript for hours before cutting out a few sentences," he said later. "Sometimes I wanted to rip in blindly and slash, but unless I knew *where*, the result would be disastrous." So the job fell to Perkins, who worked nights on it for nearly a year, reorganizing as well as cutting. When the task was finished, Wolfe said to him, "You are now mixed with my novel in such a way that I can never separate the two of you. I can no longer think clearly of the time I wrote it, but rather of the time when you first talked to me about it and when you worked upon it."

In the process of revision, the title turned into *Look Homeward, Angel*. Published late in 1929, it made Wolfe famous and for the first time injected Maxwell Perkins into the public eye.

Soldier's Pay, William Faulkner's first novel, had been published in 1926, a few months after Hemingway's *In Our Time*. The story of a soldier returning to his Mississippi home, face mutilated and memory gone, it had seemed another promising first novel and another war book, in a period which had a sufficiency of both.

Yet it won recognition. In the New York *Herald-Tribune*, Larry Barretto, who had written the soldier's-return *A Conqueror Passes*, found "the author writes with irony and pity, but he is more ironic than pitiful . . . almost a great book." Another critic noted the author's "swift, nervous talent." Others were bothered by the impressionistic writing—"he admits of no restraint and he submits to no discipline." To them parts of the novel were half-baked Joyce.

Now thitry-one, Faulkner had done considerable wandering for the offspring of an aristocratic but nonprospering family in Oxford, Mississippi, home of the state university known as Ole Miss. In 1917, after his childhood sweetheart married another man, he tried hard to enlist in the wartime air corps. Rejected because of his small stature (which always seemed even smaller because of his fine bones), Faulkner decided to try the Royal Canadian Air Force. En route he paused at New Haven to stay with Phil Stone, a five-years-older resident of Oxford, who had encouraged him to read books and write poetry. In Toronto, Faulkner was accepted by the RCAF and had just mastered flying when peace came. Thus his only rugged wartime adventure came on Armistice Day when he got drunk and landed his plane upside down on a hangar.

Returning to Oxford, he led so shiftless a life that towns-folk dubbed him "Count No 'Count," a dubious tribute to his ever-courtly manners. But while appearing to squander time, he wrote quantities of poetry and absorbed the messages of so many books that later he liked to say, "It's not Faulkner sittin' there at the typewriter . . . it's a thousand men livin' and dead."

For a time he lived in New York, where he washed dishes in a Greek restaurant and clerked in Scribner's Book Store, then managed by a lady named Elizabeth Prall. After six months, he learned from his father, who had become general manager of Ole Miss, that the job of college postmaster was open. Faulkner went home to fill it, and during his tenure also spent time in Memphis bordellos and acted as a boy-scout leader. As postmaster he was far from successful. "I didn't want to be beholden to every son of a bitch who had two cents for a stamp," he once said, explaining an almost total inertia on the job. Soon he quit to go to New Orleans, nursing vague ideas of working his way to Europe on a tramp steamer. In that city he found Sherwood Anderson in residence with a new wife—none other than Elizabeth Prall.

So the gates of New Orleans' most exclusive literary group opened wide to him. Dominated by Anderson, the circle included Roark Bradford, Oliver La Farge, George Milburn, and Hamilton Basso, with occasional visits from travelers like Sinclair Lewis, Carl Sandburg, and John Dos Passos. Faulkner charmed and mystified this sampling of the intelligentsia. A natural deference was rendered more attractive by the deep Mississippi politeness. Yet his frequent drinking bouts were frightening. How, friends wondered, could such a tiny body hold so much liquor? Conversely, was able to remain sober for long periods. Biographer Robert Coughlan thinks he took to drink only when life became unendurable. "He was not an alcoholic," he explains, "but perhaps more accurately an alcoholic refugee, self-pursued."

Until arriving in New Orleans, Faulkner had wished to be a poet. Two years before, his friend Phil Stone had paid for publication of a book of his verses called *The Marble Faun*. Yet Sherwood Anderson—whose influence on young writers was both amazing and uncanny—seemed to have so much free time for "drinkin' and talkin'" that Faulkner was inspired to try the life of novelist. In six months he wrote *Soldier's Pay*, which Anderson recommended to Horace Liveright.

Strange to relate, Faulkner repaid Anderson in the same cruel coin as Hemingway. He wrote, and allowed to be published locally, what seemed to him a good-natured parody of Anderson's writing. Anderson thought otherwise—what author likes to be parodied?

Why the gentle Anderson brought out the worst in his young protégés is a tantalizing question. Perhaps it involved his integrity, for Anderson has been called "A dedicated man with an almost holy respect for the art of writing." Yet his skill was dwindling and disappointment in him could have brought out the vicious in the talents who admired him.

With the two hundred dollars advance for *Soldier's Pay*, Faulkner took his tour of Europe, returning by steerage. He then wrote *Mosquitoes*, a satire on the New Orleans artistic-literary set. Liveright published it to small success, then dropped Faulkner from his list. Undeterred, the author wrote *Sartoris*, a mixture of war, aviation, and spiritual torment back home in an area Faulkner called Yoknapatawpha County, Mississippi. Harcourt, Brace accepted it but brought it out with reluctance.

As author of three books which had not appealed greatly to the public, Faulkner concluded (with an assist from Phil Stone) that he had been trying too hard to appeal to the public. Each of his novels had derived in some way from a successful book or author. *Soldier's Pay* showed traces of

John Dos Passos, Laurence Stallings, Larry Barretto, and the Laurence Stallings–Maxwell Anderson play *What Price Glory?* In *Mosquitoes,* he attempted a satire on the order of Aldous Huxley and (one critic said!) Ronald Firbank. *Sartoris* reflected Hemingway's influence.

Yet Faulkner did not wish to be a popular writer. By nature taciturn and noncompetitive—"an exclusive person," a friend said—he really asked no more than a faithful audience. So why not write to please himself, letting readers find him?

He was in Oxford again as, fed by new resolve, he began to concentrate on his self-created Yoknapatawpha County, in the northwest part of the state. Below the torpid surface of this community—population 15,611—lay a writhing snake pit of greed, murder, cruelty, treachery, infidelity, and incest. Of it, Granville Hicks wrote, "The world of William Faulkner echoes with the hideous march of lust and disease, brutality and death."

First he completed *The Sound and the Fury,* which showed the influence of Joyce and the Russian masters but was Faulkner nonetheless. Then he began *As I Lay Dying,* still considered by many his outstanding work. It told of the death of a hill woman and transportation of her coffin halfway across the state for burial, while a degenerate family schemes and the body putrefies. It has been said that if Hemingway created a style of writing, Faulkner conceived a landscape of fiction. His style has been called by V. S. Pritchett an "agonized prose which appears to be chewed like tobacco and squirted out."

As he labored on these two novels, Faulkner's personal life was brightened by the return of his childhood sweetheart, now a divorcée with two children. For the second time, he set out to marry her.

And so the world proceeded toward 1929, the final year of the Literary Decade. . . .

An Era Ends . . . . *Lewis* . .

Fitzgerald . . Dreiser . . Dorothy Thompson . .

Strange to say, Scott Fitzgerald and Sinclair Lewis foresaw the Depression which in late October 1929 brought a high-flying America tumbling to the ground.

On Scott's 1926 visit, and again two years later, he made melancholy note of the mood sweeping the land: "The uncertainties of 1920 were drowned in a steady golden roar." Around him he saw frayed nerves and jangled spirits adding up to "a restlessness approaching hysteria."

To him New York City was "bloated, glutted, stupid with cake and circuses." He particularly noted widespread use of the expression "oh, yeah," uttered with a downbeat inflection; to him it typified the jaded, unimpressed attitude of the nation. On a mundane level Scott found that his favorite barber had retired on paper profits to live the life of gentleman of leisure. . . . Implicit in the comments of this most sensitive of expatriates was the feeling that something had to give.

Sinclair Lewis' prophecy was more dramatic. Married to Dorothy Thompson in May 1928, he returned with her to New York four months later, and the pair went immediately to the offices of Harcourt, Brace. Suddenly Lewis stopped on busy Madison Avenue to exclaim, "Within a year this country will have a terrible financial panic. I *know*! Can't you *see* it? Can't you *smell* it? I can see people jumping out of win-

dows on this very street!" This prediction was the more uncanny because Lewis had no previous history of psychic experience. Eighteen months later, when men actually did leap
from windows, he could not recall his amazing words.

Returnees from Europe might be conscious of the pressure-
cooker atmosphere, but to Americans it seemed normal. Vincent Sheean, who attests Sinclair Lewis' moment of second
sight, goes on to say, "Except for Dorothy and Red Lewis, I
cannot remember a single acquaintance of mine in America
who perceived the shallowness of the 'prosperity' and the in-
evitability of the crash."

Assisting the country in its mass euphoria was the conviction that America surpassed the rest of the world in nearly
everything: prosperity, automobiles, movies, slang, education
—you name it! Americans felt they had won this eminence
by means of their extroverted, go-getter spirit, given them
alone by a kind of divine dispensation. Popular at the time
was "A Businessman's Prayer":

> *God of business men, I thank Thee for the fellowship of*
> *red-blooded men with songs in their hearts and handclasps*
> *that are sincere;*
> *I thank Thee for telephones and telegrams that link me*
> *with home and office no matter where I am.*
> *I thank Thee for the joy of battle in the business arena,*
> *the thrill of victory and the courage to take defeat like a*
> *good sport.*
>
> AMEN

To paraphrase another observation of Scott Fitzgerald,
proud Americans saw themselves as residents of a universe
rather than a country. This heady conviction was amply
shared by the nation's publishers, to whom the decade had
been unusually kind. More than ten thousand books aimed at
the general public would be published in 1929—Professor
Billy Phelps' words were certainly coming true! Ten years
before only half that number had been available in bookshops. High-priced limited editions might be fading away, but
people were buying regular editions—still at a usual $2.50—

as never before. Publishers intoxicated by prosperity adver-
tised their products by airplane skywriting over Manhattan.
One actually brought out a stunt volume by an author who
tied down a key on his typewriter so that he could not use a
single word requiring it; critics said the loss of a crucial letter
of the alphabet made surprisingly little difference.

Stunt books of a less eccentric variety also captivated the
public. Robert L. Ripley's *Believe It or Not* was among them;
another, J. P. McEvoy's nonnarrative *Show Girl*, an amusing
mélange of love letters, telegrams, mash notes, and sexy
sketches of pretty Dixie Dugan. Anita Loos followed the sensational *Gentlemen Prefer Blondes* with a less successful,
though still funny, *But They Marry Brunettes*.

For a time Robert Benchley and Ring Lardner, top humor-
ists, were eclipsed in public favor by the curious Yiddish
humor of Milt Gross, who wrote and illustrated (basically
he was a comic cartoonist) such gems as *Nize Baby, Hia-
watta Wit Odder Poems*, and *Dunt Esk*. Gross characters—
they bore names like Mr. and Mrs. Feitlebaum, Looey, Nize
Baby, and Mrs. Noftolis—screamed at one another in ac-
cents almost impossible to decipher—"Oohoo, Nize Baby—
ohoo—Baby—Squshlzzrrlz!! Baby, dollink, wots dees?" Who
remembers Milt Gross today?

Then, in 1929 came *Is Sex Necessary?* by E. B. White and
James Thurber. This book, stemming from the creamy-
smooth sophistication of *The New Yorker*, ushered in a new
era of humor and a lot more. Leaving behind the fisticuff fun
of Mencken and his *Mercury*, White, Thurber, Frank Sullivan, Donald Moffat, Joel Sayre, Wolcott Gibbs, S. J. Perel-
man, and other *New Yorker* contributors shaped fresh standards of American humor and new patterns of sophisticated
behavior.

In this best of possible publishing worlds, one matter
remained annoying to publishers—the continuing existence
and prosperity of the Book of the Month Club and the Literary Guild, with the first-named claiming fifty thousand
members. Making the situation worse was the demand by

book clubs for an extra 20 percent discount on all books sold them, plus the usual discount already allowed booksellers. This gave the publishers an uneasy feeling that they were being cheated of lovely revenue.

What appeared a golden opportunity to discredit the book clubs came in March 1929, when the Book of the Month Club chose as its selection *Cradle of the Deep,* by Joan Lowell, a Simon and Schuster publication. The author claimed to be a Lowell of Boston on her mother's side; the name of her adventurous Montenegran-Australian father was too complex to adorn a book jacket.

Joan Lowell was young and statuesque, with flashing eyes, a strong physique, and the ability to swim like a shark. Those who praised the girl's beauty or aquatic skills were frequently rewarded by a life synopsis which revolved around the fact that Joan had grown up aboard the four-masted schooner *Minnie B.,* captained by her father. Joan had written a few magazine articles on her seafaring experiences, and these had been submitted to Simon and Schuster as material for a book. Underlings in the firm who read her articles called them preposterous. But when Richard Simon and Max Schuster met the gorgeous gal in person, they felt sure her experiences were real. "Go home and do us a book," she was told.

Joan did, and turned in a manuscript not only replete with adventurous situations, but spiced with sexy innuendo as she told of learning the facts of life (verbally) from salty old seamen. The manuscript was given to Felix Riesenberg and William McFee, two highly respected nautical authors, to be perused for believability and nautical accuracy. Both approved it with high praise. But the reaction was different when *Herald-Tribune Books* sent a review copy to Lincoln Colcord, Down East seaman and writer. Colcord blasted *Cradle of the Deep,* professing to find on its pages impossible episodes and erroneous nautical terms. Joan claimed to be able to spit a curve into the wind; her father, she said, shot down a waterspout with a rifle; when the *Minnie B.* caught fire, Joan saved herself by swimming through miles of rough sea with a kitten on each shoulder. Ridiculing these and other exploits, Colcord got unexpected support from the president of Baker and Taylor, book wholesalers. An amateur yachts-man, this fellow told Simon the book was "the biggest hoax of the century."

Simon's reaction was to call Joan to his office, look search-ingly into her flashing eyes, and ask, "Is your book true?" She demurely assured him it was, at which the firm went ahead with plans for a publication-day party aboard the *Ile de France*. At this reporters dared Joan to spit a curve in the wind; she pointed out there was no wind that day.

Colcord hammered away, and finally a showdown meeting between the two opponents was arranged. According to *The New Yorker*, "Joan was coy at first, but as she realized she was being called a liar on count after count, she flexed her powerful biceps, invited Colcord to remove his glasses, and was barely prevented from taking a poke at him. . . . After about an hour she burst into tears." Neither then nor later did she admit her book might be a hoax.

Further exposure came as the New York *Post* delved deep into her background. Joan, it transpired was no Lowell, but rather Helen Joan Wagner, a Hollywood bit actress with a vivid imagination. Her father had indeed been skipper of a four-master, but Helen Joan had been aboard for only one voyage. At this, Simon and Schuster caved in, stating the book "had been published in good faith, not as an autobiog-raphy, but as a thrilling yarn."

In an age of ballyhoo, such a development merely in-creased public interest. Moved from nonfiction to fiction cat-egory, *Cradle of the Deep*, proceeded to sell more copies than before. But the publishers themselves were deeply upset, with Richard Simon reportedly suffering a nervous breakdown as a result. Morale at the prospering firm sank so low that for the first time in five years it failed to make a profit for the year.

During this controversy the Book of the Month Club remained serenely aloof, continuing to distribute a notorious, possibly fraudulent book. This haughty attitude infuriated John Macrae, president of E. P. Dutton and Company. In the belief that the behavior of the Book of the Month rendered both it and the Literary Guild vulnerable, he began efforts to destroy them. Hoping others would rally behind him, he announced that no more Dutton books would be submitted in advance to book clubs. Only the old-line firm of F. A. Stokes supported him, but Macrae persevered.

Next, he mailed a broadside to a thousand critics, editors, and booksellers, branding the book clubs no more than mail-order houses which tended to concentrate attention on one or two books a month to the detriment of others. The extra discount, he went on, robbed publishers and booksellers of rightful rewards. He also expressed doubts that the distinguished judges of the clubs actually picked monthly selections. Here he went too far—the Book of the Month Club sued him for libel.

The book clubs countered Macrae's other charges by stating in effect "the public wants and needs us." Pointing to a continuing rise in membership, they pictured themselves as opening new markets, finding a public the bookstores had overlooked, and creating fresh interest in current literature. The extra 20 percent discount, they claimed, was necessary for advertising and distribution.

So the situation simmered until the May convention of the American Booksellers Association in Boston. There a vociferous majority sided with Macrae, castigating book clubs as "menaces and intellectual shams, which atrophy American taste." Attacking the claim that the clubs picked the best book each month, one speaker ringingly declared, "The word 'best' implies a selection among comparable books. . . . There are many different fields represented each month."

"BOOKSELLERS VOTE TO WAGE WAR ON BOOK CLUBS" ran a headline on May 19. But how to wage it? Only two publishers had refused to submit books in advance to the clubs, and without a united front, defiance was meaningless. Thwarted, the booksellers turned to other problems. Some had installed lending (or circulating) libraries on their premises, and discriminating members rose to ask if this did not lower the standards of the bookselling profession.

A few weeks later the impressive judges of the Book of the

Month and Literary Guild offered evidence that they did indeed pick their clubs' monthly selections. With this, Macrae's most sensational charge evaporated, and he was forced to devour his words, after which the Book of the Month dropped its suit. As controversy faded, *The New York Times* editorialized about "silver-lined book clouds ahead."

By this time *Cradle of the Deep* had also vanished. A fickle public, having given the book a second wind as a work of fiction, abruptly ceased buying it. Pocketing forty-one thousand dollars in profits, statuesque Joan Lowell, née Wagner, faded from the New York scene. Behind her she left *Salt Water Taffy, or Twenty Thousand Leagues away from the Sea*, a parody of her book by Corey Ford, signed with the pseudonym June Triplett.

Critics called the Ford parody far superior to the original. Like the Dr. Traprock epics of George S. Chappell, *Salt Water Taffy* was illustrated with absurd photographs of well known writers, Manhattan *bon vivants*, and pretty girls. Two of its episodes were "I capture a baby waterspout named Gladys, and keep it for a pet" and "I am forced to swim around Cape Horn because Richard Halliburton has exclusive swimming rights to the Panama Canal."

Not all the books of 1929 were on an armchair-adventure level. The Twenties were a disappointing decade to some intellects who pondered them from a spiritual level. Walter Lippmann, brilliant at Harvard, contributor to President Wilson's Fourteen Points, editorial writer, journalist, and currently editor of the New York *World*, was one who viewed the American society with sorrow, if not alarm. In his *A Preface to Morals*, he now sifted the manifold problems of an age in which people had abandoned the faiths of their fathers. The first, or downbeat, section of his book was called "an eloquent analysis of the disillusionments of the modern world." In it, the author wrote, "It is common for young men and women to rebel, but that they should rebel sadly and without faith in their own rebellion—that is something of a novelty." Continuing, Lippmann tried to chart a way out of contemporary confusions by advocating acceptance of a "higher humanism," which would lead to a new morality.

Joseph Wood Krutch, in his mid-thirties, was one more intellect upset by the Twenties. As a youth, a reading of Shaw's *Man and Superman* had switched his ambition from engineering to literature. Now drama critic of *The Nation*, he had published books on the Restoration drama as well as the critical study of Poe. In *The Modern Temper* he applied himself to the case of the thinking individual who "having weighed and rejected the moral, aesthetic, and other values of his predecessors finds only in the pursuit of knowledge that which makes life worth living." One reviewer found it "dismal pessimism."

A curious footnote to the entire decade—and a highly successful book—was *Middletown: A Study of American Culture*, by Robert S. and Helen M. Lynd. The married Lynds had conducted a deep sociological study of a representative American city-town of 30,000 population. Eventually the name of this city was revealed as Muncie, Indiana, but more pertinent was that life in the Middle West seemed to have remained distressingly akin to what Sinclair Lewis had pictured in *Main Street* and *Babbitt*. The Lynd study was read with fascination by a large segment of the public, but proved a bitter pill for highbrows who had sought over ten years to raise the intellectual sights of the nation.

During 1929, Scott Fitzgerald fought two demons. One was his own lack of progress on the matricide novel that had engaged him on and off over the last four years. Before this year was out he would abandon it, to begin the work that became *Tender Is the Night*.

Demon number two was Zelda's fiendish preoccupation with ballet. On the family's return to Paris, she began attending morning ballet classes, taking private lessons in the afternoon, dieting strenuously, and forgetting domestic responsibilities. At the same time quarrels between the two reached depths of ugliness. Not until April 1930 did Zelda break down completely, but her incipient madness was all too apparent. Scott was helpless in such a situation. Bitter about her "dancing and sweating," he once asked caustically, "Are you under any illusion that you'll ever be any good at this stuff?" Zelda, mind choked with dreams of ballet triumphs, did not bother to reply.

When her training was finally completed, she appeared briefly with a provincial ballet company. Returning to Paris, she received an offer to do the shimmy at the *Folies Bergère*. It was a bitter touch Scott might have conceived for a novel. . . .

Nineteen-twenty-nine may well have been the happiest twelvemonth in the whole frenetic existence of Sinclair "Red" Lewis. He first set eyes on Dorothy Thompson in July 1927 at a diplomatic reception in Berlin and had instantly fallen in love with her. On second meeting, he begged her to marry him. When she laughingly refused, he vowed, "I'm going to propose to you every time I see you from now on, in public or private." Several days later the pair attended a meeting at which Lewis was asked to speak. Rising to his feet he said, "Dorothy, I love you," and sat down.

Dorothy Thompson was a hard-working foreign correspondent, filing exceptional news dispatches to the New York *Post* and Philadelphia *Public Ledger*. Radiantly beautiful at thirty-three, she found her impetuous suitor fascinating and amusing. Just divorced herself, she felt attuned to his rampant miseries. According to her, he was "destroying himself as a man, a father, and even as an artist." Gradually she began to believe that it lay within her capacity to arrest this process.

While conducting his determined courtship, Lewis wrote *The Man Who Knew Coolidge*, an expansion of a long story written for *The American Mercury*. In book form, it read like one of his long-winded monologues, and one critic saw "a dismal creation."

Next, Lewis began work on *Dodsworth*, at the same time trying to spend every moment possible with Dorothy. In late

October 1927, she left alone for Russia to cover the tenth anniversary of the Russian Revolution. A month later Lewis, having completed fifty thousand rough words of *Dodsworth,* dropped everything to join her. On their return to Berlin, she agreed to become his wife. The ceremony took place in England the following May—by then Lewis had finished the first draft of *Dodsworth.*

The couple arrived in the United States in August, taking a town house on lower Fifth Avenue and a country place in idyllic Vermont. Lewis was enormously proud of his wife's work, especially when her dispatches from Moscow were published in book form as *The New Russia.* Yet in the midst of his unaccustomed well-being, Lewis made no effort to taper off drinking. In the words of Mark Schorer, he often got "fantastically drunk," and was still not above disgracing himself in public.

Dodsworth, published in the spring of 1929, brought him added pleasure. Like *Arrowsmith,* this was a novel no one could really dislike. As if all his passion had been spent on *Elmer Gantry,* Lewis emerged this time the tolerant author of a book which dealt intelligently with the collapse of an American marriage during exposure to Europe. However, a few critics were dubious about *Dodsworth,* wondering if it might possibly signal the beginning of a downward slide in Lewis' exceptional career.

In *Dodsworth,* Lewis had for the first time written an ambivalent novel, offering in Sam Dodsworth a likable, successful Middle Westerner lucky enough to have been exposed to Yale and other aspects of eastern culture. Yet Lewis had just written of his doctor brother who had stayed in their hometown of Sauk Center, "It's a good thing he *is* determinedly Midwestern; it gives him a solidity, an integrity, likely to be lacking in those of us who always want to be some place where we ain't."

Dodsworth reflects these mixed emotions. At one time or another every creative artist seems to wish he had remained at home to become a solid citizen, and apparently Sinclair Lewis was suffering these pangs. This burgeoning admiration for qualities once despised inevitably weakened him as a novelist, creating a fissure more apparent in future works. Once he had written from strength; now it would be uncertainty.

Fran Dodsworth, Sam's wife, is equally hard to figure. Lewis had written his novel while wooing Dorothy Thompson, and it might be expected that good-looking, restless Fran would radiate features of a new love. But Fran, the "babied adult," is more like Grace Hegger. To the author, Fran is the "limited" woman finally abandoned by Sam Dodsworth for a "spacious" one. Presumably the spacious lady is Dorothy, with Grace limited. Yet Lewis lavished much loving care on the character of Fran, and some of his admirers thought her a creation as fine as Leora in *Arrowsmith*. "God kissed you when you created her," one friend assured him. Lewis suffered this tribute gladly.

At the moment dispraise of *Dodsworth* was muted, while praise rose high. As always with Lewis novels, voices were heard proclaiming it superior to its predecessors, so *Dodsworth* seemed destined to be the fifth Sinclair Lewis best seller of the decade. It hardly seemed possible that the author would never again write books as good as his major works of the Twenties, up to and including *Dodsworth* . . .

Theodore Dreiser was another whose best work lay behind. Still, this ponderous, self-approving man continued to be controversial and newsworthy until the day of his death.

With *An American Tragedy*, success had enveloped Dreiser in a bear hug. Not only did the five-dollar, double-decker *Tragedy* earn money, but his old novels began selling in new editions. The play version of *An American Tragedy*, ridiculed by Alexander Woollcott and other captious critics, nonetheless attracted audiences and for a period earned thirty thousand dollars a week, from which Dreiser received a gratifying royalty. Soon the author who had lived most of his life in unappealing semipoverty was making almost $100,000 a year, minus the paltry tax bite of the Twenties.

At first, Dreiser had been unable to credit his good fortune, only daring to venture the remark "I am likely to be rich." But as the greenbacks poured in, confidence grew, and he gleefully told friends, "I am opulent—*opulent!*" It's a measure of Dreiser, as well as the Teeming Twenties, that he accepted money for a cigarette testimonial, though he did not smoke.

If Dreiser rejoiced over the money in his life, his faithful companion Helen Richardson experienced transports of joy. This beautiful woman, just entering her thirties, bought herself an exotic wardrobe and a Russian wolfhound to set it off. Then she prodded Dreiser into renting a picturesque duplex apartment at 200 West 57th Street. When Helen finished decorating it, the premises boasted stained-glass windows, a grand piano, indirect lighting, Oriental rugs, and other appurtenances of luxury.

On the walls were nudes (girls, naturally) painted by Dreiser himself, who as an artist had a certain rugged honesty. To editor-author Manuel Komroff, the Dreiser duplex was "a cross between Gimbel's and Roxy's," but it made a perfect setting for the Thursday night parties the novelist began to give. "Is it possible," asked Fannie Hurst, as she left one, "that our host was *Theodore Dreiser?* Say what you will, I don't believe it!"

The Dreiser soirees, which began at nine thirty in the evening, never had the flair of Carl Van Vechten's parties, or the chic of publisher Condé Nast's. But celebrities flocked to them. There were always plenty of pretty girls, with the host pausing occasionally to haul one to his lap and paw her. Dreiser might lament to friends that his sexual powers were waning, but he could still bed three different girls in one day. Now he labored amidst a fresh contingent of attractive young secretaries and literary aides, plus a female press agent. It was a situation Helen Richardson continued to accept, though at times she tried to assert her independence. But for the most part she found solace in being the woman Dreiser always returned to. "[He] was my religion," she explained once. Her reward was long in coming, but a year before his death the titan grudgingly married her.

As always, Dreiser was involved in numerous writing

projects, as well as projecting an elaborate country home in Mount Kisco, New York. In 1927 he eagerly accepted an invitation from Russia to attend the decennial of the Revolution. This would, he thought, give him a chance "to revise his understanding of America." He also wished to understand Russia. Up to this time his personal brand of liberal-radical thinking had consisted in expressing general sympathy for the underdog while despising the American capitalist system. But recently he had shifted mental gears to see man's problems on a world scale. Perhaps in Russia's communist system lay the answer to human inequity and injustice.

The Russian trip was not without interesting aspects. Leaving behind five girl friends, not counting Helen, Dreiser traveled alone and in Berlin fell ill of bronchitis and an enlarged aorta. This came in the midst of the Dorothy Thompson-Sinclair Lewis courtship; nonetheless, kind-hearted Dorothy found time to nurse Dreiser. Sinclair Lewis, a man Dreiser disliked and resented, took over when Dorothy was busy. One Berlin doctor whispered to Miss Thompson that Dreiser had lung cancer. With this secret, she left for Moscow.

Dreiser soon followed, though doctors had forbidden the trip. In Moscow, he revived, unearthed a Russian girl friend, and sat back to be lionized. Dorothy Thompson, believing him fatally ill, continued her kindnesses. Dreiser repaid her by noting in his diary that she made amorous "overtures" to him. Later, in the United States, he broadly hinted at sex relations, yet this seems unlikely, for Dorothy was writing Lewis that she had wearied of "being facetiously nudged by old Dreiser, who has turned quite a gay dog in Moscow."

Determined to see more of Russia, Dreiser devoted his stubborn will to gaining a one-man tour which carried him to outposts like Yalta and Tiflis. It was an uncomfortable journey, made worse by red tape and the stupidity of guides. At its end he growled, "I'd rather die in the United States than live here."

But by the time he reached Paris, where Helen was waiting, he had begun to romanticize Russia. Says W. A. Swanberg, "For Dreiser, whose keen mind was subjugated by helpless emotionalism and deep prejudices, retrospect and reality were two different things." From now on he glowingly remembered any pleasant aspects of Russia and conveniently forgot the rest.

Back in New York, he began writing a book modestly entitled *Dreiser Looks at Russia.* Again, he was immersed in many projects and failed to give proper time to the book, though it was intended as a milestone in his career. Apparently he was unaware that Dorothy Thompson's dispatches from Russia were being put between hard covers. Dreiser's work came out two months after hers, and proved rambling, disorganized, and contradictory. Worse, it contained paragraphs, statistics and turns of phrase duplicating those of Miss Thompson. Where she wrote that the cathedrals of Moscow stood out in the drab city "like jewels in a mud puddle," Dreiser said the same. And so it went, with only minor changes in some three thousand words of Dorothy Thompson material.

Sinclair Lewis grew apoplectic at the obvious plagiarism, but Miss Thompson kept her cool. She reasoned (no doubt correctly) that Dreiser, believing her newspaper stories would be forgotten when his book appeared, had clipped them for use as research material. W. A. Swanberg takes it from there: he theorizes that Dreiser instructed one of his casual lady friends to incorporate the Thompson articles in the manuscript, and the inexperienced girl did it with only perfunctory changes.

Trapped in a dastardly act, Dreiser was magnificently unregenerate. On the theory that the best defense is attack, he first accused Miss Thompson of using information furnished by him in Moscow talkfests. When this failed to hold up, he declared that both of them had used the same Russian handouts. He made much of the fact that, because of his traveling, he had spent eleven weeks in Russia to her four. Under these circumstances, he demanded indignantly, how could she know more than he did? To friends, he dropped those meaningful hints of sex interludes.

But how to explain the identical turns of phrase? Dreiser

couldn't and never tried. Instead, he turned Olympian. "His attitude seemed to be that the whole thing was of no importance and that we could do nothing about it," said one of his lawyers, after Miss Thompson decided to sue. It turned out to be a smart tactic, for Miss Thompson shortly withdrew the suit. But it all had a bad effect on *Dreiser Looks at Russia*, which sold only four thousand copies.

With his mind still a jumble of plans and projects—the Mount Kisco house was taking more time—Dreiser lumbered on. In 1929, his *A Gallery of Women* was published in a two-volume, ten-dollar set. Dreiser considered this indiscreet, kiss-and-tell volume to be sexy and sensational, yet a lot of it had been written five or more years before and already seemed out of date. Reviewers accorded the book lukewarm praise, and sales proved disappointing.

At this low point in life, Dreiser was suddenly sustained by a fresh hope. For years he had nursed dreams of winning the Nobel Prize for Literature. Now literary gossip said the prize committee was determined to pick an American writer in 1930. Dreiser, already popular in Germany, sent his young lady press agent overseas to whip up favorable comment in other European countries . . .

Whatever the activities of the titans, the year 1929 really belonged to Ernest Hemingway. His second novel, *A Farewell to Arms*, was published then, following serialization in *Scribner's*, and it consolidated his reputation as the most influential novelist of the decade. Yet to some, the book was a surprise.

In *The Sun Also Rises*, Hemingway had posed as bold spokesman of an amoral Lost Generation, offering a shocker by his emphasis on drinking and sex. But *A Farewell to Arms*, told a story as ancient as man. Lieutenant Frederic Henry, an American ambulance driver on the Italo-Austrian front, falls tenderly and truly in love with English nurse Catherine Barkley. The two talk love, play love games, and slither between sheets. When the lieutenant is wounded,

Catherine becomes his nurse and love deepens—it is, thought Henry Seidel Canby, "amorousness lifted into deep, fierce love." Catherine gets pregnant and goes to Switzerland to bear the child; he deserts the army to be near her. A Caesarean is necessary; mother and baby die. The love story—though not the sex scenes, pregnancy, and death—stemmed directly from Hemingway's experiences in a World War I Italian hospital.

To some *A Farewell to Arms* was Romeo and Juliet all over again. On a lecture tour of the United States, Bertrand Russell saw fit to denounce it as Victorian. Yet critics felt that by his hard-boiled, he-man approach and short-sentence prose, Hemingway had spun his oft-told tale in the most modern manner. "It deals with life when the blood is running and the spirit active—and that is good enough for me," Henry Canby summed up.

More, the tender episodes contrasted powerfully with the rough behavior of soldiers, both levels supplying enough sex and profanity to get the book banned in Boston. Some thought the novel best in its thoroughly masculine description of the savagery and confusion of the Italian retreat at Caporetto. Others preferred the poetic idiom of the final tragic dialogue between the star-crossed lovers, a section Hemingway said he rewrote seventy times.

Time's critic saw total triumph—"infused with the chaotic sweep of armies and tenderly quiescent love. . . . In its sustained, inexorable movements, its throbbing preoccupation with flesh and nerves rather than fanciful fabrics of intellect . . . it fulfills the prophecies that his most excited admirers have made about Ernest Hemingway."

Still, there can be sourness in the fruits of success. *A Farewell to Arms* may have brought Hemingway his desired eminence as heavyweight champion of the literary world, but it was not *the* war novel of 1929. *Farewell* sold ninety thousand copies, excellent for a novel. But the top-selling fiction work of the year was *All Quiet on the Western Front,* which sold 300,000, including Book of the Month copies, and was hailed as the finest war novel of the decade.

Written by Erich Maria Remarque, a fellow of Hemingway vintage who quit school to join the German army, the book was titled *Im Westen nichts Neues* (Nothing New in the West) in the original. Its enormous success in Germany, England, and America, might have been due to its essential simplicity. For this novel pictured war as hell (and the trench warfare of World War I the most hellish ever) with none of the subtlety and symbolism Hemingway at times inserted into his prose.

Rather than battling the Allies, Remarque's Boche soldiers fought an ever-present Death. The author conveyed war's ghastliness in part by an atmosphere that readers almost tasted. Said one reviewer, "The net result is feverish horror. There is a vivid, merciful unreality about the book. To be permeated by horror is to be destroyed spiritually. That is what the book tells." With all this went the soldiers' feeling that they were being betrayed by generals, fat-cat munitions makers behind the lines, and the almighty Hohenzollerns. The same brutal cynicism was to be found in another antiwar import of the year—Stefan Zweig's *Strange Case of Sergeant Grischa*.

End-of-the-decade fiction also included a type of sex novel which adumbrated the anything-goes sizzlers of the Sixties and Seventies. This provokes the intriguing notion that lacking a Depression and a second world war to intervene, the country might have attained its era of sex permissiveness long before the Sixties.

In 1929 publishers were convinced that at last they were on the verge of defeating the heretofore powerful forces of censorship. Indicative of this belief was the wild bidding for a book called *The Well of Loneliness*, by Radclyffe Hall. A superior lesbian novel with a Foreword by Havelock Ellis, this had been published and banned in merrie England. Nonetheless, it was purchased by Alfred A. Knopf, who designed it into one of his distinguished Borzoi books. Then he decided not to publish it.

Immediately other American firms clogged the cables with importunate offers. That of Donald Friede, of Covici-Friede, was one of the most unusual in publishing annals. Friede promised a ten thousand dollar advance against a 20 percent royalty. This sum would remain the author's even if the book were suppressed in America. In addition, Friede promised to protect the book by hiring censorship-lawyer Morris Ernst, whose zeal would be stoked by a bonus of twenty-five cents on each copy sold. Finally, the novel would retail at five dollars, instead of the usual two-fifty, vastly increasing the author's profit.

The offer was accepted, and Covici-Friede became publishers of the hot-to-handle *Well of Loneliness*. Donald Friede first acquired the handsome Knopf books, offering them as a ten-dollar limited edition. Regular editions were cannily printed in New Jersey; if vice-crusader John S. Sumner struck in New York, books could still be printed and distributed from its sister state. As expected, Sumner took action, describing the novel as obscene. With this, sales of the five-dollar edition, already excellent, became doubly so. One of Morris Ernst's strategems was to seek support from well-known persons who thought the book literary rather than prurient. Sinclair Lewis obliged by calling it "almost lugubriously moral." Eugen Boissevain, husband of Edna St. Vincent Millay, wired, "Will not some true Christian teach Mr. Sumner to abuse himself instead of us and get rid of all this public nuisance?"

Even so, Friede, who personally sold the book to Sumner, was tried and found guilty in lower court. Yet the publishers' belief that the walls of censorship might be crumbling proved right. For, on appeal, three judges of the Court of Special Sessions ruled *The Well of Loneliness* not to be obscene.

Around this test-case novel revolved a cluster of lesser works which also forecast the unabashed sexuality of thirty years hence. The titles of Viña Delmar's novels—*Bad Girl, Loose Ladies, Kept Women*—were always naughtier than her books; yet people bought them as much for the titles as for the author's indubitable story-telling gifts. Carmen

Barnes' *Schoolgirl*, Helen Grace Carlisle's *See How They Run*, Donald Henderson Clarke's *Millie*, Maxwell Bodenheim's *Replenishing Jessica*—these and others shoved sex to the limits of the time.

Most daring of all was *Ex-Wife*, an autobiographical novel wherein the lady author informed the world that predatory males considered pretty divorcées the fairest of game. "They used to bring me violets," the heroine sighs, "but now they buy me gin." The author of *Ex-Wife*, published anonymously at first, turned out to be Ursula Parrott, who went on to earn $120,000 a year writing titillating books and magazine fiction. *Ex-Husband*, published in the wake of successful *Ex-Wife*, proved male writers able to outdo females in salaciousness.

In late October, the American stock market buckled and broke. On the afternoon of the twenty-third, $5 billion fell off market valuations within five hours. By eleven o'clock the next morning, every bank in the city was technically insolvent, having lent millions on stocks for which no price was offered.

This Depression, intermittent at the beginning, was unusual in that it first hit the wealthy and well-to-do. Thus book sales afforded a unique barometer of economic conditions. It was possible to anticipate the worst as *Dodsworth*, having sold 100,000 copies, stopped selling in midcareer. Thomas Wolfe's *Look Homeward, Angel*, published early in October to fine reviews, sold a disappointing seventeen thousand copies.

William Faulkner's *The Sound and the Fury* was another casualty. By now a married man with two stepchildren, Faulkner decided drastic action was necessary to salvage his writing career and set out to find the most lurid sex situation possible for his next book. He came up with the nightmarish saga of coed Temple Drake, thrill-hungry flapper gone wrong, who is abandoned by a drunken boyfriend, then physically violated by means of a corncob, which brings satisfaction to the perverted character called Popeye. Temple winds up in a Memphis bordello—all this was the genesis of *Sanctuary*, the novel that put Faulkner on the literary map. When published two years later critics recoiled from its "obscene and bestial decadence," but the public bought copies in droves.

Faulkner was not aware that Ernest Hemingway, temporary resident of Key West, had read one of his novels and again found bitterness in fruits of success. From that moment on, the acknowledged champ considered Faulkner a better novelist than he was.

Never in history has a full-fledged era ended so suddenly—or with such devastating effect—as the Roaring Twenties after Depression struck. Artistic folk, always sensitive, felt all the early vibrations. In *Exile's Return*, Malcolm Cowley recounts that drinking turned desperate rather than dizzy, and that numerous marriages and friendships broke up. People began having nervous breakdowns, something easy to avoid in the halcyon Twenties. One man said his psychoanalyst's anteroom was so crowded with authors and publishers as to resemble a literary cocktail party.

With the exception of Ernest Hemingway, Gertrude Stein, Ezra Pound, and a few others, expatriates began to flock back to the United States, revealing the guilty secret that funds from home had maintained many of them abroad. Even Harold Stearns returned, to marry a woman of wealth and write his memoirs.

Writers lost money like everyone else. Theodore Dreiser, for one, dropped at least seventy-five thousand dollars in the market crash. In his autobiography, Burton Rascoe gives a classic picture of the literary man gradually entrapped in the web of Wall Street. One of his friends, a successful stock operator, said to him, "I'd like to make some money for you, if you'll let me." Rascoe let him and soon became sufficiently involved in money making to trade for himself. The subheads of his chapters detail the unhappy process: "Unwittingly I Become a Stock Market Gambler" . . . "Everybody's Doing It" . . . "Black Wednesday" . . . "End of an Era" . . . "My paper fortune had shrunk in two and a half days," Rascoe laments.

More than money vanished with the Twenties. Nearly everyone prominent in the Literary Decade had left the better part of his life in that era. True, Alfred A. Knopf continued to be Manhattan's most distinguished publisher, while Carl Van Vechten quit novel writing to become an outstanding portrait photographer, and Thornton Wilder achieved glory as novelist and playwright. Among his works are *Our Town* and the adaptation on which *Hello, Dolly* is based. But not all the others fared so well.

H. L. Mencken, who had done so much to invigorate the decade lost much of his strenuous spirit to become crotchety and hidebound, culminating his career as a hater of FDR and the New Deal; in 1930, the perennial bachelor amazed friends by taking a bride. George Jean Nathan remained the glossy boulevardier but never seemed much at home in the theater of the Thirties and Forties, though he still loved night life; he too married but waited longer than Mencken.

Sinclair Lewis, so content in 1929, stayed the husband of Dorothy Thompson for ten years more, with the last period between them stormy; he died desolate and alone in Italy in 1951. Theodore Dreiser survived until 1945, when he breathed his last at age seventy-four; two major novels, *The Bulwark* and *The Stoic*, came out in his final years. Joseph Hergesheimer, reputed earner of $500,000 all told from *The Saturday Evening Post* alone, kept on as one of the nation's most prosperous authors, but never wrote another novel as popular as *Cytherea* or as good as its predecessor, *Linda Condon*. James Branch Cabell, author of twelve volumes in the Twenties, sliced his name to Branch Cabell and produced the book of essays, *These Restless Heads*.

Ernest Hemingway went from Paris to Cuba to live; he married twice more (four wives in all), wrote *For Whom the Bell Tolls* and other notable novels, served enthusiastically as a correspondent in the Spanish Civil War and World War II, and in 1961 committed suicide in his native land. Scott Fitzgerald died in Hollywood in 1940 without writing a novel better than *The Great Gatsby*; standing before his coffin, Dorothy Parker murmured, "The poor son of a bitch." Zelda survived him by seven years; inmate of various sanitariums, she died when one of them caught fire—"her second death," someone said.

Louis Bromfield, reestablished in his native Ohio, became an outstanding agriculturist-author and wrote *The Farm*, perhaps his most heartfelt book. Edna Ferber produced *Cimarron* and other novels, each seemingly more popular than the one before; the ambitious lady who lived her early working years in hotels wound up with a chateau-*cum*-swimming pool in Connecticut. Horace Liveright, predicatably, went broke in the Wall Street crash and died almost friendless a few years later. Richard Halliburton kept performing his incredible adventuring feats and died (somewhat mysteriously) in the midst of one.

Burton Rascoe became a best-selling author-literary critic with *Titans of Literature* and other volumes. Whimsical Christopher Morley eventually jolted the world by producing the daring novel *Kitty Foyle*. Ben Hecht continued to write books, but his main interest turned to Hollywood script writing, at which he was tops. For Ernest Boyd the Twenties had been the ideal decade; he never was so much himself thereafter. Dorothy Parker lived until 1967, marrying the same man twice; the passage of time brought no surcease to her inherent melancholy.

In various ways, the Twenties represented the best of times to each of these talents. And, as the century turned thirty, all could look back and see how much their efforts had contributed to changing the cultural atmosphere of America. Ten years before, Harold Bell Wright and Zane Grey had seemed important writers to a large segment of the American public; now only the young read them. Books and authors, not to mention publishers, had played a vital role in the battle to banish Puritanism and Victorianism from the American scene, and in so doing raised the standards of native literature and life. Doing this, they had also managed to have a lot of fun.

In the early Twenties, Joseph Hergesheimer had donned a soothsayers' cap and predicted for American writers:

> *I [see] them penetrating the entire fabric of American life and exposing, with the acid of their supreme experience, countless rotten threads and false designs.*

Here, indeed, was a prophecy that came true. . . .

Epilogue

"There are no second acts in American lives," Scott Fitzgerald said, in an oft-quoted remark. Nor was there a second act to the Literary Decade, though two additional scenes—or curtain calls—remained.

The first came on November 5, 1930, when word reached Sinclair Lewis that he had won the Nobel Prize for Literature. Three members of the Swedish Academy had voted, with a single vote going to Dreiser and the other two to Lewis largely because of the "gay virtuosity and flashing satire" the Swedes detected in *Babbitt*.

The award became a front-page event, since Lewis was the first American to receive it, and resulted in a burst of excitement reminiscent of the Roaring Twenties. The author was at first incredulous, then delighted, and finally a trifle shamefaced, graciously informing reporters that Willa Cather deserved the honor more than he did. Dreiser, of course, was beside himself—"almost suicidal with rage," a friend said.

Naturally the American public was pleased that a countryman had at last won an award which could well have been bestowed on William Dean Howells or Mark Twain. Even so, the Lewis choice did not seem popular with either public or literary community; it was as if, in these early days of Depression, both groups realized Lewis had typified a bygone era which had probably contributed to the current distress. The financial benefits involved in the award came to about forty-eight thousand dollars, and most letters of congratulation from the general public included requests for a loan or outright gift of some part of it. In addition, Lewis' first wife filed for an increase in alimony.

As for the literary world, Ludwig Lewisohn has said that "something like a groan went up from other writers" when the news was announced. The list of those who omitted to congratulate Lewis is far more interesting than the roster of those who did. William Lyon Phelps sent bubbling congratulations but, Lewis noted bitterly, his was the only voice heard from Yale. Sherwood Anderson, Lewis Mumford, Ernest Boyd, and others clung firmly to the belief that Dreiser should have won the award. William Seabrook, a man who had no reason to be fond of Dreiser, nonetheless said, "Dreiser will be granite when Lewis is dust." It was the feeling among the literary.

One voice raised in protest was that of the American Academy of Arts and Letters, an encrusted outfit which had labored hard to keep the Genteel Tradition alive through the distractions of the Twenties. Its head, Dr. Henry Van Dyke, told reporters the Lewis award was "an insult to America." Lewis, who should have given a horse laugh, instead let this gnaw at him during his moment of triumph.

At the end of November, Lewis and his wife embarked for Stockholm where he was to accept the honor in a speech before the Swedish Academy. With him the author carried a little book titled *Swedish in Ten Lessons*. At cocktail parties and dinners preceding the awards, the American proved to be the most colorful and informal of the 1930 recipients, a favorite of the press as well as other winners and their wives.

After being presented to the King of Sweden and dining off gold plate, Lewis rose on December 12 to deliver his acceptance speech. Looking slightly uncomfortable in white tie and tails, he exposed his resentment over the reaction of America to his award. In a neat blend of irony and backhanded compliment, he asked members of the Swedish Academy to imagine how men like Dr. Van Dyke might have responded had an author other than himself been chosen:

> *Suppose you had taken Theodore Dreiser.*
>
> *Now to me, as to many other American writers, Dreiser more than any other man, marching alone, usually unappreciated, often hated, has cleared the trail from Victorian and Howellsian timidity and gentility in American fiction to honesty and boldness and passion of life. Without his pioneering, I doubt if any of us could, unless we liked to be sent to jail, express life and beauty and terror. . . .*
>
> *Yet had you given the prize to Mr. Dreiser, you would have heard groans from America; you would have heard . . . that his style is cumbersome, that his choice of words is insensitive, that his books are interminable. And certainly respectable scholars would complain that in Mr. Dreiser's world, men and women are often sinful and tragic and despairing, instead of being forever sunny and full of song and virtue, as befits authentic Americans. . . .*
>
> *And had you given Mr. James Branch Cabell the prize, you would have been told that he is too fantastically malicious. So would you have been told that Miss Willa Cather, for all the homely virtue of her novels concerning the peasants of Nebraska, has in her novel, "A Lost Lady," been so untrue to America's patent and perpetual and possibly tedious virtuousness as to picture an abandoned woman who remains, nevertheless, uncannily charming, even to the virtuous, in a story without any moral; that Mr. Henry Mencken is the worst of all scoffers; that Mr. Sherwood Anderson viciously errs in considering sex as important a force in life as fishing; that Mr. Upton Sinclair, being a Socialist, sins against the perfectness of American capitalistic mass production; that Mr. Joseph Hergesheimer is un-American in regarding graciousness of manner and beauty of surface as of some importance in the endurance of daily life; and that Mr. Ernest Hemingway is not only too young but, far worse, uses language which should be unknown to gentlemen. . . .*

The speech was no great success in his homeland, for Lewis obviously included the reading public as well as the

Academy of Arts and Letters in his barbs. The fact that he had been the most-read author of the past decade was forgotten while his compatriots branded him an ungrateful fault finder.

Nor had the great honor done much to change Lewis as a person. Looking back over the period since news of the award had arrived, Lewis decided that his publisher did not respond with sufficient jubilation. So he abruptly quit Harcourt, Brace, his faithful publisher over ten years of fame.

The final scene—or curtain call—of the Literary Decade occurred in mid-March 1931 when Ray Long, editor of *Cosmopolitan*, gave a dinner for the visiting Russian novelist Boris Pilnyak. Compiling the list of guests, Long said, "We must have our Nobel Prize winner." Another invitation went to Theodore Dreiser, who had known Pilnyak in Moscow.

It would be the first meeting between these two men since Dreiser's plagiarism and Lewis' selection for the Nobel Prize. On this evening, Lewis was not a gracious winner. Obviously he had been drinking before his arrival, and now he proceeded to lap up more. One guest recalled, "He stood eating tiny sausages and drinking, drinking, drinking."

When Dreiser entered, he spotted his rival and walked over to say, "Congratulations, Lewis." With that, the Nobel Prize winner made a circle of two bony fingers, lifted them to puckered lips, and emitted the unpleasant sound then called the Bronx cheer, the bird, or the razzberry. Dreiser retired in no visible disarray.

As the most famous author present, Lewis was called upon to make the first postdinner speech. He rose to say, "I am glad to meet Mr. Pilnyak, but I do not care to speak in the presence of a man who has plagiarized three thousand words from my wife's book on Russia. Nor do I care to talk before two sage critics who objected to me as the Nobel Committee's selection of me as America's representative writer." This last referred to Heywood Broun and Arthur Brisbane who, for wildly differing reasons, had protested when he won the prize. The toastmaster hastily called upon folksy Irvin S. Cobb to cool the atmosphere by recounting a few stories. Matters were not improved when the guest of honor spoke. Through an interpreter Pilnyak made many flattering references to "Père Dreiser," but hardly mentioned Lewis at all.

When the dinner ended, Dreiser made a beeline for Lewis, shoving him into an anteroom. There he snapped, "You made a statement about my taking stuff from your wife's book. I know you are in ignoramus, but you are crazy. You don't know what you are talking about!" He then demanded an apology. Lewis refused, and Dreiser slapped him resoundingly across the face.

The Nobel Prize winner made no attempt to hit back. Instead, he said, "Theodore, you are a liar and a thief." With this, Dreiser slapped him again.

Friends appeared to pull the two battlers apart. But word of the fracas reached reporters, and for several days the set-to between America's literary titans made news throughout the world. Dreiser righteously proclaimed, "Rash and unwarranted insults were rewarded by two slaps in the face." Turning bellicose, he promised that next time he would use both hands. Lewis was also ambivalent. To one group of reporters he branded the affair "outrageous and scandalous." To another he said, "I'm just a country hick living on a farm, and every time I leave I get into trouble." One New Yorker sat down and composed a poem titled "The Slap Heard 'Round the World," which was printed in newspapers.

And so, to the echo of slaps to the face of the foremost writer of the decade, delivered by the hand of the foremost author of the century, the Literary Decade departed down the corridors of time.

Author's Note

My book deals with the commercial publishing scene of the Twenties, centered in mid-Manhattan. Any who feel I neglect Greenwich Village, or avant-garde writers, are referred to my book *The Improper Bohemians*, which deals exclusively with the scene below 14th Street.

This is—I hope—a popular work. In a sense, I have tried to write it from the outside looking in—that is, to recapture the excitements of the Literary Decade as they appeared to the intelligent, book-and-author-conscious person alive at the time. In other words, to the man or woman more interested in such controversies as the one over *Trader Horn* than in Dada or the New Humanism.

In my years as editor and author, I have met (and sometimes known) many of the persons mentioned here. I have interviewed others for the book; their names and comments are to be found in the text. Thanks for special services go to Professor Edwin Arthur Hill of the Bernard M. Baruch College of the City University of New York, to Mrs. Ad Schulberg, my literary agent, to Ned Calmer, and Guy Repp.

The novels read in the course of writing are mentioned on these pages, in some cases amply. Following are the nonfiction books on which I depended:

Bibliography

Adams, Franklin P., *Diary of Our Own Samuel Pepys*. New York: Simon & Schuster, 1935.

Adams, Samuel Hopkins, A. *Woollcott, His Life and His World*, New York: Reynal & Hitchcock, 1945.

Amory, Cleveland, and Frederic Bradlee (eds.), *Vanity Fair*. New York: Viking, 1960.

Angoff, Charles, *Henry L. Mencken, A Portrait from Memory*. New York: Yoseloff, 1956.

———— *World of George Jean Nathan*. New York: Knopf, 1952.

Baker, Carlos, *Ernest Hemingway*. New York: Scribner, 1969.

Boyd, Ernest, *Criticism in America*. New York: Harcourt, Brace, 1924.

———— *H. L. Mencken*. New York: McBride, 1927.

———— *Portraits*. New York: Doran, 1924.

Brooks, Van Wyck, *Days of the Phoenix, The 1920's I Remember*. New York: Dutton, 1957.

Brown, John Mason, *Worlds of Robert E. Sherwood*. New York: Harper, 1965.

Cabell, James Branch, *As I Remember It*. New York: McBride, 1955.

Clark, Emily, *Innocence Abroad*. New York: Knopf, 1931.

Cleaton, Irene and Allen, *Books & Battles, American Literature 1920–30*. Boston: Houghton Mifflin, 1937.

Collins, Joseph, *Taking the Literary Pulse*. New York: Doran, 1924.

Cooke, Alistair, *Talk About America*. New York: Knopf, 1968.

Cowley, Malcolm (ed.), *After the Genteel Tradition*. Carbondale: Southern Illinois University Press, 1965.

———— *Exile's Return, A Literary Odyssey of the 1920's*. New York: Viking, 1951.

Dell, Floyd, *Intellectual Vagabondage*. New York: Doran, 1926.

Dolmetsch, Carl R., *Smart Set, A History and Anthology*. New York: Dial, 1966.

Dos Passos, John, *Best Time*. New York: New American Library, 1966.

Erskine, John, *Memory of Certain Persons*. New York: Lippincott, 1947.

Fadiman, Clifton, *Party of One*. New York: World, 1955.

Farrar, John (ed.), *Literary Spotlight*. New York: Doran, 1924.

Ferber, Edna, *Peculiar Treasure*. New York: Doubleday, 1939.

Fitzgerald, F. Scott, *Crack Up*. New York: New Directions, 1945.

───── *Stories of Scott Fitzgerald*. New York: Scribner, 1951.

Forgue, Guy Jean, *Letters of H. L. Mencken*. New York: Knopf, 1961.

Friede, Donald, *Mechanical Angel*. New York: Knopf, 1948.

Gallico, Paul, *Confessions of a Story Writer*. New York: Knopf, 1946.

Goldberg, Isaac, *The Man Mencken*. New York: Simon & Schuster, 1925.

───── *Theatre of George Jean Nathan*. New York: Simon & Schuster, 1926.

Hapgood, Hitchins, *Victorian in the Modern World*. New York: Farrar & Rinehart, 1930.

Harriman, Margaret Case, *Vicious Circle*. New York: Rinehart, 1951.

Haverstick, John (ed.), *Saturday Review Treasury*. New York: Simon & Schuster, 1957.

Hecht, Ben, *Child of the Century*. New York: Simon & Schuster, 1954.

Hellman, Geoffrey, *Mrs. De Peyster's Parties and Other Lively Studies*. New York: Simon & Schuster, 1963.

Hellman, Lillian, *Unfinished Woman*. Boston: Little, Brown, 1969.

Hemingway, Ernest, *Moveable Feast*. New York: Scribner, 1964.

Hoffman, Frederick J., *The Twenties, Writing in the Postwar Decade*. New York: Viking, 1949.

Hutchens, John K. (ed.), *American Twenties, A Literary Panorama*. New York: Lippincott, 1952.

Kellner, Bruce, *Carl Van Vechten and the Irreverent Decades*. Norman: University of Oklahoma Press, 1969.

Kemler, Edgar, *Irreverent Mr. Mencken*. Boston: Little, Brown, 1950.

Kunitz, Stanley, *Authors Today and Yesterday*. New York: Wilson, 1933.

───── *Living Authors*. New York: Wilson, 1931.

Land, Myrick, *Fine Art of Literary Mayhem*. New York: Holt, Rinehart & Winston, 1962.

Lewis, Grace Hegger, *Half a Loaf*. New York: Liveright, 1931.

───── *With Love from Gracie*. New York: Harcourt, Brace, 1955.

Lewisohn, Ludwig, *Expression in America*. New York: Harper, 1932.

Loos, Anita, *Girl Like I*. New York: Viking, 1966.

Manchester, William, *Disturber of the Peace, A Life of H. L. Mencken*. New York: Harper, 1950.

May, Henry F., *End of American Innocence*. New York: Knopf, 1959.

Merz, Charles, *Great American Bandwagon*. New York: John Day, 1928.

Mizener, Arthur, *Far Side of Paradise*. Boston: Houghton Mifflin, 1949.

Morris, Jo Alex, *What a Year!* New York: Harper, 1926.

Morris, Lloyd, *Postscript to Yesterday*. New York: Random House, 1947.

Overton, Grant (ed.), *Mirrors of the Day, 1926–7*. New York: Stokes, 1928.

———— *Women Who Make Our Novels*. New York: Doran, 1918.

Phelps, Robert, and Peter Deane, *Literary Life*. New York: Farrar, Straus & Giroux, 1968.

Phelps, William Lyon, *As I Like It*. New York: Scribner, 1923, 1924, 1926.

———— *Autobiography with Letters*. New York: Oxford, 1939.

Piper, Henry Dean, *F. Scott Fitzgerald, A Critical Portrait*. New York: Holt, Rinehart & Winston, 1965.

Powys, John Cowper, *Autobiography*. New York: Simon & Schuster, 1934.

Rascoe, Burton, *Before I Forget*. New York: Doran, 1924.

———— *We Were Interrupted*. New York: Doubleday, 1947.

Rosenfeld, Paul, *Men Seen, Essays on Fourteen American Moderns*. New York: Harcourt, Brace, 1921.

Schorer, Mark, *Sinclair Lewis*. New York: McGraw-Hill, 1961.

Seabrook, William, *No Hiding Place*. New York: Lippincott, 1942.

Sedgwick, Ellery, *Happy Profession*. Boston: Little, Brown, 1946.

Singleton, M. K., *H. L. Mencken and the American Mercury Venture*. Durham, N.C.: Duke University Press, 1962.

Sklar, Robert, *F. Scott Fitzgerald: The Last Laocoön*. New York: Oxford, 1967.

Slocombe, George, *Tumult and the Shouting*. New York: Macmillan, 1936.

Smith, Harrison (ed.), *Main Street to Stockholm, Letters of Sinclair Lewis, 1919–1930*. New York: Harcourt, Brace, 1952.

Sullivan, Mark, *Our Times, The Twenties*. New York: Scribner, 1935.

Stokes, Horace (ed.), *Mirrors of the Year, 1927–8*. New York: Stokes, 1929.

Swanberg, W. A., *Dreiser*. New York: Scribner, 1965.

Towns, Charles Hanson, *So Far, So Good*. New York: Messner, 1945.

Turnbull, Andrew, *Scott Fitzgerald*. New York: Scribner, 1962.

Untermeyer, Louis, *Another World*. New York: Harcourt, Brace, 1939.

Van Gelder, Robert, *Writers and Writing*. New York: Scribner, 1946.

Van Doren, Carl, *Many Minds*. New York: Knopf, 1924.

Wharton, Edith, *Backward Glance*. New York: Appleton, 1934.

Wilson, Edmund, *American Earthquake*. New York: Doubleday, 1958.

———— *Axel's Castle*. New York: Scribner, 1948.

Woodward, William, *Gift of Life*. New York: Dutton, 1947.

Worthington, Marjorie, *Strange Case of William Seabrook*. New York: Harcourt, Brace, 1966.

Magazines: *The American Mercury, The New Yorker, Time, Smart Set, The New York Times Book Review*.

Index